D1118723

Ambition
and Privilege

Ambition and Privilege

The Social Tropes of
Elizabethan Courtesy Theory

by
Frank Whigham

University of California Press

Berkeley • Los Angeles • London

University of California Press
Berkeley and Los Angeles, California

University of California Press, Ltd.
London, England

Printed in the United States of America

1 2 3 4 5 6 7 8 9

Library of Congress Cataloging in Publication Data

Whigham, Frank.
    Ambition and privilege.
    Bibliography: p.
    Includes index.
    1. English literature—Early modern, 1500–1700—
History and criticism.   2. Courtesy in literature.
3. Great Britain—Court and courtiers.   4. Literature
and society—Great Britain.   5. Politics and literature—
Great Britain.   6. Social classes—England—History—
16th century.   1. Title.
PR428.C64W5   1984   820'.9'355   83-12638
ISBN 0-520-05104-1

For my mother, who taught me to read,
and my father, who taught me to work.

Contents

Acknowledgments

Part of this study appeared in another form in the Spring 1983 issue of *New Literary History* (vol. 14); I thank the editors for permission to reprint it here. I also wish to acknowledge the kindness of two publishers that have allowed me to quote from their publications: from *Spenser: Poetical Works*, edited by J. C. Smith and E. de Selincourt (Oxford: Oxford Univ. Press, 1912), reprinted by permission; and from *Studies in Philology*, vol. 77, no. 5, Texts and Studies, Copyright 1980, The University of North Carolina Press. Reprinted by permission.

The seeds of this book were sown by those with whom I first explored Renaissance studies: Shirley Bishop, Don Wayne, Richard Hicks, Ward Tonsfeldt, J. R. Mulryne, T. K. Dunseath, Leonard Barkan, Ron Martinez, and Louis Montrose. Some of these friends have left the academy (to its loss), but I am bound to them all for both past and present guidance. My colleagues at Claremont Graduate School have shared with me their varied commitments to the study of nonliterary texts, from Albert Friedman's work on the semiotics of burglary, to William C. Spengemann's explorations of travel narrative and autobiography. I have tried to emulate their examples. Others have given aid in many ways, great and small. I am grateful to Harry Berger, Jr., Ted Brown, Aaron V. Cicourel, Pat Delana, Michael Harper, Ann R. Jones, W. T. Jones, Richard C. McCoy, Catherine Mushel, Brenda Rosen, Bob Shephard, Peter Stallybrass, Jim Swan, Leonard Tennenhouse, and especially Johanna Smith. I am also indebted to Doris Kretschmer, Mary Lamprech, and an anonymous reader, all of the University of California Press. Thanks finally, for my book and for all else, to Jackson Cope, Jill Layne, and Charles Young.

Claremont
May, 1983

Foreword

Since the early 1970s, a good deal of scholarly attention has been focused on the Elizabethan court; much dormant material has been brought to life, and the application of modern social theory has brought major advances in our understanding of this complex institution. We are now more alert to the determinations of many literary texts written by and for courtly readers, especially as they function in relation to the social and political pressures of courtly life. However, this new understanding has yet to be applied in detail to that body of literature most specific to the court—courtesy literature. This corpus has thus far been dealt with largely in idealist terms: it has been thought that the courtier made his life a work of art with the help of these texts and used his powers to guide the court toward a higher morality. Efforts of this sort no doubt were made; many courtiers might well have so described themselves. But this model does not provide a comprehensive view of the functions of courtesy literature at court.

In addition, I think, we must view courtesy literature as having an intricate social purpose combining poetry and politics, philosophical speculation and social combat, ritual pageantry and ambition. I believe courtesy literature helped create and sustain the court's view of its own virtue and centrality—the dominant ideology of the Elizabethan ruling elite. The actual workings of this ideological service were of course extremely complicated. The court was simultaneously an arena of conflict and a mart of opportunity as well as a radiant center of order. I think we can fruitfully construe these interrelated functions by focusing on the crucial issue of social mobility. The received sense of personal identity, seen as founded on God-given attributes such as birth, was slowly giving way to the more modern notion that the individual creates himself by his own actions. This new view was enticing to those on the rise, but it threatened those who resisted sharing their positions or who feared they would be displaced. The latter proposed the distinctions found in courtesy theory in order to maintain their preeminence; the former read the courtesy books, hoping to avoid being so distinguished. The effect of this practical intellectual struggle was to articulate a sophisticated rhetoric, indeed an epistemology, of personal social identity—a new understanding of *how people tell who they are*. The texts that articulated this struggle thus combined practical action and creative intellectual exploration. They were both tools and the kinds of activity we now describe as literature, history, and philosophy.

This study, then, treats Elizabethan courtesy literature as a repertoire of actions invoked by, and meant to order, the surge of social mobility that occurred at the boundaries between ruling and subject classes in late sixteenth-century England. This repertoire formed slowly and unevenly, first coming into view among the ruling elite as they absorbed the pressures created by the new sense of personal merit proposed by Italian humanism. The first chapter focuses on the situation of the ambitious courtier at the time these pressures arose and the consequent development of Elizabethan courtesy literature.

Notions of status began to assume new modes of exhibition in this tense context, and so we must inquire into the rhetorical production and interpretation of courtly signs of status. Chapter II, "Rhetorical Semiotics at Court," examines the ways in which all aspects of courtly life came to carry symbolic messages about status, poses a dialectic between social performer and audience, and specifies some mechanisms of adjustment between rigorous codes of value and supple modes of interpretation.

The next three chapters detail the vocabulary and grammar of three systems of tropes of status: tropes of social hierarchy (justifying stratification into ranks of gentle and base); tropes of personal promotion (imputing value, through praise or flattery, to the self, superiors, or allies); and tropes of personal rivalry (assaulting the value of rivals and inferiors with blame or slander). Chapter III deals with techniques that stipulate an individual's membership in the elite group and then claim privilege and power for the individual by asserting the superiority of the group. Chapters IV and V reverse this structure, dealing with tropes that stipulate the ruling elite's entitlement as a class and argue for the individual's inclusion in or exclusion from that privileged class.

This way of subdividing the subject, though it may seem knotty at first, is meant to be the simplest possible. Other partitions are feasible, such as division by speaker or addressee, or by individual courtesy writer or generic literary structure. Analysis can be made of social rituals such as greetings or apologies, or of other kinds of ritual such as games or jokes. A rhetoric of bodily demeanor, as in the work of Norbert Elias and Edward Hall, might be constructed. There are still other categories, but all of these schemes either leave gaps or overlap confusingly. So I have founded my analysis on the ways *all* tropes of courtesy work, for group or for individual, with praise or with blame. Though some overlap remains, such broad and simple categories allow me to cover a wide variety of historical texts; to explain how the idea of hierarchy itself was maintained; and to unfold the ways in which individual status might be located along this axis of rank.

My organization will, then, focus attention on four subjects. First, a specific historical situation: the English Renaissance transition between medieval and modern social formations, reflected in the new locus of mobility between ruling and subject classes. Second, the grammar of a particular set of symbolic actions. Third, a thesaurus of tactical tropes adapted for those actions. Fourth, a set of rules for interpreting and reinterpreting them. I believe that collation of these four subjects will help us to construe an extended historical event of great importance for its own age and for ours.

Any study of this kind necessarily dangles, not only between historical and literary investigation as they are traditionally conceived but between traditional forms of investigation generally and newer forms of analysis of text and social action. Much of what follows is archival in character, bringing to light phenomena previously unconsidered. Some of these perceptions obviously help to revise our understanding of the Elizabethan court; others must count as trivial by received criteria. But such dismissals are themselves determined; we need these buried facts, and we must consider who buried them and why. In many cases, as will become clear, I think that the Elizabethan gravediggers' descendants are still hard at work. In many others, needless to say, the efforts of traditional historical and literary scholarship are indispensable guides to this region of the past, and it is to this fund of data that I seek to contribute. In any event, the corpus of courtesy literature, small and distinctive, offers a convenient opportunity to anatomize the operations of a discourse of power whose modern form has become natural, obvious, and therefore largely invisible.

I have generally retained original spelling in my citations from Renaissance texts, except where I have used modernized editions. I have, however, silently altered the long *s* and expanded the macron.

Euerie pragmatician castes about for life, and scoures the coast to the purpose. Jt importes euerie negotiatour, discouerer, intelligencer, practitioner, and euerie wittie man continually to cast abowt, & scowre the coast. Still & still more & more.

Gabriel Harvey, marginal note transcribed by John L. Lievsay from Harvey's copy of Lodovico Domenichi's *Facetie, et motti di diverse persone* (1571). In Lievsay, *Stefano Guazzo.*

Oh what a difference is there betweene wants, and aboundance, betweene preferment, and standing at a stay, betweene imployment, and idlenesse? whereas before I walked unre-garded, now I sitte at ease admyred; and how euer the heart, is corrupted, I am sure of an obsequious ceremony, and cheerefull countenance; where as before I was scarce welcommed to any, I am now entertained of all; and in steed of fretting my selfe for lacke of presents to giue my friends, am now made cheerefull with many gratuities, euen from my enemies: whereas before I could not preuent necessities with great paines taking, and trouble, I now supply euen wantonnes with cheerefulnes and pleasures. So that the feare is as great to be corrupted with felicitie, as the vexation was greeuous to be tormented with adversitie.

Thomas Gainsford, *The Secretaries Studie.*

If all societies and, significantly, all the "totalitarian institutions," in Goffman's phrase, that seek to produce a new man through a process of "deculturation" and "reculturation" set such store on the seemingly most insignificant details of *dress, bearing,* physical and verbal *manners*, the reason is that, treating the body as a memory, they entrust to it in abbreviated and practical, i.e., mnemonic form the fundamental principles of the arbitrary content of the culture.

Pierre Bourdieu, *Outline of a Theory of Practice.*

1. Courtesy Literature and Social Change

The preface to Thomas Wilson's *Arte of Rhetorique* presents an account of the origin of civilization. Life after the Fall was savage and depraved; law was unregarded, "the earth vntilled, societie neglected ... some like brute beastes grased vpon the ground: some went naked: some roomed like Woodoses: none did any thing by reason, but most did what they could by manhood."[1] In the midst of this moral chaos, "God still tendering his owne workmanshippe" gave his elected ministers reason and utterance, "that they might with ease win folke at their will, and frame them by reason to all good order." This God-given gift was to repair the damage wrought by our first father; the gift was not, however, the Christ, but Eloquence—not the Word, but words. This complex of intellectual and oratorical power makes all things possible through the winning of men's minds with ease and at will. And such power comes not from submission and humility, as does Christ's; instead, "I thinke him most worthie fame, and amongst all men to bee taken for halfe a GOD." Wilson's vision shifts the emphasis from God's creative powers to human articulation. Although the gift comes from God, it is exercised by men, and its exercise elevates them to the status of demigods, not through suffering but through speech.

Wilson's hymn to human rhetoric is not so generalized as Pico's *Oration*, which lauded *Man*'s self-determination. Wilson's eloquence enables *selective* elevation, in a zero-sum world worthy of Machiavelli:

> What man I pray you, beeing better able to maintaine himself by valiaunt courage, then by liuing in base subiection, would not rather looke to rule

like a Lord, then to liue like an vnderling: if by reason he were not perswaded, that it behoueth euery man to liue in his owne vocation: and not to seeke any higher roume, then wherunto he was at the first appointed? Who would digge and delue from Morne till Euening? Who would trauaile and toyle with ye sweat of his browes? Yea, who would for his Kings pleasure aduenture and hassarde his life, if witte had not so won men, that they thought nothing more needfull in this world, nor any thing whereunto they were more bounden; then here to liue in their duetie, and to traine their whole life according to their calling.

Although Wilson intends to voice the dominant Elizabethan ideology, his account of rank as *achieved* brings into view patterns of exploitation and submission revealingly at variance with the tenderly organic ligaments of the traditional body politic. He makes it possible to ask new questions about the origin of social structure.

Wilson's rhetorical division of humans into haves and have-nots is internally contradictory. The superiors in his originary scenario are God's chosen ministers, restoring an order of His making. But Wilson then suggests that *any* man would live like a lord rather than an underling if he could; that lording derives from persuasion; and that instruction in persuasion is shortly to follow, available to anyone with wit and the purchase price. Rhetoric is presented as a power open to many applications. Wilson no doubt meant his instruction to further the careers of the queen's public servants, modern counterparts of his primitive elect ministers. But the idea that those who rule do so with, and because of, their rhetorical powers also suggests that one with rhetorical powers may hope to rule, or at least be powerful, or at least gain some access to power and its assorted privileges (say, not having to dig and delve). Most important of all, Wilson is ready to transmit these skills to the reader. The presumptive link between rhetoric and the current God-given order of things snaps when the Wilsons of the age, with fully conservative self-consciousness, convert the tools of rule, of domination and self-determination, into a commodity packaged for the open market of the literate.

A corollary to this internal discrepancy reveals rhetoric's fundamental indeterminacy of application. If rhetoric maintains rule by persuading subjects to submit, may it not be that subjects are *merely* persuaded to submit, to those who have merely rhetorical powers? Wilson enabled his readers to attain an awareness, however foggy, of the inorganic exploitation in his picture of persuaders living like lords on the "trauaile and toyle" of those in "base subiection." This realization puts into question not only the Elizabethan reader's own status but that of his superiors as well. Wilson makes possible a new conception of the hierarchical social order: not as a set of sealed ranks, nor even as an order based on merit (another new strategy with its own problems), but as a system dominated by those who can convince others that they ought to submit. He effectively uncouples the existing order from transcendent authority and refounds it on the sheerly formal, learnable, vendible skills of persuasion.

Wilson closes his offer of aid by invoking God's grace, which he gives "vnto al such as call vnto him with stretched handes": "I purpose by his grace and especiall assistence, to set forth such precepts of eloquence ... that the vnlearned by seeing the practice of others, maie haue some knowledge themselues, and learne by their neighbours deuise, what is necessarie for them selues in their owne case." This domestic relation depicts what Michel Foucault calls the "capillary" form of power, "the point where the power reaches into the very grain of individuals, touches their bodies and inserts itself into their actions and attitudes, their discourses, learning processes and everyday lives."[2] For Wilson writes not just of God's purposes, but of one's "neighbours deuise." And although the workings of such powers are often hidden in the obvious and banal, they also—indeed, thereby—govern the sources of social order. Treatises like Wilson's, seen collectively as a cultural document, confirm Foucault's view that "there are manifold relations of power which permeate, characterise and constitute the social body, and these relations of power cannot themselves be established, consolidated nor implemented without the production, accumulation, circulation and functioning of a discourse."[3] Foucault has for some time been exhuming such discourses buried in recent centuries, focusing both on the precise historical detail of lost specializations (an example relevant to this study is the system of heraldry) and on the equally lost "popular" knowledges of local acquaintance (governing, for instance, the nuances of personal interaction between unequals in a hierarchical society). "With what in fact were these buried, subjugated knowledges really concerned? They were concerned with a *historical knowledge of struggles*. In the specialised areas of erudition as in the disqualified, popular knowledge there lay the memory of hostile encounters which even up to this day have been confined to the margins of knowledge."[4]

Renaissance courtesy literature offers a prime specimen of such a subjugated or marginal knowledge. Historians have dismissed it, owing to its "soft" character, its evidentiary imprecision compared with the bonier fossils of, say, constitutional history. And literary scholars have habitually seen its subject under the ameliorative sign of "the poetry of conduct,"[5] erasing the traces of struggle by a familiar reification of the poetic. But what is needed with this body of texts is, to paraphrase Kenneth Burke, a sociological criticism that assembles and codifies the lore of courtesy as a repertoire of strategies, tools for such tasks as "selecting enemies and allies, for socializing losses, for warding off evil eye, for purification, propitiation, and desanctification, consolation and vengeance, admonition and exhortation, implicit commands or instructions. . . . "[6] Courtesy literature is indeed "equipment for living" and requires an analytic mode that applies "both to works of art and to social situations outside art."[7] We must inquire into application as well as intellectual coherence and moral and aesthetic matters. For courtesy is a systematic activity like Pierre Bourdieu's ritual practice:

> Understanding ritual practice is not a question of decoding the internal logic of a symbolism but of restoring its practical necessity by relating it to the real conditions of its genesis, that is, to the conditions in which its functions, and the means it uses to attain them, are defined. It means, for example, reconstituting—by an operation of logical reconstruction which has nothing to do with an act of empathic projection—the significance and functions that agents in a determinate social formation can (and must) confer on a determinate practice or experience, given the practical taxonomies which organize their perception.[8]

An account of the practice of Renaissance courtesy, unlike a description of the ritual practices of traditional undifferentiated societies, must confront the existence of native codifications—courtesy books. These texts are crucial to "the real conditions of . . . genesis" of the practical discourse of courtesy, because they make explicit (and so spread wide) "the practical taxonomies which organize . . . perception" of the social world. This corpus is not open to Bourdieu's charge of theoreticism (here applied to accounts of honor):

> However close it may come to the logic of practices (and to the extent that it does), the abstract diagram which has to be constructed in order to account for that logic is liable to obscure the fact that the driving force of the whole mechanism is not some abstract principle (the principle of isotimy, equality in honour), still less the set of *rules* which can be derived from it, but the sense of honour, a disposition inculcated in the earliest years of life and constantly reinforced by calls to order from the group, that is to say,

> from the aggregate of the individuals endowed with the same dispositions, to whom each is linked by his dispositions and interests.[9]

In fact, the corpus of Renaissance courtesy literature began to develop at a time when an exclusive sense of aristocratic identity (closely entangled with, and resting upon, the traditional ideas of honor of which Bourdieu writes) was being stolen, or at least encroached upon, by a horde of young men not born to it. This historical locus requires a double adaptation of Bourdieu's formulation. First, his concept must be relocated to a differentiated society, in which honor is a notion specific to the ruling elite, not shared by all males. Second, there is a further shift to a period during which that structuration had begun to decay. Movement across the gap between ruling and subject classes was becoming increasingly possible, and elite identity had begun to be a function of actions rather than of birth—to be achieved rather than ascribed.

In this twice-removed context, the sense of self, of membership in the ruling elite, is no longer necessarily "a disposition inculcated in the earliest years of life," except perhaps for those established (and besieged) aristocrats who sought to resist the incursions from below. For many others, such elite identity was a mode of being that could be acquired, taken on in adulthood—a commodity like Wilson's that could be *bought*, by means of courtesy books. Such men were precisely in the market for what Bourdieu calls a repertoire of rules, a "representation of action which is forced on agents or groups when they lack practical mastery of a highly valued competence and have to provide themselves with an explicit and at least semi-formalized substitute for it in the form of a *repertoire of rules*, or of what sociologists consider, at best, as a 'role,' i.e., a predetermined set of discourses and actions appropriate to a particular 'stage-part.'"[10] This kind of discursive system is forced not only upon the anthropologist visiting a traditional society, but upon the social climber in Elizabethan England, who seeks to pass for a native aristocrat. But the texts of courtesy theory were written in response to *internal* determinations; they were not the alien inquiries of the extracultural visitor who "has no place (except by choice or by way of a game) in the system observed and has no need to make a place for himself there."[11] In fact, courtesy theory was precisely a tool for "making places" in the social order and was used for this purpose by Elizabethans on both sides of the struggle. First promulgated by the elite in a gesture of exclusion, the theory was then read, rewritten, and reemployed by mobile base readers to serve their own social aggressions. Both purposes are decisively Elizabethan.

Given such a post-traditional situation, it is necessary to inquire into the circumstances of the "native" production of theoretical formulations and to seek to define and explain the functions of such texts, as means of satisfying social needs. I shall be arguing that the principal function of Elizabethan courtesy literature (different in operation for different social groups) was the government of the abrupt sixteenth-century bridging of the gap between ruling and subject classes. In so doing I will be trying to "restore the practical necessity" of the literature by resituating it in the social context from which it derived its deep structures and which it in turn reshaped. I will focus principally on the *resources* of the theory, with reference to the needs to which they were addressed. I reserve for another study the examination of documented daily practice, excepting only the ways in which the promulgation of theory was itself a practice. Before turning to the theoretical texts, however, it is useful to consider some quantitative evidence of the structural shift from a rigid to a fluid ruling elite.

Renaissance courtesy literature arose during what Lawrence Stone calls "the century of mobility, 1540–1640," during which "English society experienced a seismic upheaval of unprecedented magnitude."[12] A full discussion of this surge of social mobility is beyond the reach of this study, since many questions of data and definition continue to be debated. But some general outlines are clear and may be recapitulated here.

Stone's divisions of English Renaissance society offer a convenient grid.[13] The populace was divided into two fundamental ranks, gentle and ungentle—according to freedom from or obligation to perform physical labor. These ranks were further partitioned into six categories:

1. Dependents on charity and live-in servants and apprentices
2. Living-out laborers (rural and urban, agricultural and industrial)
3. Husbandmen, yeomen, artisans, and shopkeepers
4. Lesser gentry
5. County elite: squires, knights, and baronets
6. Peers

In addition, Stone specifies four "semi-independent occupational hierarchies"—merchants, lawyers, clergy, and administrators—which
offered "rapid escalators" for upward mobility. These occupational
sets are difficult to relate precisely to the sixfold vertical hierarchy;
the problem is one of "trying to describe a society whose legal system
and status system were based on possession of land at a time when
non-landed skills, wealth and power were increasingly significant."[14]
Presumably, though, specialists in various forms of intellectual work
cluster toward the upper end of the scale.

During the sixteenth century the ease of movement up and down
all of these ladders, as well as the relative sizes of the various groups
and of the gaps between them, shifted considerably. In particular, as
will become clear, the elite increased distinctly in size relative to the
subject classes, and vertical social mobility became much more common. Such changes were in fact widespread, if unevenly so, throughout the culture, but attention here will focus mainly on the social elite,
producers and consumers of courteous writings and behaviors.

Until the late fifteenth century, birth was the principal determinant
of rank, the natural conduit for the self-evident. Individual skill, education, and rhetorical self-presentation might enhance the clarity of
identity, or even improve the local conditions of life, but alteration of
social rank by personal effort (least of all at the crucial gap between
elite and subject classes) was quite uncommon. But nearly a century
later, Wallace MacCaffrey tells us, "in the intensely rank-conscious
world of late Tudor England, there was an unceasing scramble to
cross the dividing line which separated gentlemen (the 'common sort
of nobility,' as Camden called them) from the mere yeoman or free-
holder."[15] This scramble was a concern to those on both sides of the
line. As Ruth Kelso realized long ago, while "those who lacked the
title [of gentleman] were busy trying to acquire it . . . those who had it
were anxious to resist encroachment."[16] During the sixteenth and
early seventeenth centuries, the relatively static social structure
founded upon self-evident birth-based status was seriously disrupted—not least, perhaps (as will be argued in this study), by the
very texts that were designed to govern the scramble.

The causes of this complex increase in social convection are manifold. In addition to the European pressures of the Reformation toward a new sense of the personal, and the rise of intellectual self-
determination as a result of humanism and print phenomena,[17] there

are numerous causal patterns specific to England. As far as political advancement was concerned,

> Henry VII had opened the doors of political opportunity to a wider range of men than before, particular to the landed gentry. His son continued this policy, and after 1529 vastly expanded the rewards and opportunities open to the successful politician. These monarchs went far in altering the qualifications for a political career. The factious war-lords of the fifteenth century had required the brutal skills of the armed retainer, half-soldier, half-gangster: now it was the suppler skills of the courtier, suave and persuasive, or the administrator, clear-headed and literate, which were in demand. At the same time there occurred what might be called the "nationalization" of politics. The person of the monarch became the focus of a single, national political world with centripetal force powerful enough to draw into its orbit all rivalries, personal, local, or dynastic. Thus, centralization of political life accompanied a new sophistication in the political arts and a striking growth in the number of their practitioners.[18]

The political arts of self-depiction grew necessarily more important at a single central court where universal personal acquaintance could not be counted upon, as had been the case at the earlier local courts. Into this vacuum of impersonality flowed the arts of courtesy, as we shall see later. But these years saw more material determinations of status rise to prominence. Late in his reign Henry VIII reversed earlier policy and began a generous distribution of new titles. An even greater impetus for mobility into the elite came with the dissolution of the monastic holdings. The division of such lands among the gentry and yeomanry greatly enriched and enlarged these groups, whose members at once sought official ratification of their new status. "Unless many heralds' visitations are uniformly misleading, the century which followed the secularising of church lands saw in every shire a remarkable multiplication of gentle families and of the more substantial yeomen-farmers from whose ranks new gentry were constantly being recruited."[19]

The rapid dispersion of landed wealth offers the basic documentary evidence that "this period saw a phase of unprecedented individual mobility, upwards and downwards"; these transactions reached a peak around 1610 and after, being 250 percent higher than in the 1560s.[20] Such mobility was given added impetus by the political free-for-all of the 1550s, which extended further the spoliation of the church and tossed political primacy back and forth among warring camps under Edward and Mary. It was this swirling scene that Elizabeth had to order when she came to the throne; without much in the way of coercive governmental power, she had to seduce the swelling political class, rather than subdue it. Many of her labors were ideological, of course—a kind of performance for which the young queen was marvelously well equipped. But she had material capacities at her disposal too:

> There were hundreds of offices in her gift, and others which could be diverted to her use by the device of recommendatory letters or verbal orders, sometimes amiable in tone, sometimes hectoring, but at all times difficult, if not dangerous, to resist. [Many of these offices could be exercised by deputy, increasing the number of people who might be satisfied by them, and so were hungry for them.] There were also royal lands to be leased or sold, or to be granted as reward for services; a source of great wealth, and most eagerly solicited. Finally, there were all those grants by letters patent, whether charters, licenses, monopolies . . . which conferred some benefit on the recipient.[21]

The competition for these privileges was intense, but the hope was that "by the expert sharing of those gifts . . . at its command, the government could secure the continuing goodwill of the politically preeminent classes."[22] Needless to say, these lures, grasped or not, gave rise to much activity among the ever-growing group of ambitious have-nots.

At the outset of Elizabeth's reign, then, the government faced both a disrupted governing class flushed with increased pressures from carrot and stick alike, and a growing "horde of aspirants," as Stone calls them,[23] who sought material enrichment and social ratification from a queen who strove to please nearly everyone. Little wonder, then, that between 1540 and 1640 "there was a remarkable increase in the number of the upper classes, which trebled at a period when the total population barely doubled. The number of peers rose from 60 to 160; of baronets and knights from 500 to 1,400; of squires from perhaps 800 to 3,000; of armigerous gentry from perhaps 5,000 to around 15,000."[24] These figures of course reflect the notorious "inflation of honors" by James, of which Stone has given such a detailed view in *The Crisis of the Aristocracy*.[25] Elizabeth's resources gradually shrank, and she grew more and more parsimonious with age; the hunger for reward thus increased in inverse relation to its likelihood. When James, also penurious but not parsimonious, sought to buy his way into his new English subjects' hearts by selling honors and offices, the rush of the ambitious (who had been kept waiting in the wings by Elizabeth) redoubled, resulting in another swelling of the politically active classes. This process at once enlarged the effective elite (both established and would-be) and smeared its reputation, as Gervase Holles complained:

> It was the constant custome of the Queene to call out of all counties of the Kingdome the gentlemen of greatest hopes and of the best fortunes and families, and with those to fill the most honourable roomes of hir household servantes; by wch she honored them, obliged their kindred and allegiance, and fortified hir selfe. But when most of those rooms were possest by such trotting companions the better sort of the gentry declined the Court as scorning their fellowship. Hence it followed that in a little time the Court was in a manner wholly composed of theis Scots and such inconsiderable persons as favourites preferred or mony introduced.[26]

Too many suitors competing for too few rewards inflated the cost while deflating the value. Whether or not we agree with Holles's estimate of this swollen group, swollen in size it certainly was.

The composition of this group must be specified more precisely than it is in Holles's venomous passage. It was relatively very limited in size when compared with the larger population units. The currently definitive estimates of the total Elizabethan population, based on the complex "back-projection" operations of E. A. Wrigley and R. S. Schofield, suggest a growth from 2.984 million to 4.109 million between 1561 and 1601.[27] Similarly current estimates of the London population in 1600 suggest a range from 160,000 to 180,000.[28] With these numbers we must compare Stone's estimates of the increase of armigerous gentry and ranks above, which suggest a broad aristocracy of perhaps 12,000 to 15,000 at the turn of the century.[29] A more conservatively conceived, actively political elite, according to Mac-Caffrey, but one that still included "younger sons and . . . those other aspirants just ready to enter the political lists," would number about 2,500.[30] He suggests by another calculation that "the Crown was able to dispose of about 1200 places worth a gentleman's having and as many again of humbler consequence. Allowing for a considerable amount of pluralism, especially among the minor keeperships and stewardships, there must have been at least a thousand gentiemen-placemen at any given moment in Elizabeth's reign."[31] By even the most generous of these calculations, the elite appears miniscule in relation to the subject classes, but it had, needless to say, a disproportionate influence on the culture, not least through the exemplary functions of its enticing privileges. It is for this reason that although

Elizabethan comment is unreliable regarding actual demographic shifts, owing to a misleading preoccupation with the lives of the elite, it precisely records perceptions, especially ideological ones. Similarly, although the elite was numerically small, shifts in access to it that to us seem relatively tiny loomed large to contemporaries. They should loom equally large in our judgments of Elizabethan ideology; the ideological corpus we are to study in this book was created in order to govern such shifts of power and privilege, changes that are nearly imperceptible when viewed in terms of total-population demographics.[32]

The interplay between demographic fact and public perception may be very complex. For instance, the rich and the poor were becoming increasingly polarized economically, because of the price revolution and the growing economic value of technical skills. At the same time, these processes made for greater parity between nobles and gentry.[33] To one stationed at the lower boundary of the elite, on either side, the good life might well have seemed both nearer and farther away. To take another example, the apparent retreat into rarefaction that the demographic polarization would seem to have entailed must be weighed against the increased dispersion of the elite: "For the first time in history the majority of the population were living directly under the eye of a member of the ruling elite."[34] Again, we must imagine a closer and more enticing view of the increasingly distant. The exact relations are very knotted; what is clear is that the increase in actual social mobility distinctly altered the shared perceptions of the social world.

We should also consider the typological makeup of those who were ambitious or privileged. MacCaffrey divides the clientele of the Elizabethan political opinion managers into four types: "the established magnate for whom politics is a secondary but essential part of life; the daring aspirant, soaring for the greatest prizes; the plodding placeman seeking a secure living; [and] the zealot, the dedicated agent of the Divine Will."[35] Of these, "the greediest and most restless were those with the least in hand and the most to wish for—the great army of younger brothers, or the jostling crowd of lesser gentry, men with little patrimony or none at all, either threatened with the loss of status or desperately anxious to attain it."[36] For all such men, high and low alike, "the gentlemanly profession of serving-men" was a locus of security and prestige, opening out laterally at all levels of public service. And so it gave rise to the only apparently paradoxical scene of a court thronged with suitors begging for a chance to "serve" their royal mistress. Successful self-donation brought fortune to both individual and lineage; at the same time, these myriad acts of grasping submission constituted a collective obeisance that reaffirmed the ideological power base of the royal presence.[37] In turn the queen strove to reward, and so to control, all her servants throughout the elite.

It is important to stress that the queen was only *central* to this scene; she was not in effect its sole constituent. In too many discussions the institution of patronage is made to resemble the protestant theological universe: the near-divine patron seems equidistant from all suitors and is their sole point of reference. In fact, of course, access to the queen was limited, and much of her largesse was distributed by courtiers and functionaries, who formed a many-layered matrix of mediation and themselves demanded wooing, from below as well as from above. Elizabeth was by no means the sole audience for the courteous and self-seeking offer of service; she was only the original source of privilege. Most actions of self-presentation flowed between individuals of *adjacent* ranks, seeking and awarding patronage at all levels of intimacy and degrees of distance from the throne at the heart of the court. When we think of suitors and patrons, we should emphasize the *activities* that defined them, not the reified roles they occupied permanently. Courtiers of all ranks were by turns (even, in a mixed three-tiered group, at once) suitors to their superiors and patrons to their inferiors. The emphasis should fall not on the queen, who was only the ultimate end point of such suits, but on the activity that constituted and reconstituted the web of local bonds among courtiers of all subranks, and in so doing, reconstituted the categories of rank themselves.

As we might conclude both from MacCaffrey's picture of the new verbally oriented retainer, courtly or bureaucratic, and from Stone's "rapid escalators" of law, church, city, and administration, most of the new modes of social self-elevation required substantial education. The most elevated sons continued to be tutored at home (though in the newer humanist mode), as had long been the case. But in the 1530s there was a remarkable invasion of the universities by established and would-be gentry.[38] These inaugural years saw two symmetrical developments: the eviction of Rome and the advent of Italian humanist educational theory. A series of statutes culminating in the Act of Supremacy displaced the canon law, and in 1535 Cromwell forbade the awarding of such law degrees, thus abolishing an entire profession and the educational structure that fed it.[39] At the same time the monastic colleges were dissolved, and the Regius professorships and royal colleges were endowed.[40] These changes derived ultimately from Italian humanism's central notion of a unitary intellectual, social, and political elite participating actively in power and privilege.[41]

Three elements can be discerned in the educational program. The first is a recapitulation of the knightly ideal of the medieval polity, stressing the physical exercises of battlefield and court. The new second and third elements are a focus on modern courtly manners and on subjects seen as specific to politics: moral and political philosophy, history, law, modern languages, and the like.[42] These ideas flowed from Italy to England in the sixteenth century and changed the shape of English education. Kenneth Charlton summarizes the process, showing "how what has been called civic humanism, classically expressed in the writings of Bruni and Alberti, was assimilated in those of Elyot; how the refinements of court life, characteristic of late fifteenth-century Italy, became known in England largely by way of translations; above all how it came to be recognized, though not without opposition, that an educated governing class, made ready by its education to serve the prince and the common weal, was a prime need in the modern State as it was developing during the sixteenth century."[43] So the ruling classes of the English Renaissance came to share a political and intellectual and stylistic self-concept, rather than the limited military one of the armed knight. Sir Thomas Elyot's "governor" was a gentleman, a fluent denizen of the urban court, whose textual hero was not Lancelot but Cicero. The combative chivalric ideology of moralized force was altered by new cooperative pressures of nationally centralized life; problems of power once solved by force were now submitted to a rule of words, of laws and principles that often seemed to the old order to be effete fraud and trickery. This new system created new social employment for intellectual skills even as it monopolized the roles of potency in public life. The philosophical program of the Italian humanists specified a link between such intellectual work and leadership and called for a wider participation in power than had been common in England. English adoption of these ideas aroused a presumption of national destiny in the young man at the university.

Daniel Javitch has suggestively traced the progressive frustration of this expectation as it percolated from fourteenth-century Italian republics to the Elizabethan monarchy.[44] The republics had validated the myth of actual government by intellectuals, but as a result of the rise of despotic rule in the fifteenth century it was recast in terms more acceptable to those in control. The humanists began instead to produce works of generalized moral guidance, less annoying to rulers now grown from peers to patrons. This "advice to princes" literature spread laterally to generate a wide range of abstract and theoretical comment on what was at this time seen not so much as government as "life at court." But even this distanced format found a hostile reception, and so a second removal took place, into an expressly fictional realm. This fictional fictiveness allowed the would-be social servant to avoid culpable reference to the real actions of real rulers, while still employing the powers his education had taught him to see as his defining capacities. He had to work through techniques of sublimation and indirection. If his patrons regarded such fictions as entertainment rather than counsel, he was at least not silenced, and there was plenty of classical precedent for the stoic endurance of repression. In fact, of course, he must often have felt not repressed but fulfilled. Virgil the poet was as powerful a model as Cicero the engaged orator, and his Aeneas repeatedly had to set aside his personal desires for the good of the state.

The fit between humanist ideals and English educational actuality has also been questioned. Charlton and Hugh Kearney pose objections to the notion that much change took place in actual educational procedures or in political advancement. Each stresses the continuation in the sixteenth century of late medieval religious instructional modes and goals.[45] But Charlton does think that the new theory actually motivated the striking increase in gentry enrollment,[46] and Kearney credits the increased gentry attendance with significance in terms of perceived status, though not of actual political power.[47] Such views are quite consistent with the fact of the new *aspirations* that accompanied the increase in social mobility outside the university. We cannot separate the ideological from the practical, for what we have here is the rise of a new sense of aristocratic identity, quite as politically factual as the actual holding of an office or the completion of a degree or the practice of a profession. For one thing, the absence of detailed specialization during the formal educational experience (the "serious" pursuit and completion of a particular course of study) in some ways matches the lack of specialization in actual royal service; according to MacCaffrey, beyond the law and the military, "professional expertise was little in demand."[48] More generally, one may question the dismissive formulation that, in the absence of "real" progress toward a degree or professional career, the universities "increasingly provided a useful bridge between schooling and the inns of court or travel, or where these were not contemplated themselves acted as finishing schools."[49] For this function of "finishing" involved "the fashioning of a gentleman or noble person in vertuous and gentle discipline," as Spenser put it in the letter to Raleigh: the indoctrination of a more and more widespread group with an ideology of their political significance and its daily manifestation in a courtly life-style. Hence the popularity of Castiglione's *Book of the Courtier*, "which became in time almost a second bible for English gentlemen."[50] Such cultivation of style was itself a political action, which might either help accomplish or substitute for actual political advancement.

It is in the English context of such conflicts, between ambition and its limits, that we must situate the mentality of many young men from the universities and Inns of Court. The expulsion of the Roman church had opened many doors, and the new educational theory published that fact, fueling ambition with moral injunctions. But supply rapidly eclipsed demand, and by the 1630s, Stone calculates, 600 educated young men were leaving the universities each year without entering the professions.[51] Richard Mulcaster, Spenser's teacher and headmaster of the famous Merchant Taylors' School, may have spoken habitually of those young gentlemen "whose ordinary greatness is to govern our state and be public pillars for the prince to lean on and the people to stay by,"[52] but such greatness was not really ordinary. And in fact Mulcaster was aware by 1581 of the dangers of this overproduction, for he pointed out "that too many learned be too burdenous, that too few be too bare, that wits well-sorted be most civil, that the same misplaced be most unquiet and seditious. . . . To have so many gaping for preferment, as no gulf hath store enough to suffice, and to let them roam helpless, whom nothing else can help, how can it be but that such shifters must needs shake the very strongest pillar in that state where they live, and loiter without living?"[53] The fact that many such "shifters" did not matriculate or graduate or enter the professions for which they were nominally studying need not demonstrate the absence of "seriousness of purpose," as Charlton suggests.[54] (Indeed, Mulcaster's conservative fears may imply the reverse.) Degrees often led to less ambitious clerical posts, which conferred less status and were usually occupied by men of lesser rank.[55] Stone's researches also suggest some degree of inverse relation between social rank and matriculation.[56] James McConica provides the right perspective, I think, with which to view the jostling army of younger sons and other aspirants. He notes that "for many members of Tudor England's propertied class, the colleges of Oxford and Cambridge must have made more generally available a kind of gentleman's education that had long been associated with private aristocratic households, and that had little or nothing to do with the acquisition of academic degrees."[57] A good deal of serious purpose must be imputed to those who sought to achieve for themselves the styled identity specific to the governing class, as McConica makes clear.

> Plainly, many [gentlemen-commoners] made their way into the professions, including the traditional callings of university-trained men: the church, medicine, and law. [But] it is clear too, if only from the number admitted who did not matriculate, that other motives were at least equally important. . . . Some came to find patronage connections, some to acquire the elementary skills of acceptable literacy; others benefited from the provision (statutory or extra-statutory) for studies in the rhetorical arts or humanities. Even scholastic exercises contributed to the fundamental skills needed for advancement in society, the disputation by its training in logic and debate, and the declamation as a set piece designed to show rhetorical and literary proficiency. The declamation may indeed have been the chief receptacle for humanist learning, so closely tied to the rhetorical arts.[58]

We may discern a hint of this sort of ambitious study in a complaint of Matthew Parker to William Cecil in 1565 regarding protestant disputation at St. John's College, Cambridge: "If your honour will hear their challenges ye shall hear such cumbrous trifles and brabbles that ye shall be weary. . . . Scholars' controversies be now many and troublous; and their delight is to come before men of authority to show their wits."[59] Even religious instruction was steeped in the tones of courtly suit.

Education at the Inns of Court, it should be said, offered the same diverse fruits—professional, practical, and stylistic. "The increasing responsibilities placed on J.P.s and the extraordinary growth of litigation were the two principal factors behind the invasion of the Inns of Court by the nobility and gentry. Once the habit was formed, however, attendance at an Inn began to acquire a social *cachet* of its own and the powerful inducement of social snobbery lent weight to the other, more practical considerations."[60] The Inns of Court attracted the ambitious—the would-be snobs, in effect—as well as the established elite, once membership came to be seen as a sign of rank.

"When it was customary for 'gentlemen of the best quality' to join the inns, . . . gentlemen of somewhat lesser breed and those who wished to pass as gentlemen naturally followed suit."[61] Then too, of course, nonprofessional residence was common (and became more common during the early seventeenth century): "The serious law students; the sons of the gentry, sent with the hope that they would pick up sufficient legal expertise to free them from servile dependence on their inferiors and fit them for the service of the commonwealth; the place-hunters, fortune-seekers and social climbers— all mingled together at the schools of dancing, fencing and music scattered around the inns, to acquire the non-academic accomplishments which befitted the role of the gentleman."[62] Finally (and here the Inns differed from the universities), "their geographical location made them ideally suited to introduce young men to the exciting world of London, already the mecca of ambition and talent, the kingdom's administrative, commercial, cultural and political hub. The inns provided convenient communal accommodation midway between City and Court. For most young gentlemen who wished to spend some time in London, an inn of court was the logical place to stay."[63] In other words, the Inns were also inns, though quite exclusive ones. (The Inns' historian, Wilfrid Prest, estimates that "no more than a quarter of the members admitted to the inns [during the period 1590–1640] could have come from non-gentry or non-peerage families . . . [and] even this estimate is almost certainly overcautious."[64]) At the Inns, then, even more than at the universities, nominally nondirected study would very often have masked a specific round of training in the skills and styles of aristocratic life, and such activities must be counted as a principal ideological matrix for the mentality of the Elizabethan ruling elite.

We may close this survey of the social and educational demographic patterns of the English Renaissance elite with Stone's summary statement that "between 1570 and 1650 secondary and university education had been running wild, resulting in a free-for-all competitive struggle uncontrolled by the existing elite, which produced a surplus of qualified men for available elite jobs."[65] This struggle derived not only from "the arguments of the sixteenth-century humanists and educators, Colet, Elyot, Mulcaster and others," but from "the new social ideals set out by Castiglione."[66] Intellectual, social, political, and stylistic gestures clashed in the arena of competition for status. The ruling elite, its numbers swollen not only by those assuming the new positions at court but by the much larger number of those who came to share its discourse in hopes of sharing its privileges, adopted a new notion of its characteristic appearance. In this context the codifications of Elizabethan courtesy literature came to perform several complexly related functions, to which we now turn.

The pressure from below of so many able young men attempting to enter the ruling elite, to "serve the state" and to reap the fruits of such service, caused the established aristocracy much anxiety. What the humanist youth saw as public service (and opportunity), the established courtier saw as contamination and competition. The first employment of courtesy literature was the repression of such mobility. This had been its original function: the collective depiction of the ideal courtier in Castiglione's *Book of the Courtier* was, we are told, designed programmatically "to disgrace therfore many untowardly Asseheades, that through malapartnesse thinke to purchase them the name of a good Courtier." ("Per reprimere adunque molti sciocchi, i quali per esser prosuntuosi ed inetti si credonò acquistar nome di bon cortegiano.")[67] This social problem, and the ideal's curative function, were recognized even before the book was printed, as Bandello's lament reveals: "It seems to me that a multitude apply themselves to the art of courtliness [*cortegiania*], but very few learn its proper exercise. In the courts of various princes, here in Italy as elsewhere, many are found who profess to be courtiers; but if you examine them diligently, you find that they hardly know the meaning of the word. One certainly hopes that our signor Count Baldassare Castiglione will expose the error of these slight courtiers, by having his *Cortegiano* printed."[68] This understanding obtained in England too, as the earl of Oxford's preface to Bartholomew Clerke's 1571 translation of Castiglione into Latin suggests. Oxford lauds Castiglione's "delineations in the case of those persons who cannot be Courtiers, when he alludes to some notable defect, or to some ridiculous character, or to some deformity of appearance."[69] Necessarily, of course, the complementary effect of these proscriptions was to teach the members of an endangered aristocracy how to reascribe to themselves the self-evident ascriptive status their forebears had enjoyed, by the personal affirmation of the signs that disgraced the assheads.[70] These gestures were to structure the disturbing social convection that had begun to typify life at the margins of power in sixteenth-century England.

However, the self-undercutting capacities of this reascriptive rhetoric were not sufficiently understood. The circulation of the texts would have had to have been restricted for the recuperation to be effective. For all too many of the assheads could read, and in fact they soon learned to use the elitist texts for their own purposes. A rudimentary awareness of this danger can be discerned in I. Kepers's preface to "the curteous and beneuolent Reader," which accompanies his translation of Count Annibale Romei's *The Courtiers Academie* (1598). Kepers, like many courtly writers, feared "deprauation" by "malignant eies."

> Translation therfore in generall . . . hath bin thought altogether a thing, not only vnnecessary, but further preiudicial . . . knowledge being an ornament, most befitting those noble or honorable, who command, ignorance agreeing best with the vulgar sort, who be subiect and obey: it is therefore requisit (say they) that high wisedome, and excellent workes, shuld be concealed from common sight, lest they through equall experience, and knowledge in things (according to the ordinary conditions thereof) puffed up, shake off likewise that humility of spirit, which shuld comprehend them vnder the obedience of laws and magistrates.[71]

But Kepers justifies his translation by saying that realms have often been reduced from chaos to order by the translation of Plato, Aristotle, and Plutarch: "people well instructed, know best how sweet a thing it is to liue vnder gouernment" (sig. A3v). What Kepers presents as an argument from sweetness, John Ferne derives from a generous severity, discounting the affront to those below:

> Vnto all mechanicall artisans, and churles broode, this worke might come without any acceptation, bycause she pictureth out their base and servile conditions, much inferior to the shining and franke estate of gentlenesse, vnto whose malignant toongs, I disdaine any other reply, then those texts and reasons set downe in this present booke, when any such thing falleth into discussion. And heerein I would haue them all vnderstand, how gently I haue delt with them, in that I haue not opened vnto our Gentry and Nobles, the one halfe of those seuere lawes and constitutions, both prouinciall and imperiall, iustly layd vpon that base and obscure state of the vngentle, bycause I would not haue them altogether troden vnder foote, in this our common wealth, since that by the customes of our nation, and the lenitie of our soueraigns, they are suffered to enioy a greater freedome of life, then in any other nation.[72]

Kepers and Ferne share the mission of maintaining hierarchy and believe their books will repress the unworthily ambitious; the harshness of Ferne underlies Kepers's "sweetness." However, this dream was not to be. Instead, a notion theorized by Foucault came into play. "Rules are empty in themselves, violent and unfinalized; they are impersonal and can be bent to any purpose. The successes of history belong to those who are capable of seizing these rules, to replace those who had used them, to disguise themselves so as to pervert them, invert their meaning, and redirect them against those who had initially imposed them; controlling this complex mechanism, they will make it function so as to overcome the rulers through their own rules."[73] The counter-Renaissance suspicions of Kepers's elite critics proved more prophetic than his own humanist confidence. Courtesy literature seems effectively to have discouraged social humility and aroused ambition; like Wilson's *Arte*, these texts did not persuade those below of the sweetness of "living under."[74]

Yet we must not misconceive these ambitious young men. The scholar's predilection is usually to fasten analysis on the successful, the noteworthy, or the brilliant, or on the practices of high-serious activities such as Poetry.[75] But if we are to get at the typical character of the rhetorical life at the Renaissance court, we must work with a more elastic notion that includes the achievement of just such aspects of the good life as the courtly butterfly cherished: comfort, prestige, entertainment, a sense of personal superiority. Butterflies have for too long been merely sneered at, as caterpillars; we need instead a notion of the *ordinary courtier*. The motor of life at court was the pursuit of power and privilege, and we must be sensitive to the serious (not high-serious) privileges of this order. For these were goals shared by famous, infamous, and trivial courtiers alike, all of whom sought them by means of the same humanist rhetorical postures. Even setting aside the fact that much of our "great" literature was probably written quite consciously for such readers (think of the young Donne at the theater),[76] we should reconsider these lives for what they tell us about the dialectical tensions of rhetoric. Such rhetoric both *maintained* and *altered* the status quo; it was at once conservative and disruptive. Life at the margins of power and privilege gave full scope to these various modes of rhetorical behavior, and so constitutes an unusually rich object for the study of shifting notions of social being.

The humanist student had all too often been promised and denied not only the chance to serve at a high level of government, but also the expected material reward for his services. Enticing analogies between the modern courtier and Roman senators or prince-tutors like Aristotle bore little resemblance to the careers of men modestly endowed in intellect and patronage. Even so exceptional a young servant as Sidney was denied the chance to exercise his will to powerful service (and, as the biographies of Greville and Osborne reveal, it was this will that was seen to typify his public identity).[77] Some who encountered such obstruction moved elsewhere, toward the manufacture of ideology for the established, or the would-be, or for the disestablished, whose failure could be mystified as a progression away from the grubbing for temporal power and toward some transcendental ideal of pastoral or Neoplatonic society. And yet another group, traditionally regarded as failed or trivial, must also be reconstrued, for its chosen task was to provide a courtly environment pleasing to those in power and comfortable to themselves. This group includes the Osrics and Guildensterns (to say nothing of Goneril's Oswald), with whom we enter the realm of another sort of service. They were products of the same educational system and were driven by similar ambitions for a life of influence and respect at the courts of princes, but they lacked the moral seriousness or individual impact that has traditionally made such figures seem worthy of study at this distance. Satiric depictions can blind us to the probability that most young Elizabethan hopefuls were as much like these figures as like Sidney or Castiglione (whose harried letters home from court contained endless requests for money and clothing).[78] We now habitually find some of these figures admirable and others not so, but we must nevertheless learn to read the actions of all of them if we are to comprehend the networks of stress and opportunity that governed their lives, and the powers and weaknesses imposed upon them by their tools of "the trade and maner of courtiers" (*la forma di cortegiania*) (pp. 15/79).

These tools can, by another division, be seen to perform two kinds of functions: the securing of interests and the relieving of strain.[79] The former includes the established courtier's goals of repressing mobility and reascribing absolute status; it also embraces the mobile man's rewriting of the rules to power his own project. But severe strains accompanied the gradual readjustment of his goals—from giving direct advice to princes to presenting fictive allusion, and finally perhaps to providing mere entertainment (not to mention the worst case, total failure). A final central employment of the tropes of courtesy was to relieve these strains, by postponing, accounting for, or mystifying the various levels of personal failure. This unevenly rewritten awareness produced weird phenomenological mixtures of arrogance and paranoia, each factor deriving from a desperate need for coherence, between the normative humanist expectations of the university and the murky and resistant realities of court life as lived. Jonas Barish describes the basis for integrating these systems in his examination of La Rochefoucauld, where he suggests (in paraphrase) that "we . . . come to form our own best audience. . . . Our efforts to hoodwink the rest of the world amount to a prolonged essay in self-deception. . . . Life [is] a delusion imposed on the actor by himself, a desperate tactic by which he tries to foist a certain sense of himself onto himself, with whom he is far more likely to succeed than with others who lack his reasons for cooperating, and who are engrossed in similar designs on their own selves."[80] The texts we shall analyze can be seen as offering not only strategic codifications for social conflicts but also scripts for such dramas as these, modes of construing a life of strain so as not only to gain public rewards but to render failure tolerable.

A brief examination of Gabriel Harvey's case will reveal all of these interests and strains in one example. Harvey exhibits in sharp relief the various dialectics between weakness and repair, motive and means, ambition and alienation, that characterize the arena in which social ambition was worked out. Harvey's case also conveys vividly both courtly anxiety (in his case nearly legendary) and its self-defensive recasting. J. R. Woodhouse sees the "uncertainty of privilege and status" as a "tragic threat" surrounding the greatest figures and works of the Italian Renaissance. (He means here those of the courtly life.)[81] Although one hesitates to use the label "tragic," lives like Harvey's do seem deeply pathetic, especially in the disproportionate, obsessive, yet fruitless deployment of courtly postures. Neither Harvey nor many others possessed the confidence of Bacon's awareness that "if behaviour and outward carriage be intended too much, it may pass into a deformed and spurious affectation[,] . . . a great thief of more serious meditation."[82] On the other hand, even such a cold-hearted observer as Guicciardini allowed in the end that substantial power could be derived from such pursuits.

> When I was young, I used to scoff at knowing how to play, dance, and sing, and at other such frivolities. I even made light of good penmanship, knowing how to ride, to dress well, and all those things that seem more decorative than substantial in a man. But, later, I wished I had not done so. For although it is not wise to spend too much time cultivating the young toward the perfection of these arts, I have nevertheless seen from experience that these ornaments and accomplishments lend dignity and reputation even to men of good rank. . . . Moreover, skill in this sort of entertainment

opens the way to the favor of princes, and sometimes becomes the beginning or the reason for great profit and high honors.[83]

The difficulty was to balance these elements properly; any reader of Harvey knows his problems with this task. He expended enormous effort in courteous artfulness, reflexive and critical alike, and was relentlessly disappointed. His loyal friend Spenser strove to aid him in his pain, literally rewriting the failures as pastoral alienation above the fray.

> Haruey, the happy aboue happiest men,
> I read; that, sitting like a looker-on
> Of this worldes stage, doest note, with critique pen,
> The sharpe dislikes of each condition;
> And, as one carelesse of suspition,
> Ne fawnest for the fauour of the great,
> Ne fearest foolish reprehension
> Of faulty men, which daunger to thee threat:
> But freely doest of what thee list entreat,
> Like a great lord of peerelesse liberty;
> Lifting the good up to high Honours seat,
> And the euill damning euermore to dy;
> For Life, and Death, is in thy doomefull writing!
> So thy renowme liues euer by endighting.[84]

Harvey did of course have the obligatory literary ambitions of the young humanist, and indeed he lives for us chiefly on such grounds (thanks to Spenser, not to his own "doomefull writing"). But he did not relish this particular revision of his fate, fearing above all the role of wallflower, "vncovth vnkiste." Like Elyot, he rejected the role that Spenser nominally welcomed.[85] Instead he exhibits the deformations of humanist ambition, by mocking it in others and parading it in himself.

"What Newes al this while at Cambridge?" he (typically) asks himself, and he answers with a veritable fugue on the social changes that Sir Thomas Wyatt called "newfangleness."

> All [are]inquisitiue after Newes [as is Harvey himself, in view of his own question], newe Bookes, new Fashions, newe Lawes, new Officers, and some after Newe Elementes, and some after newe Heauens, and Helles to. Turkishe affaires familiarly knowen: Castels buried in the Ayre: muche adoe, and little helpe: Iacke would fain be a Gentlemanne: in no age so little so much made of, euery one highly in his owne fauour, thinking no mannes penny, so good silver as his own: Something made of Nothing, in spite of Nature: Numbers made of Ciphars, in spite of Arte ... as of olde

Bookes, so of auntient Vertue, Honestie, Fidelitie, Equitie, newe Abridge-
mentes: euery day freshe span newe Opinions: Heresie in Diuinitie, in Phi-
losophie, in Humanitie, in Manners, grounded much Vpon heresay: Doc-
tors contemned: the Text knowen of moste, vnderstood of fewe: magnified
of all, practised of none: the Diuell not so hated, as the Pope: many Inuec-
tiues, small amendment: Skill they say controlled of Will: and Goodnesse
mastered of Goods ... Olde men and Counsailours amongst Children:
Children amongst Counsailours, and olde men: Not a few dubble sacred
Tani, and chaungeable Camelions: ouer manye Claw-backes and Picke-
thankes: Reedes shaken of euerie Wind: Iackes of bothe sides: Aspen
leaues: painted Sheathes, and Sepulchres: Asses in Lions skins: Dungle-
cockes: slipperye Eles: Dormise: I blush to thinke of some, that weene
themselues as fledge as the reste, being God wot, as kallowe as the rest:
euery yonker to speake of as politique, and as great a Commonwealths
man as Bishoppe *Gardner*. ... And wil you needes haue my Testimoniall of
your olde Controllers new behauior? A busy and dizy heade, a brazen forehead: a ledden braine: a woodden wit: a copper face; a stony breast: a
factious and eluish heart: a founder of nouelties: a confounder of his owne,
and his friends good gifts: a morning bookeworm, an afternoone malt-
worm: a right Iuggler, as ful of his sleights, wyles, fetches, casts of Legerde-
maine, toyes to mocke Apes withal, odde shiftes, and knauish practizes, as
his skin can holde.[86]

This spasm of envious invective delineates the have-not's view of the
world. Dominated by ambition and repression, contorted by the techniques of reascription, this perspective is conveyed in the unmistakable tones of arrogant self-reassurance so typical of Harvey. His own
pirouetting implicates him helplessly in his own criticism, of course;
he is as ambitious and pushy as the rest. In this light his satiric acidity
indicates sheer envy, the scab of injured merit.

Lest this be thought to be merely the hothouse world of university
life, Harvey's literal subject, it should be noted that the university was
the chief nursery of the court, as humanism in another key dreamed it
should be. As we have seen, its gentry populace was continually
wooed by the government, along with the rest of their rank: "Elizabeth and her ministers were sensitive to every nuance of public feeling, every tremor of discontent, within the limited range of the politically active classes," according to MacCaffrey.[87] Williams shows that
the universities in particular were rhetorical arenas with a courtly
audience: Elizabeth's government "encouraged the concentration of
power within the hands of oligarchies in each university—as it did
also in the towns—since a small group of senior men was more likely
to respond favourably to pressure than were assemblies of young

dons."[88] Pressure on these men, and patronage of many of those nominally under their control, "was continually exercised throughout the reign."[89] Joan Simon shows how this pressure was perceived: "In 1579 the Cambridge vice-chancellor and heads registered a strong protest with their chancellor [Burghley] at the crown's interference whereby 'the rewards of merit and studiousness are withheld, scholars being induced to look for preferment to the favour of courtiers rather than to their true deserts at the hands of the university.'"[90] The court was the focus of power for both students and faculty and functioned as the principal audience for many of their deeds. Harvey was correct, if a bit extreme, in perceiving the court as the dreamland of the university, the telos to which all action there was dedicated, however falsely or vainly. And his moralistic tone, such as it is, is not unique to him. Ascham thought the fall from proper virtue sufficiently advanced by 1563 or so to say: "Tyme was, whan I dyd reioyce to see the court, in manye respects lyke to the vniversitie: and I am now evyn as sorye, to hear say, yt the Vniversities be ouer lyke to the court."[91] This comment suggests that the two zones were equally riddled by the pressures of convection.

The have-not's obsessive scornfulness, what we might call sour grapes, is only one of many tactics open to the ambitious novice and his established or displaced superior. Many other ways of construing and manipulating the shifting currents of the cultural center—ingratiation, insult, dismissal, anesthesia, and so forth—will be examined in due course. But what should be stressed at this point is that many of these tactics, or many of their uses, were finally self-defeating, since they were aimed at making possible one social action (of the speaker) while refrigerating the frame against further convection by others. The use of artful reascriptive tools against the old order reveals that order's vulnerability to attack; restorative maneuvers that assault the mobile or reground the ascriptive frame reveal the frame's basis in human art.[92] Nonetheless, work is a great healer for one and all, and the available tropes were used by all sides, with predictably erosive effects. The aim of this book is to consider the workings of these tactical weapons, which brought about, as technological advance often does, a profound rewriting of the articles of battle.

Having surveyed the whirl of courtly self-assertion, we should now review the set of tools for ordering it (though they might as easily be seen as devices for maintaining its revolutions at speed). Again Harvey is a principal source of information. "Schollars in ower age," he says, are "rather active then contemplative philosophers . . . and of all thinges in the worlde [detest] that spitefull malicious proverbe, of greatist Clarkes, and not wisest men."[93]

> And nowe of late forsoothe to helpe countenaunce owte the matter they have gotten Philbertes Philosopher of the Courte, the Italian Archebys-shoppies brave Galatro [*Galateo*], Castiglioes fine Cortegiano, Bengalas-soes Civil Instructions to his Nephewe Seignor Princisca Ganzar: Guat-zoes newe Discourses of curteous behaviour, Jouios and Rassellis Emblemes in Italian, Paradines in Frenche, Plutarche in Frenche, Frontines Stratagemes, Polyenes Stratagemes, Polonica, Apodemica, Guigiandine [Guicciardini], Philipp de Comines, and I knowe not how many owtland-ishe braveryes besides of the same stampe. . . . You can not stepp into a schollars studye but (ten to on) you shall litely finde open ether Bodin de Republica or Le Royes Exposition uppon Aristotles Politiques or sum other like Frenche or Italian Politique Discourses.[94]

And in the midst of the catalog of newfangledness quoted earlier he notes: "*Matchiauell* a great man: *Castilio* of no small reputation: *Petrarch*, and *Boccace* in euery mans mouth: *Galateo* and *Guazzo* neuer so happy: ouer many acquainted with *Vnico Aretino*: The French and Italian when so highly regarded of Schollers? The Latine and Greeke, when so lightly?"[95] Mark H. Curtis provides confirmation of this unofficial curriculum, in a survey of the private libraries of Elizabethan university students who died while in residence.[96] His survey corroborates Harvey's lists and adds Elyot, Ascham, and Camden, among others, as being commonly read.

It is obvious that these readings are meant as "equipment for living" the life of a courtly mover, or at least that they register the desire for such a life. Before we turn to a detailed consideration of just how they were read and applied, it is useful to ponder just what sort of corpus they constituted. Thomas Greene has pointed out that such books were a genre unto themselves; he calls it the *institute*,[97] a treatise governing the formation or transformation of an individual or social construct (such as the state or family). Nor is the corpus only generically homogeneous. Javitch has appropriately drawn the conclusion that despite their varied historical and intellectual points of origin, these texts were, for English readers, effectively contemporary.[98] Although the positions articulated by the authors and their interlocutors varied considerably, Harvey's and Curtis's lists make it clear that the books were taken from the same shelf, and were seen as composing a unified and coherent curriculum, by their first English readers. (Evidence from edition counts corroborates this effectively Elizabethan provenance.[99])

I propose to homogenize the conceptual materials of courteous practice one step further, by arguing that most of the major texts were *formally* pliant to incremental use in social debate and self-presentation. We must emphasize text rather than author, as Javitch notes, and reception rather than promulgation. But further, I believe, the arguments made in these texts were actively (not contemplatively) read, repeated, and enacted in a thoroughly discontinuous way that makes contradictions within or between individual texts insignificant, if not irrelevant. Bourdieu's discussion of what he calls the "synoptic illusion" offers analogies.

> Just as genealogy substitutes a space of unequivocal, homogeneous relationships, established once and for all, for a spatially and temporally discontinuous set of islands of kinship, ranked and organized to suit the needs of the moment and brought into practical existence gradually and intermittently, and just as a map replaces the discontinuous, patchy space of practical paths by the homogeneous continuous space of geometry, so a calendar substitutes a linear, homogeneous continuous time for practical time, which is made up of incommensurable islands of duration, each with its own rhythm, the time that flies by or drags, depending on what one is *doing*, i.e., on the *functions* conferred on it by the activity in progress.[100]

I conceive Renaissance courtesy theory similarly, as a corpus of strategic gestures that is coherent as practiced even though discontinuous among its textualizations (and sometimes contemplatively continuous within them). Dekker's parodic courtesy book, *The Guls Horn-Booke*, describes the would-be courtier as "he that talkes all *Adage* and *Apothegme*": this seems to me fairly literally credible, given Burke's observation that "the rhetorical striving for advantage is usually conducted in a very piecemeal way, with refutations of a purely opportunistic and catch-as-catch-can sort."[101] We must expect frequent citations out of context, for one might have to perform one moment as a repressive superior and the next as a clandestine arriviste. The operation will always have the force of the analytic utensil specified by Burke as the proverb. Quite to the point here is Burke's demonstration of the way in which opposed proverbs (e.g., "out of sight, out of mind" and "absence makes the heart grow fonder") are tools for dealing with different problems, not contradictory halves of a contemplative whole.[102]

Whatever organic program may have governed the composition of a courtesy text, its use often involved atomization by a reader who needed tools for many different purposes. As Bodin astringently observed, "it is one thing to reason of degrees and dignities in the assemblie of wise men; and another thing to doe it in the presence of the vulgar sort, and scumme of the people."[103] The field of textual data being studied here contains many contradictions, both within and between texts, but they are irrelevant to the *uses* of the theory, actions addressed to various audiences or goals. Various claims were made, for instance, as to the function of virtue in determining rank; established and mobile Elizabethans alike would deploy arguments on either side as need arose, without feeling either devious or conspiratorial—indeed, without sensing any contradiction at all. The textual corollary of this fact is that the enabling corpus, internally dissonant in contemplative terms, is coherent in practice *in service of this flexibility*. Applications of the devices will vary in the widest way imaginable, but the instrumentalities remain a coherent set.

The texts formally invite such particulate consumption. Most obviously, the numerous dialogues show interlocutors doing with the text's agenda just what the reader will do with it; just as Fregoso, say, might quote Aristotle incrementally, for different purposes on different occasions, so may the reader quote Castiglione, ad hoc. The dialogue form regularly exhibits this segmentation, from Plato onward, and in Castiglione,[104] Jovius's *Worthy Tract*,[105] Guazzo's *Civile Conversation*,[106] Ferne's *Blazon of Gentrie*, Romei's *Courtiers Academie*, and of course the *Parnassus Plays*.[107] Another set of relevant writers used an even more incremental format, the epigrammatic series. Guicciardini's *Ricordi* are explicitly antiprogrammatic,[108] as well as epigrammatic. Raleigh's *Maxims of State* are also discontinuous and are designed to be flexible; he calls them "mysteries" and "sophisms."[109] Bacon's *Essays*, many of which deal with courtesy, form another quasi-epigrammatic set.[110] They constitute an essential text, having been reprinted more often than any other secular work of the Renaissance.[111] Still other courtesy texts offer a limiting example of fragmentation, being perforated wholes primed for disassembly. Some present full-blown arguments for positions taken incrementally in dialogues, such as Elyot's *Book named the Governor*,[112] the anonymous *Institucion of a Gentleman*,[113] della Casa's *Galateo*[114] (in fact a dramatic monologue), Gilbert's *Queene Elizabethes Achademy*,[115] and Ascham's *Scholemaster*.[116] A related option is offered by Puttenham's *Arte of English Poesie*;[117] his courtesy injunctions purport to be merely by-products, and he also exploits the inorganic discontinuity of his intellectual program (for reasons to be noted later). What Bacon says about apothegms may be said of all the various incremental units of these courtesy texts: "They serve not for pleasure only and ornament, but also for action and business; being, as one called them, *mucrones verborum*,—speeches with a point or edge, whereby knots in business are pierced and severed. And as former occasions are continually recurring, that which served once will often serve again, either produced as a man's own or cited as of ancient authority."[118] The texts were adapted for the needs of the moment: for game, for courtly self-display, and for political interaction—purposes that frequently overlap. They are blades or goads for the cut and thrust, or the prodding, of the personal politics of courtly life. And they have epideictic force to register either the courtier's creativity and penetration or his education.

The requisition of these tools from the storehouse of courtesy writings requires a mode of reading specific to the applied science of courtly activity; Thomas Blundeville makes this mode of review explicit in his *True Order and Methode of Wryting and Reading Hystories*:

> In our reading, we must not onely consider of them, but also note them apart by themselues in such order, as we may easily finde them, when soeuer we shall have neede to vse them. And the order of such examples, would not be altogither according to the names of the persons, from whence they are taken, which order some writers do commonlye vse in the tables of theyr bookes, but rather according to the matters & purposes whereto they serue . . . which [common] places are to be founde, ordered, and disposed, not before wee begin to reade, but whylest wee continue in reading. . . . And by considering vnder what title euery example is to be placed (for the ready finding thereof) wee shall greatlye helpe our memorie.[119]

The construction of such "tables" entails treating one's reading as raw material—matter and tools to build with according to need.

In effect, then, all of these texts function as commodities, in two ways. First, each offers a specimen of its author's worth, epideictically; many criteria are at work here besides interior intellectual ones. Second, each offers itemized concepts that may be traded anew by its consumer. For, as we shall see, the Renaissance conversation in which such coin was spent was often organized by the canons of the *querelle*, wherein the conduct of argument was *primarily* epideictic and formal, rather than substantive. In such a case ideas as quotable segments of texts may be analyzed in terms of exchange value rather than use value. Emilia Pia makes it clear that sheer philosophy is not welcome at Urbino evenings (Castiglione, pp. 200/358), privileging the incremental value of clear and witty "good points" over the complex extended structures of developed argument (which, when allowed to go on at all, is seldom allowed a firm resolution). Shooting from the hip is the order of the evening, and "mots" rather than argument are preferred. This reemphasizes from another direction the idea of weaponry, and so points to the status of these texts as enchiridions (from the Greek *encheiridion*, a small hand-held object— hence *manuals*, or, equally, *daggers*). Jovius's *Worthy Tract* is explicitly introduced as an enchiridion;[120] Guicciardini's ultrapragmatic family *Ricordi*, unpublished during the Renaissance, have the status of a concealed weapon; and W. H. Woodward reports that Sir Philip Sidney "carried [Castiglione's *Courtier*] ever in his pocket when he went abroad."[121] As both analyses and weapons, these texts both depict and enact the exercise of power and privilege in a world dominated by the social rhetoric of courtesy.

One other context of these texts suggests that the corpus articulates the hidden. As national centers began to grasp to themselves the determination and licensing of actions of all sorts, the conceptual screens of bureaucracy fell between ordinary people and the practices of their everyday lives. The denizens of the court quickly discovered the lucrative role of intercessor, of translator, of priest to these secular mysteries. Access to the sources of power involved procedures that became stylized rites to the outsider; he would see that they were conspicuously (if opaquely) ordered and would seek such a guide or interpreter. The rites internal to the structure might be church Latin, legal code, or secretary hand; many kinds of interpretive barriers arose to block the new communicational demands. If we imagine Renaissance courts to be less logically organized than our own governments (probably a fantasy); if we realize that the servants of the court (not yet modern bureaucratic officials) worked in rapidly varying capacities from one day to another;[122] and if we see the various zones of power as actively reflecting the personalities and preferences of their immediate masters, then the court becomes ever more mysterious, interpretation ever more necessary. Richard Lanham has pointed out the poetic character of bureaucratic prose in our own day.[123] Bureaucrats during the Renaissance likewise delighted in songs of obscurity that brought fees for the penetrating talents of a cryptologist.[124] The texts we are to examine were the operations manuals for many of these figures, "inside dope" for threading through the mazes of power.

In a famous passage in *A Rhetoric of Motives*, Kenneth Burke elaborates the mode of interpretation proper to literature viewed as equipment for living. He argues by analogy from the fourfold scriptural hermeneutic of Aquinas, in which anagogical meaning signifies "what relates to eternal glory."

> Since we are looking for elements of "social mystery" rather than of "celestial" mystery, hence our term, "socioanagogic." The new equivalent of "moral" or "tropological" criticism would probably be found in a concern with the poem as a ritual that does things for the writer and reader: reforming, stabilizing, heartening, purifying, socializing, and the like. Any sense in which one order is interpreted as the sign of another would probably be the modern equivalent of the "allegorical." . . . Allegorical and moral senses lead into the socioanagogic insofar as the emphasis is placed upon the hierarchic mystery (the principle of secular divinity, with its range of embarrassment, courtship, modified insult, standoffishness . . . its scenic embodiment in the worldly equivalent of temples, ritual vestments, rare charismatic vessels and the like). In brief, the socioanagogic sense notes how the things of books and of the book of Nature "signify what relates to worldly glory."[125]

In succeeding chapters I attempt to apply this secular criticism to the universe of courtesy literature. Burke's socioanagogic hermeneutic at its simplest reconstructs a mode of perception familiar to all denizens of the Elizabethan court, an everyday way of taking for granted the radiations of self-evident structures of rank and merit. In the next chapter I present an extended review of the Elizabethan version of this semiotics of worldly glory and thus provide the interpretive frames for this and more complex readings of the tropes inventoried in the chapters that follow.

2. Rhetorical Semiotics at Court

We have seen that the advent of widespread social mobility stimulated the established members of the aristocracy to conduct, as if for the first time, a rhetorical defense of their exclusive right to power and privilege. They mustered a complex array of ideological maneuvers, many of which were soon co-opted by the mobile. Thus most weapons were soon used for most of the different tactical purposes of this battle zone, whether for mobility or repression, by established or would-be aristocrats against equal, superior or inferior, whether competitor or ally. Because of this confusing variety, the tools of courtesy are conveniently anatomized by function rather than by user or purpose. Consequently, the following three categories of tropes will be examined: tropes that illustrate the elite's entitlement by class, tropes of promotion and compliment, and tropes of combat and rivalry. Before turning to these divisions, however, we must consider the semiotic operations of the rhetorical arena where the tropes were deployed, for their production and interpretation were subject to systemic determinations. Emphasis will be placed upon the symbolic operations of manner; the asymmetrical power relations between audience and performer (shaped both by the audience's government of epistemology and morals, and by the techniques of audience management); and the reification and sale of personal image.

For established and mobile Elizabethans alike, public life at court was governed by a rhetorical imperative of performance (*esse sequitur operare*: identity derived from behavior).[1] Elite status no longer rested upon the absolute, given base of birth, the received ontology of social being; instead it had increasingly become a matter of doing, and so of *showing*. Those who would maintain their privileged position now had to constitute their own fundamental difference from their ambitious inferiors, in their own minds as well as in those of their rivals, while stifling if possible not only the latter's accomplishments but even their dreams. On the other side, those who would rise aimed to make themselves indistinguishable from their future peers, if possible by persuading those peers themselves. Normative criteria for elite identity, whether used for inclusion or exclusion, mobility or repression, provide us with the elite's nominal view of itself. The question then is, how were the criteria applied?

The principal strategy of self-manifestation in such a frame is the ostentatious practice of symbolic behavior taken to typify aristocratic being. The gentleman is presumed to act in certain ways; the limiting case would have it that only a gentleman *can* act in those ways. But the symbolic referent here is ascriptive identity, an identity that by definition cannot be achieved by human effort. As a result there arose a basic governing principle of the display of *effortlessness*, Castiglione's *sprezzatura*, designed to imply the natural or given status of one's social identity and to deny any earned character, any labor or arrival from a social elsewhere. In this trope we may discern, adapting certain suggestions of the *Tel Quel* group, the rise to theoretical consciousness of the reification of the subject, insofar as such behavior involved "the effacement of the traces of production on the [subject]."[2] The "natural" self is here recognized, perhaps for the first time, as a product, and soon with the aid of courtesy books, becomes a commodity. This pose implies that the rhetorical manifestation of typical aristocratic virtues was not a demonstration of desert, for this would entail the status being contingent rather than absolute. The desired sense was that a noble or gentle man would of course possess and manifest such virtues, but that they followed from and were natural functions of his social position—not that if he were to possess and manifest them, he would then so belong. (By the same token, membership in inferior classes was also absolute, hence inescapable—the obverse of noncontingent elevation.) This means that useful effort *can* be expended, if it is hidden; the rhetorical radiations of identity will then be seen as natural and absolute. Symbolic manifestations do not prove, but identify or mark. Thomas Middleton's satiric depiction of Sir Bounteous Progress reveals this structure of perception clearly: "There's a kind of grace belongs to't [aristocratic hospitality], a kind of art which naturally slips from me, I know not on't, I promise you, 'tis gone before I'm aware on't."[3] (The satire lies, of course, in having the ambitious Sir Bounteous *proclaim* such a self-image—to a visiting nobleman's footman!) Theoretically speaking, then, if rank cannot be grasped voluntarily, its fundamental manifestations will be seen as unchosen, simply self-expressive, not aimed to transmit information or to persuade a witness: in short, as not rhetorical.

However, the established aristocrat cannot allow rank to depend on such status. Meritocratic arguments for social elevation tend to ground such status in substantive powers such as martial force or organizational ability. Such arguments legitimate social mobility by positing a prior hierarchy of merit; the meritorious inferior can then claim the right to relocate. Aristocratic ideology had to deal with this disruptive fact; he who would occupy exclusively the position of established aristocrat must de-emphasize not only his own efforts at self-manifestation but the substantive efforts of those below. One solution was to emphasize *manner* rather than matter: others may be found who can do the things a gentleman does, but they cannot do them *properly*. The difference in kind remains visible, but it becomes one of style rather than substance. I. M., the author of *A Health to the Gentlemanly Profession of Serving-Men* (1598), specifies in just these terms the incapacity of the base to perform the duties of the gentleman-follower:

> Would they [employers in the good old days], thinke you, haue been contented, to haue entertayned a man that could onely haue caried a Dysh, giuen a Trencher, or caried a Rapier after them? No, they did not onely require this to be done in decent and comely maner, which none, no not one of them [lower-class servants] which is obiected [claimed to be], fitte enough for this profession, can do as is required, but much more he must ouer and besides the qualities before in him required, be able to giue entertaynement to a stranger in decent and comely maner, delyuer a Message discreetely and wisely to a Potentate, Maiestrate, or meaner person, to talke and discourse with his Maister vpon forraine or domesticall affayres, nay much more then I can expresse.[4]

This emphasis makes substantial parity irrelevant to the ontological social categories. Like the gentle servant, the base servant *can* deal with dish, trencher, and rapier, but not in the proper style. The modifiers label the essentials: decent, comely, discreetly, wisely. The substantial resemblance becomes mere externality, leaving the absolute difference alive and well in the zone of style. What counts is the new usurping servant's lack of style. The core of the job resides in the nuances: subtleties of delivery, audience discriminations, and the like. The passage does suggest the substantive capacity to talk knowingly of public affairs, which might well imply university training, but the bulk of the absolutist distinctions are projected in terms of style.

This strategy works through the inferential movement from stylistic action to ontological conclusion. And if this step is usually a leap, if the basis of the conclusion remains obscure or partial, so much the better. For the kind of aristocratic difference thus established cannot be factually disconfirmed. Sartre's account in *Anti-Semite and Jew* of the prejudicial definition of personal identity offers a paradigm for this vague superiority. Sartre explains how the dominant elite creates its own identity, along with that of its subject class, by deriving the former from the latter. For the anti-Semite, "the Jew contaminates all that he touches with an I-know-not-what execrable quality . . . 'Jewishness,' a Jewish principle analogous to phlogiston."[5] The vagueness of this notion of Jewishness is its major power; it cannot be undercut because it is impervious to fact or experience, present only to intuition. And it has a reflexive capacity to define its promulgator equally imperviously. "By treating the Jew as an inferior and pernicious being [the anti-Semite says], I affirm at the same time that I belong to the elite. This elite, in contrast to those of modern times which are based on merit or labor, closely resembles an aristocracy of birth. There is nothing I have to do to merit my superiority, and neither can I lose it. It is given once and for all. It is a *thing*" (p. 27).[6] Like the Jew and the anti-Semite, the aristocrat has "that certain something" that cannot be achieved or escaped because it is never fully defined or specified. The anti-Semite, like the aristocrat, reasons this way "because of a longing for impenetrability" (p. 18). His superiority, like his inferior's baseness, is ontologized by being obscured.[7]

So courtly stylization arises not only to deflect effort and its powers but to render perfection indeterminate. Nuance and oblique subtlety of manner, like effortlessness, become goals. And as this subtilization takes place, the role of audience ratification increases in importance. Although logical criteria can seem to transcend group ratification, with magical criteria the group reasserts its power. In the absence of clear theoretical frames one can test performance only by reference to the collective arbitrator. The Jew knows he is "Jewish" not by reference to the logical constituents of "Jewishness" but from the jeers of the crowd. And so a further rhetorical goal of the pressure toward nuance is to invite public imitation doomed to failure. The courtier is to act, says Castiglione, "with such conveyance of easinesse, that who so heareth him, may conceive a good opinion of him selfe, and thinke that he also with verie little adoe, might attaine to that perfection, but when hee commeth to the proofe, shall finde him selfe farre wide" (pp. 57/141).[8] At the level of conception rather than of action, we may see this as the exhortation to the courtier's "perfect understanding," which is to be such that "all men wonder at him, and hee at no man" (pp. 129/249).[9] Distance is maintained by the continuous display of inimitable nuance and manner. And so a large repertoire of techniques develops, based on the symbolic exploitation of substantive actions both great and small.

The range of this repertoire marks an advance over the chivalric ideology that humanist self-display replaced, for the new tools of the trade could be displayed equally well in war or peace. A huge new area was thus annexed for public self-affirmation: if all actions can be made adverbially symbolic of wit and understanding, all can attest to desert or elevation. No longer is the opportunity for meaningful self-display infrequent, or to be found only in the inconvenient thick of battle. In addition, it becomes a good deal less expensive; virtue resides on the tongue tip as well as on the sword point or in the purse. Only the imagination imposes limits to this kind of opportunity.

As a result of such flexibility, symbolic purposes come to dominate, or at least tint, substantive ones in all aspects of everyday life. Substantive activities continue, of course: one still eats, or carries trenchers. But no act remains without symbolic weight or allusion to status. And if this possibility is universal, if the ritual, formal, ceremonial, or stylistic radiations of any act require scrutiny and forethought, preoccupation with interpretive matters becomes common. How, one asks, can I make this look good, or good on me? All substantive actions become subject to self-depictive symbolic imperatives. And an equally hypertrophic attention is required for interpreting others' actions; one views others as one presumes to be seen oneself. (Is he doing that because I am watching him?) In this context, Puttenham names the figure of *allegoria* "the Courtier" and also variously calls it the figure of fair, *beau*, or false semblant (pp. 299, 158, 186).[10] The crowning capacity of the courtier is, he says, "cunningly to be able to dissemble" (p. 299). If neutral exposition is habitually presumed to be impure persuasion, then the capacity to register "literal" meanings is seriously impaired. Style has become opaque and demands penetration; transparency— the obvious—is revealed as one more fiction, requiring analysis and situation before it can be accepted.

The rhetoricized character of courtly life thus carries a toll of indeterminacy that Kenneth Burke deftly captures when describing the continual double asymmetry of the power relations between performer and audience. "The artist who relies upon smartness as a mark of 'urbanity' may be "socially inferior" to the 'ideal public' he is courting. Yet he is 'professionally superior,' and courts as an 'ideal public' many persons he would unquestionably despise in the particular. Yet again, as soon as you thus set him up, you must recall (as with the Arabian Nights relation) that the artist-entertainer is the servant of the very despot-audience he seeks to fascinate."[11] Each side of the dialectic confers both a sense of power and a sense of abjection. In intellectual history more attention has traditionally been paid to the positive component of this relation: the human capacity for self-elevation (that is, quite often, for dominance). Pico and Ficino posit a model in which man's peculiar glory lies here, in his performative life. The Marlovian overreacher represents a somewhat more limited view of this ideal. But in these cases Man or Superman is at issue, not individual unheroic humans. Burke speaks to the character of the ordinary lived human experience of performance, by noting the obverse of the heroic potential—the performative life as *predicament*.

It is explicitly from this unstable public arena that courtly identity is to be derived. Guazzo contends that the experience of conversation begets self-knowledge: "By meanes of civil conversation, a man may not onely cleere himselfe of cowardly abjection [*viltà*], and vaine presumption, but besides, cloath himselfe with the knowledge of himselfe. For if you consider it wel, the judgement which wee have to knowe our selves, is not ours, but wee borrow it of others" (1:115).[12] Conversation offers the opportunity to forestall potential accusations, by others or by oneself, of the "cowardly abjection" that may result from "solitarinesse, and . . . want of experience in the affaires of the world. Which causeth, that into a base mind, there entreth the distrust of his owne doings, and the feare of other mens judgement" (1:112). To fly from conversation is to risk being seen as base: only the bumpkin fails to enjoy such give-and-take. If this is "cowardly abjection," then fear of the conversation of city life would offer self-knowledge of baseness prima facie (and display of such fear would summon the judgment of others to the same effect, becoming a potential cause of fear in itself). This judgment, says Annibale, is to be trusted, as external and therefore unbiased information. For one thing, "the eye sees not itself but by reflection," as Achilles and Ulysses agreed. For another, we have a tendency to deceive ourselves as to our virtues and inadequacies, a bias others do not necessarily share.

On the whole, merely seeking out conversation can dismiss the charge of such dodging abjection, but to do so risks incurring Guazzo's other charge, of "vaine presumption." For one may be unwelcome, and one's (apparent) peers will have an investment in continually monitoring incursions. This interest can be seen in the self-defining actions of Castiglione's Duke Guidobaldo in the ordering of his court:

> Hee set his delight above all thinges to have his house furnished with most noble and valiant Gentlemen, with whom hee lived verie familiarly, enjoying their conversation.
>
> Wherein the pleasure which hee gave unto other men was no lesse, than that he received of other, because hee was verie well seene in both toongs, and togither with a loving behaviour and pleasantnesse hee had also accompanied the knowledge of infinite things. And beside this, the greatnesse of his courage so quickned him, that where hee was not in case with his person to practise the feates of Chivalrie [owing to ill health], as he had done long before, yet did he take verie great delight to beholde them in other men, and with his wordes sometime correcting, and otherwhile praising every man according to his deserts, he declared evidently how great a judgement hee had in those matters.
>
> And upon this at Tilt, at Tourney, in playing at all sorts of weapon, also in inventing devices in pastimes, in Musicke, finally in all exercises meete for noble Gentlemen, every man strived to shew himselfe such a one, as might deserve to bee judged worthie of so noble assembly.
>
> Therefore were all the houres of the day divided into honourable and pleasant exercises, as well of the bodie, as of the minde. (Pp. 19/84–85)

Such an arena requires continual performance before and judgment by one's peers and superiors, whose own reputations are seen to rest not only on performance but also on their abilities as judges. The registration of discriminations is a necessary ingredient in performative self-projection: failures of others are necessary to the judge's success. The denizen of Duke Guidobaldo's court was thus continually and stressfully on trial no matter what he was doing at any given moment. Such subjection to criticism was a constitutive element of the courtly atmosphere. So, at any rate, thought such a native as Raleigh: "Publicke affaires are rockes, private conversacions are whirlepooles and quickesandes. Itt is a like perilous to doe well and to doe ill."[13] Here Pico's heroically self-fashioning man recedes before a man whose identity comes close to being a pure commodity, produced (however self-consciously) for conversational consumption. If all utterance in this context comes to have primarily epideictic force; if the manifestation of style transcends issues of substance; if subjects of conversation increasingly become querelles; if conversation is not listened to but watched; then the power relation between speaker and hearer becomes skewed normatively toward the audience. Speech and other significations reveal not power but powerlessness, a pleading with the audience for a hearing, for recognition, for ratification.[14]

It is important not to misunderstand the character of this theoretically dominant audience. Quite often its confident superiority was a myth. For each member of the audience, supposedly empowered by the skewing of Burke's balance beam, was himself subject to the same unsettling pressures of dependency on audience. The members are united in their individual isolation before the same audience of others, trying to act as others do, modeling their behavior on the codes presented to them. But this presentation derives from no real normative other; each turns to all others, aiming to imitate a confident example present only in the imaginative projection of the ultimate Other who "knows what he is doing."[15] One can in some cases imagine the capture of an adequate Other paradoxically through self-estrangement; Stephen Greenblatt suggests that Thomas More's ultimately ironic self-presentation commits him "to asking himself at all times 'What would "More" say about this?'"[16] More's referential locus is presumed to be his own existential project (however unstable), and so he retains an internalized Other to whose judgment he has, as it were, immediate access. But in many more ordinary cases, the typical courtier's dominant Other will be the embodiment of a nonexistent "public opinion," readable in the mirroring responses of witnesses but dangerously evanescent. In fact, no one is in charge here.

Paradoxically, this evacuated authority had an infinite allure; it was continually sought after and continually defended against. However, all such seduction and evasion were undermined in advance. For the responses of two audiences were required for an act to be properly ratified. One needed from the elite either acceptance or the parity of rivalry, and from inferior classes, the differentiating recognition of either abjection or resentment. But insofar as either group might be suspected of contamination by the other, the force of audience ratification would be obscured. The approbation of a noble could be clouded by knowledge of his false pedigree hiding newcomer status; conversely, deference might seem to be mockery if irony were suspected. And, as this way of putting it suggests, the interpretive insecurity of the individual in conversation could render all these external data dubious, because they rested upon possibly self-serving interpretation.

For Guazzo this was the very impulse behind the need for conversation. He saw conversation as a laboratory that allowed the discovery of truth about the fallen self by cauterizing the contaminations of self-flattery: "If hee bee faulty any way, by frequenting the companie of others, [he will enter a situation where] one or other . . . if not in way of good will, yet in manner of mockerie, or of scorne, or of spyte [*se quon in segno d'amore . . . al meno in atto ò di beffa, ò di sprezzamento, ò di ingiuria*], or by one way or another, will make him to understande his fault" (1:115/135). But conversation might be divested of precisely this force by the operations of a common courtly mechanism that Puttenham called *paradiastole*, in his modern English the "soother" or "curry-favell." (The element "curry" is connected with the currycomb, and with "clawing," the Elizabethan slang equivalent of our term "stroking." We still speak of "currying favor.") Puttenham's use of the figure emphasizes recuperation: to "make the best of a bad thing, or turne a signification to the more plausible sense . . . such moderation of words tend[s] to flattery . . . as, to call an vnthrift, a liberall Gentleman: the foolish-hardy, valiant or couragious: the niggard, thriftie: a great riot, or outrage, an youthfull pranke, and such like termes" (pp. 184–85). But the concept has greater reach than this. For Castiglione's Count Ludovico it is two-edged, cutting in both directions: "Thus doth everie man praise or dispraise according to his fancie, alwaies covering a vice with the name of the next vertue to it, and a vertue with the name of the next vice" (pp. 31/102). And Guazzo notes the critical usage: "If you be affable and courteous, you shalbe called a flatterer" (1:38).[17]

This master trope governs evaluation, positing a matrix in which praise and blame, flattery and slander, interpenetrate absolutely. The basic function of the trope is the ongoing adjustment of public information by redescribing an utterance or action in such a way as to reverse the polarity of its meaning. Depictive assertions may be seen as positively or negatively valued, and as true or false (deserved or undeserved). A criticism, for instance, can be ameliorated: a "literal" description of the "fact" of prodigality in the spendthrift can be defused by terming the quality "liberality" and so converting the criticism to praise. At the same time, such a conversion deflects attention from the substantive remark to the character of the critic; not only is the spendthrift "really" a liberal gentleman, but the critic is a slanderer. One may similarly turn an unwelcome compliment to a lie by calling it flattery and thus brand its maker a lickspittle. Of course the flatterer may then deploy the matrix himself, to ward off this attack. The matrix throws all such questions into a realm of politically determined textuality.

It may help to situate this frangible idea of the literal by locating it in relation to the newly reified "literal" meaning of scripture. In discussing Tyndale's *The Obedience of a Christian Man*, Greenblatt makes the following suggestive observation:

> In its long concluding sections, the *Obedience* turns from an analysis of the responsibilities of rulers and subjects to an attack on the four-fold method of scriptural interpretation, an attack mounted in the name of what Tyndale calls "the literal sense." ... Tyndale's "literal sense" is the expression of a powerful *confidence*: it is easy to understand Scripture, its meaning lies directly in front of us, competing interpretations are perverse mystifications. There is no need of advanced degrees, the mastery of difficult languages, the juggling of arcane symbolisms, prodigious memory, an expensive library; the truth is as accessible to a shoemaker as to a theologian, perhaps more accessible, for the latter has been poisoned by popish sophistry.[18]

This sense of the literal is meant above all to enfranchise. Greenblatt writes movingly of the effect of the Reformation's bifurcation of Christianity as the creation of two demonic churches—Catholic and Protestant.[19] The "confidence" of Tyndale's literal reading dismisses and curses received Catholic understandings, just as More's abomination of Tyndale's heresy is figure to the ground of his Catholic faith. What the figure of paradiastole brings to this opposition is the potential for awareness of relativized multiplicity. If for Henry Peacham the elder, as for Tyndale and More, the trope is monovalent, opposing "the truth by false terms and wrong names," for the sardonic modernist Puttenham it is merely a tool for the articulation of similarity and difference.[20] The studied complexity of courtly life is designed by the elite to rebuff the invader by denying his sense of reality and his confidence in his own interpretive powers. Tyndale, on the other hand, aims with his literalist tool to rend that greater popish court where eternal treasures are secured, booty stolen from those outside the walls and concealed behind veils of false consciousness. These oppositions are homologous, and the interpretive modes are explicitly class-affiliated: obscurantism is the code of the religious and courtly ruling elites; disruptive literalism is that of the unruly oppressed, ambitious for social and religious mobility.[21]

That courtly conversation was dominated by the conventions of paradiastole means that such conversation could not convey literal fact; it thus lost its epistemological force. One reason, of course, is that perception in general was impaired. At the outset of his remarks on the ideal courtier, Castiglione's Count Ludovico raises the issue of paradiastolic ambiguity: "In everie thing it is so hard a matter to know the true perfection, that it is almost unpossible, and that by reason of the varietie of judgments" (pp. 31/102). This haze fogs the entire domain of *cortegiania*; more particularly, the access to *self*-knowledge is impaired. Critical evaluations that Guazzo thought would offer an "objective" perspective on the self were frequently (often preconsciously) defused by the self-protective imputation of rivalry, jealousy, or slander. But the process works in the opposite direction too: positive feedback might be reluctantly (either "realistically" or "paranoiacally") discarded as flattery or self-delusion. As the theoretical force of the audience response becomes increasingly valorized, so the need grows for reactive and self-protective (and paranoid) interpretation. Self-judgment is undercut, but so too is audience response, when both audience and performer are ruled by the self-serving prescriptions of courtesy. When all audience members are also peformers, judgments become performances and are subjected to reinterpretive pressures. The result is an inversely proportionate relation between the intensity of self-projection and the reliability of audience reaction. The harder an individual tries to turn the system to his own advantage, the more quickly he undercuts its power. The kaleidoscopic relations between praise and blame, flattery and slander finally shift uncontrollably at every turn.

The erosion of trust in private judgment stimulated a spiraling theoretical exploration of the way in which value derived from rhetorical foundation, an exploration that began with an obsessive awareness of the presence of an audience as such. Every man at the court of Urbino saw his task as striving "to shew himselfe such a one, as might deserve to bee judged worthie of so noble assembly" (pp. 19/84). Of course this audience became internalized and thus was continually present. Castiglione judges that "such as thinke them selves neither marked, seene, nor knowne, and yet declare a stoute courage, and suffer not the least thing in the world to passe that may burthen them [*che possa loro esser carico*, i.e., that might arouse disparagement; "di biasimo," Maier glosses], they have that courage of spirite which we seeke to have in our Courtier" (pp. 36/110). The punctilio in this case is almost paranoid; it invades and dominates even those private moments when actions are supposedly most unperformed. The ideal courtier is never offstage.[22]

In this apprehensive atmosphere the rationalist mapping of audience ratification lent a certain calm (occasionally vulnerable to sarcastic puncture, according to Javitch's reading of Philibert de Vienne's satiric encomium *The Philosopher of the Court*[23]). Several theorists offer this instrumental tranquilizer, taming audience oppressiveness by defining and explaining it. Count Annibale Romei, for instance, has one of his interlocutors in *The Courtiers Academie* distinguish between the honest and the honorable man as follows: "By a man of honor . . . I meane all those whatsoeuer they bee, good or wicked, who haue not lost the good opinion that the worlde conceiued of them" (p. 100).[24] Romei separates honor from traditional morality, founding it sheerly on audience ratification. Guazzo makes a more general claim, situating the whole ethical status of men in a rhetorical field. Annibale says: "When I name the good, I meane not onely that excellencie of goodnesse, which is not any way imperfect, and which is in a manner as rare on earth as the Phoenix: but I include in that number, all those which are well reported and reputed of in the world, and which approch so neare as they can to that excellencie" (1:58). Annibale's criterion of ethical repute then posits three categories of sociomoral status: the desirable, the intolerable, and the tolerable.

The first sort includes the usual excellent beings as well as those reputed to be so (the "good" just mentioned). The intolerable are those "who for their apparent faultes are pointed at with the finger, and holden for infamous . . . which beare a marke in their forehead, and are openly knowne to bee dishonest . . . [who] for notable cause are hated of the worlde . . . [who are] holden for infamous . . . which have an evill report . . . [which have] reprochfull names given them, that most men . . . thinke it a great shame to bee seene among them" (1:58, 61). These one is to fly, "but for others [the tolerable—those well reputed], though as a Christian you ought to flie them, yet as a Courtier, you cannot keep you from them: not so much for the great number of them, as for the error of the world, which esteemeth them in the rowe of the tollerable. To be short, wee ought to consider that our name dependeth of the general opinions, which have such force, that reason is of no force against them" (1:60–61). Some of these tolerable ones are "farre more wicked then those whom you have spoken of [among the intolerable: heretics, usurers, harlots, hangmen,

Jews], albeit by their dissembling hypocrisie, they are accounted of every man for honest men" (1:61–62). Annibale's explicit rationale for accepting even these truly wicked ones is this: "It is a common saying, That he which is evill and taken to bee good, may doe muche mischiefe, and no man thinke him to bee the worker of it. Notwithstanding, I put these same in the number of the tollerable: for though it trouble your conscience to come in their companie, yet you give no occasion of mislike to the worlde, for that they are not reputed evill, and in this point wee ought to satisfie rather others than our selves, and to give place to the common custome" (1:62). Theoretical moral status is not absent, but it is explicitly subordinated to audience judgment, which is made visible in reputation. One must act as if reputation were accurate, whatever one knows to the contrary. Public opinion takes precedence over private moral perception, and not only because one is known by the company one keeps. For if one were to refuse the force of another's reputation, one would "give occasion of mislike to the worlde," apparently by arrogantly denying a collective judgment. (Fregoso says that fame "seemeth to arise of the judgments of many" [pp. 123/241].) One must trust others' reputations because one's own rests on such exhibited trust: "Our name dependeth of the general opinions." Even epistemology thus becomes instrumental to the achievement of reputation. We are to believe in others as we would be believed in—even if we know them to be unworthy.

Such demotion of the transcendental is defended in various ways. Annibale elsewhere observed that "to be acceptable in companie, we must put of as it were our own fashions and manners, and cloath our selves with the conditions of others, and imitate them so farre as reason will permit . . . touching the diversitie of the persons with whom wee shall be conversaunt, wee must alter our selves into an other: according to that olde saying, The heart altogether unlike, and the face altogether like to the people" (1:105). To be "acceptable in companie" is no mere social grace—it amounts to being adequately civilized. In this view, following accepted morality is directly conducive to civilized conduct.

Annibale also makes a pragmatic point: "For that perfect and vertuous men are rare in the world, with whom we might live to our heartes desire, wee ought not to reject the companie of any, so that hee have in him any shewe of vertue and goodnesse" (1:104). The case is even clearer for Giovanni della Casa, who argues that grace and charm are necessary to proper social interaction, and even to morality: "Without [gracefulness] even goodness has no beauty and beauty has no charm" ("Senza la qual misura eziandio il bene non è bello e la bellezza non è piacevole").[25] He goes on to order these priorities. "This is by itself sufficient reason why all forms of vice are in themselves obnoxious, for vice is ugly and degrading and those who value self-restraint and sobriety are offended and disgusted by the impropriety of it. It follows that the first rule for all who wish to make themselves pleasant to others is to avoid vice.... All [vices] without exception make a man unwelcome in the company of others because, as I told you before, they are at variance with it."[26] From della Casa's angle, vice is reduced to a social indelicacy. By the same token, if virtue were not pleasant, it would be contraindicated. Moral categories are dominated by stylistic ones.

Not only does reputation determine the frame in which virtue is judged, it is epistemologically necessary for the public reception of virtue. Romei notes that "though it be in our power, to make our selues worthy of honor, yet is it not in our power to receiue or possesse it: seeing through the ingratitude or ignorance of them, in whose hands iust distribution lieth, we are oft times deceiued ... if the vertuous man haue not Fortune for his companion, he cannot haue pessession of honor: ... vertue without fortune, is of it selfe vnto it insufficient" (p. 114). And Ferne roots nobility *etymologically* in repute: "The word *Nobilitas* ... is deriued of the verbe *Nosco*, to knowe.... A Gentleman or a Nobleman is he ... which is knowne, and through the heroycall vertues of his life, talked of in euery mans mouth" (p. 4).[27] Virtue can exist, in a pure form as it were, but it is mute until known and registered by its enfranchising audience.

What all this suggests is that at least the public sort of virtue known as "estimation" (and perhaps, for Guazzo anyway, a more inclusive sense of goodness) is radically dependent on the eye and voice of the audience. A fundamental sort of value, social indeed but far from being mere appearance, resides in one's reputation. Perhaps only by means of this conduit can nominally transcendent virtue appear, not only to the world but perhaps even to the self. Finally the strongest demonstration of this ontological displacement is the very fact of the enormous body of technique devised for the conquest and management of audience—"comely demeanours" so potent that "who so speaketh with [the courtier], or yet beholdeth him, must needes beare him an affection for ever" (Castiglione, pp. 33/105).[28] In fact the courtier was forever on the lookout, scouring the coast, for evidence of the *impact* of his initiatives. All such tactical fantasies are grounded in the existential social project of life on display, a practice summarized in the asymmetrical persuasion that ends *All's Well That Ends Well,* a play obsessed with wooing hostile audiences. In the Epilogue (line 6), the king's final words are: "Your gentle hands lend us, and take our hearts." The courtier offers up his heart in just this way, in exchange for the loan of gentle applause.[29]

Certain of the courtier's techniques have a general, rhetorical application calling for attention in this section. First among these is the strategic awareness of the status of the audience. One may perform before one's (present or future) peers, members of the elite, or before the inferior classes with an eye to the enactment of superiority. One may display class affiliation in the performance of public duty or seek publicity through the private display of wit. Or one may enact the self in a mixed audience, using the proper form of address to each group before the other, either literally (say, in a public square among churls and gentlemen) or nominally (alone with one sort in commenting upon the other—as in peasant jokes). The preferred arena is, of course, the presence of the prince, who is not only the original source and final arbiter of reward, but also the source of social place itself (of the categorizations rather than of the attendant privileges). What Puttenham calls the queen's "rayes" inform each of her subjects of his proper location in the social universe: "Out of her breast as from an eye, / Issue the rayes incessantly / Of her iustice, bountie and might." This radiance "makes eche subiect clearly see, / What he is bounden for to be / To God his Prince and common wealth, / His neighbor, kinred and to himselfe" (p. 100). For those who would relocate, this point of origin of "location" is the place to start. The basic rhetorical consequence of this fact is made clear in Castiglione's famous battlefield example: "Where the Courtier is at skirmish, or assault, or battaile upon the lande, or in such other places of enterprise, he ought to worke the matter wisely in separating him selfe from the multitude, and undertake notable and bolde feates which hee hath to doe, with as litle company as he can, and in the sight of noble men that be of most estimation in the campe, and especially in the presence and (if it were possible) before the very eyes of his king or great personage he is in service withall" (pp. 95–96/200–201). This in-

junction suggests that private ambition must take precedence over
public duty; the warrior who seeks his prince's eye above all else
places rhetorical concerns above, say, following orders (perhaps to
fight elsewhere, away from the prince's eye) or acting in accord with
military strategic concerns.[30] As an arena for the demonstration of
audacity, the battlefield provides a powerfully existential intensity
or recalcitrance against which the courtier-warrior can exercise
himself, over which he can triumph. For the theater of war sum-
mons an audience of the highest rank.

Similarly, at court "the winning of support was quite as important
as the conduct of business."[31] Eclipse may await those ignorant of this
priority. Romei knows

> some gentlemen . . . vertuous, prudent, and of great desert, yet for that they
> haue (as wee sayde) bin euer colde, and not vrged fortune, nor sought the
> honors they deserued, liue in their Cittie without any renoume: wherevpon
> by Court impostors, this their modesty is esteemed pusillanimitie, not to
> say plain stupidity: whereas on the contrary, euery day we see men of smal
> desert, raised to great honors, by hauing beene audacious, and assaying all
> means, as wel lawfull as vnlawful, but specially in procuring to themselues
> their fauor, that could bestow on them honor or riches. (P. 115)

Failing through lack of initiative to grasp the attention of the proper
audiences risks displacement by "Court imposters." The courtier
should "worke the matter wisely" to maximize the impact of the
figure he cuts, and an essential step toward this goal is to select his
audience hierarchically. Castiglione makes the priorities explicit: before estimable nobles is good, in the prince's vicinity is better, directly
before his eyes best of all. But what counts most is the location of all
three tiers in the enclosure of the ruling class.[32]

Guicciardini offers a less extreme version of this advice, workaday
counsel for grasping courtly opportunity. "If you frequent the court of
a prince, hoping to be employed by him, keep yourself constantly in
view. For often, matters will arise suddenly; and if you are in sight, he
will remember you and commit them to your trust, whereas if you are
not, he might entrust them to another" (C94).[33] Guicciardini recognizes the zone of visibility surrounding the prince and recommends
keeping oneself steadily in the limelight—but for substantive rather
than for formal opportunity. The difference between Castiglione and
Guicciardini here raises the question of exactly what such self-expo-
sures display. Castiglione imagines "notable and bold feates"; Guicciardini, simple availability and convenience. But Bacon, in his essay

on "negociating," mines deeper on this point than either, suggesting what the employer might see: "It is better dealing with men in appetite, than with those that are where they would be."[34] The display of ambition *as such* can attract the potential patron—not the Christian humanistic virtue but the pagan *virtu* of the courtier—his energy, his drive, his hunger, the power that masters him—which can be harnessed by another.

It is of course the continual display of such "virtues" that gives the court its hothouse character. Although the recreative evenings at Urbino may suggest the convivium as the typical vision of the locus of courtesy, we must remember the gladiatorial aspect too. Guazzo captures this vividly.

> The desire to maintaine and increase their wealth, and to mende their estate, will not suffer men to stande ydle with their handes at their gyrdels, whiche you shall plainely see, if you once set your foote in the Court of some Prince, where you shall see an infinite number of Courtiers assemble together, to talke and devise of many matters, to understande the newes of the death or confiscation of the goods of some one, to seeke to obtaine of the Prince, eyther promotions, goods, pardons, exemption, or priviledge for them selves or others: and before they will crave suche thinges, to proceede thereto by meanes, and to practise the favour of the Secretaries, and other Officers. And you shall have there besides, other good fellowes, conspyring together, and secretly devising howe to bring some Officer into the disfavour of his Prince, that hee may bee put from his office, and some other placed in his roome. (1:117)

Where the prince's presence is finite and one must press a suit before intermediate figures, the pressure emanates hydraulically throughout the courtly hierarchy, theatricalizing all strata. If very few attained the heights of a Leicester, with his £1000 annuity, the possibility of such reward was an intermittent reinforcement defining the entire court as a rhetorical arena. (There were, of course, occasions for performance before a base audience: Castiglione admits that the opportunity for reputation exists "among the multitude, unto whom a man must sometim apply him selfe" [pp. 42/118]. But for the most part the privileged audience for courteous behavior was the ruling group at court.)

This restricted focus caused certain problems. For one thing, there was the danger of cloying the palate of the audience: "Continuance goeth nigh to give a man his fill, and taketh away the admiration that men have of thinges seldom seene" (pp. 42/119), says Castiglione. For another, the narrow path to preferment was clogged with hostile competitors. Bacon says that "they that are glorious must needs be factious. . . . Honour that is gained and broken upon another hath the quickest reflection; like diamond cut with facets."[35] Elizabeth habitually took advantage of this compulsion, disciplining the crush of power seekers by orchestrating factions. Sir Robert Naunton saw this procedure as "the principall note of her Reign . . . that she ruled much by faction and parties, which her self both made, upheld, and weakened, as her own great judgement advised."[36] MacCaffrey offers a modern view of this arrangement.

> At the best this [system] made for a frenetic atmosphere of pushing competition; at the worst it might have degenerated into a chaotic scramble for favour in which all considerations of political common sense and administrative efficiency would have vanished. Something like this was to happen in James I's time. Under Elizabeth, however, a rough system, a pattern of order at least, emerged. The Queen's own wisdom provided the basis for it. By refusing to limit her confidence to a single favorite, she kept open a number of channels to her bounty; and she made it plain that in return for that bounty she expected hard work and loyal service. In this way a destructive, even dangerous competition among the magnates for the royal confidence was avoided.[37]

Competition was channeled and institutionalized, reminding everyone that all roads led to the queen. In a context of underemployment and oversupply, all the stations along this road were rhetorical stations, with the queen as the ultimate audience.

Although this institutionalizing helped organize and control competition, it must often have intensified the scramble as well, strengthening the pull to rhetorical combat. The prince's intervention had to be very delicate, lest the combative forces get out of hand. Raleigh thought that the better sort had to be carefully rewarded: not too much, for fear of producing the overmighty subject; not too little, for fear of widespread factional resentment.

> To that end, not to load any with too much honour or preferment, because it is hard even for the best and worthiest men, to bear their greatness and high fortune temperately, as appeareth by infinite examples in all states. The sophisms for preventing or reforming this inconvenience are to be used with great caution and wisdom. If any great person be to be abated, not to deal with him by calumniation or forged matter, and so to cut him off without desert, especially if he be gracious among the people; which besides the injustice, is an occasion many times of great danger towards the prince. Nor to withdraw their honour all at once, which maketh a desper-

ate discontentment in the party, and a commiseration in the people, and so begetteth greater love towards him.... But to use these and the like sophisms; viz. to abate their greatness by degrees, as David, Joab, Justinian, Bellisarius, &c.; to advance some other men to as great or greater honour, to shadow, or over-mate the greatness of the other; to draw from him by degrees his friends and followers, by preferments, rewards, and other good and lawful means; especially, to be provided that these great men be not employed in great and powerful affairs of the commonwealth, whereby they may have more opportunity to sway the state.[38]

This tactical stance shows that the lives of subsidiary folk were often managed for purposes that only reflected the standing of their betters. One bridles the great subject by manipulating his followers. Bacon sums up the theory this way: "In favour, to use men with much difference and election is good; for it maketh the persons preferred more thankful, and the rest more officious; because all is of favour."[39] The promoted one's assessment of his fate would have had to have been very subtle. Promotion might mean nothing about the self, and everything about one's affiliates.

Just as one's perceptions of the audience were bound to be ambivalent, so the act of speaking was itself problematic.[40] Courtly conversation (especially with the queen) would indeed supply knowledge, both of the self and of others, but all such "information" was conditioned by the rhetoric of advantage. Such pressures must frequently have overdetermined speech in public, making both speaking and interpreting difficult. The courtier must often have quailed before the decision whether to risk speech or to sit quietly. Vigorous speech probably often seemed the best avenue. Guazzo observes that "as money well imployed, turneth both to the commoditie of him that receiveth it, and likewise of him that disburseth it: so woordes well considered, bring profite to the hearer, and prayse to the speaker" (1:121). This parallel is directly quantitative: "Seeing in companie wee commonly devise of diverse thinges, leaping from one matter into another, there is nothing, in my judgement, that doeth us more honour, or maketh us better liked of, in good companie, then to be readie at all assayes, and have a mouth for every matter" (1:225). Conspicuous expenditure is extended from money to words to wit, a breadth typical of the stereotypical "Renaissance man." In part this process must have been a ramification of the oratorical virtue of *copia*, of which Walter Ong has written.[41] But it would also be, at a more inclusive structural level, a response to the general hypertrophy of rhetorical consciousness.

Speech was always tactically attractive, but silence had its positive side too. "It addeth no small reverence to men's manners and actions, if they be not altogether open," says Bacon.[42] Guazzo's Annibale agrees, going somewhat further to speak of the desire for speech as an appetite, potentially self-betraying.

> The ignorant man of weake understanding, which hath neede to keepe silence, is mervaylously delighted to heare him selfe speake: and suche force hath this fault, that alwayes those whiche knowe least, covet to speake most. Seeing then to stay the tongue, and use the eare, are the hardest things that may bee, it behooveth our patient to frame him selfe to brydle his appetyte, withstanding his owne will, and inuring himselfe by little and little, to keepe the mouth more shut, and the eares more open. Which hee shall no sooner doe, but hee shall perceive that in companie hee shall get the good will and favour of others, as well by giving eare curteously, as by speaking pleasantly. (1:120)

If free speech is risky, however, so also is pusillanimous silence. If the cheeky underling often claims to "have a mouth for every matter," so on (somehow) other occasions will the true aristocrat. If the humble individual invites by his silence the epithets of "sot" and "fool," the silent aristocrat may ipso facto confirm his own status. Behavior cannot be pinned to a single signification. So all forms of conversational behavior are risky: opportunity and pitfall look the same. The potential participant must assess the opportunity, his capacity to take advantage of it, the relative benefits of silence and speech, and the various possible reactions of his audience to both choices. And each of these assessments is as usual vulnerable to multiple paradiastolic manipulations. This infinite regress leans finally toward the negative, because it is impossible to banish doubt.

But even this fact has a positive side, for the uncertainty can count as hope. "The politic and artificial nourishing and entertaining of hopes . . . ," said Bacon, "is one of the best antidotes against the poison of discontentments."[43] Prior to disillusionment, a lower status can seem simply the prologue of things to come—necessary dues to pay before entry. The continuing pains of courtly conversation may seem instrumental to success, rather than signs of failure. Since labor is associated with both pain and results, the pain can be taken as a sign of impending result.

If one elects to speak, he may try to govern the rhetorical situation by observing two principles. The first is the idea of decorum—adjustment of the approach to the particular situation. Its converse is the action of delay—the denial of simple or immediate comprehension to the members of one's audience, so as to make them work for it. Each principle of control is not only an exercise but an exhibition of power: the first over the self, the second over the audience. (Paired, they echo Burke's structure of double dominance.) Puttenham posits several synonyms for the term *decorum*: decency, seemliness, comeliness,[44] pleasant approach. With regard to each of these, "the election is the writers, the iudgement is the worlds" (p. 263). (Although he says of this issue of decorum that it "resteth in writing, speech and behauiour" alike [p. 264], I will for the moment conflate these areas.) Decorum specifies the ascendance of the audience as arbiter. The performer becomes protean in submission, as Puttenham's partition shows. "By reason of the sundry circumstances, that mans affaires are as it were wrapt in, this [*decencie*] comes to be very much alterable and subiect to varietie, in so much as our speach asketh one maner of *decencie*, in respect of the person who speakes: another of his to whom it is spoken: another of whom we speake: another of what we speake, and in what place and time and to what purpose. And as it is of speach, so of al other our behauiours" (pp. 263–64). The range and cathexis of these stances are especially varied at court.

> It is decent to be affable and curteous at meales & meetings, in open assemblies more solemne and straunge, in place of authoritie and iudgement not familiar nor pleasant, in counsell secret and sad, in ordinary conferences easie and apert, in conuersation simple, in capitulation subtill and mistrustfull, at mournings and burials sad and sorrowfull, in feasts and bankets merry & ioyfull, in housdhold expence pinching and sparing, in publicke entertainement spending and pompous. . . . A Iudge to be incorrupted, solitarie and vnacquainted with Courtiers or Courtly entertainements . . . contrariwise a Courtly Gentleman to be loftie and curious in countenaunce, yet sometimes a creeper, and a curry fauell with his superiours. (Pp. 292–93)

Each of these vigorous postures manifests the performer's rhetorical facility.

The same can be said of the opposite tactic of delay or challenge or puzzle.[45] Here the performer imposes a negative mediation between himself and his audience, relating to them through blockage. Imagining a knight coming to joust dressed as a shepherd, Fregoso sees the misleading as a source of pleasure, augmenting the grace of the act: "The minde of the lookers on runneth forthwith to imagin the thing that is offered unto the eyes at the first shew, and when they behold afterwarde a far greater matter to come of it than they looked for under that attire, it delyteth them, and they take pleasure at it" (pp. 99/206). Earlier Fregoso treated writing in a similar way:

> If the words that the writer useth bring with them a litle (I will not say difficultie) but covered subtiltie, and not so open, as such as be ordinarily spoken, they give a certaine authoritie to writing, and make the Reader more heedefull to pause at it, and to ponder it better, and he taketh a delyte in the wittinesse and learning of him that wryteth, and with a good judgement, after some paines taking, he tasteth the pleasure that consisteth in hard thinges.
>
> And if the ignorance of him that readeth bee such, that he can not compasse that difficultie, there is no blame in the writer, neither ought a man for all that to thinke that tongue not to bee fair. (Pp. 51–52/132–33)

The aesthetic of reception challenges not the performer but his audience, offering either the pleasure of eventual comprehension or the pain of disenfranchisement as competent witness. The tension between these possibilities thus measures both aesthetic and social force.

Fregoso on horsemanship combines the contrasting elements of decorum and mystery, in a mixed model that can be extended to all rhetorical radiations of power during the Renaissance:

> If [one is] to shew feates of Chivalrie in open sights, at tilt, turney, . . . or in any other exercise of the person, remembring the place where he is, and in presence of whom, hee shall provide before hand to be in his armour no lesse handsom and sightly than sure, and feede the eyes of the lookers on with all thinges that hee shall thinke may give him a good grace, and shall doe his best to get him a horse set out with faire harnesse and sightly trappings, and to have proper devices, apt posies, and wittie inventions that may draw unto him the eyes of the lookers on as the Adamant stone doth yron. (Pp. 96/201)

The courtier seeks to control others' eyes as though with a lodestone, but he does so "remembering the place where he is, and in presence of whom." His devices, posies, and inventions are to be witty and challenging, dominating audience response; at the same time, they are to be proper and apt, decorously fitted to their occasion and audience — and so controlled by the expectation of judgment ratification. This power simultaneously commands and ingratiates.

We should not conclude this survey of the broader frames of audience management without noting that such skills can be sold, that is, performed for profit on another's behalf. This deployment of symbol-using skills is familiar today in advertising and public relations, both of which are based on the sale of intellectual labor. Such labor first became a commodity when the conduct of hierarchy and government became a matter of persuasion; many intellectual formations had worked to this purpose earlier, of course, but the decay of ascriptive hierarchy brought such operations to the cultural consciousness. Penry Williams offers an account of the pressures that created this function and that, in turn, began to be organized by it.

> With the increasing significance of communications, the importance of propaganda, the growth of paperwork, and the premium put upon information, the old-style aristocrat was at a disadvantage in Tudor politics. Important as the shires might be, the court was the real centre of politics and the skills required to manipulate it were highly professional. Men who wanted to make their way in the political world had to adopt the outlook of the court and to nurture roots in court life as well as in the shires. All this gave the Crown an opportunity for building its own bodies of supporters in· the regions and establishing courtly values there. At the same time the demands being made by government upon the administration of the shires called for an elite different in its capacities from the old regional aristocracy. The Crown sought to train such an elite and to insert it into the crucial areas of power.[46]

In this protobureaucratic context, depiction becomes a commodity. For as an attaché, a secretary, or a house or factional poet, one hired out one's verbal skills for the purpose of attesting to the power of an employer and his interests.[47] This attestation might take several forms. The production of overt encomiums was quite common. One might also ghostwrite texts intended to be passed off as the productions of one's employer; or one might produce texts to be attributed to his influence or support or sponsorship. All such actions would have the second-order epideictic function of depicting the depicter.

In their search for employment, intellectuals often presented samples of such skill. In his several prefaces to *The Posies* (the ameliorative edition of the scandalous *A Hundreth Sundrie Flowres*), George Gascoigne makes this gesture openly. To "the reverend divines" he argues,

> as I seeke advauncement by vertue, so was I desirous that there might remaine in publike recorde, some pledge or token of those giftes wherwith it hath pleased the Almightie to endue me: To the ende that thereby the

vertuous might bee incouraged to employ my penne in some exercise which might tende both to my preferment, and to the profite of my Countrey. . . . For full proofe of mine earnest zeale in Gods service, I require of you (reverende) most instantly, that if hereby my skill seeme sufficient to wade in matters of greater importance, you will then vouchsafe to employ mee accordingly. Surely you shall finde me no lesse readie to undertake a whole yeares travaile in anie work which you shall thinke me able to overcome, than I have beene willing heretofore to spende three houres in penning of an amorous Sonnet.[48]

In the later preface addressed "to the yong gentlemen," Gascoigne repeats this plea, hoping to "yeeld [the world] yet some part of mine account in these Poemes. Wherein as he may finde great diversitie both in stile and sense, so may the good bee incouraged to set mee on worke at last" (1:14).

Similar gestures appear in the second of *The Parnassus Plays*, which were written by Cambridge University students around 1600. These plays explore the commodity value of university education in Tudor England. They depict what sorts of jobs such education might command (and not, I believe, the aspirations only of would-be poets, as is sometimes thought[49]). As such they furnish an interesting catalog of employments for the humanist intellectual. (It should be said by way of orientation that the first play, *The Pilgrimage to Parnassus*, reveals the obstructions and temptations encountered by students on their way to the university; the second, *I Return from Parnassus*, tells the tale of the graduates' attempts to find legitimate employment; and the third, *II Return*, chronicles the unsavory jobs they take when these attempts fail.) One of the graduates, Ingenioso, seeks patronage from a potential Maecenas, offering professional praise and pleading that the patron "take in good part . . . youre owne eternitie, my pains, wherin in the ages to come men shall reade youre prases and giue a shrewde gess at youre vertues" (*I Return*, lines 297–99).[50] When the patron smugly concedes his own magnanimity, Ingenioso epideictically plays on the patron's phrase, in lavish self-displaying praise:

Patron: . . . when I am deade I know not what will become of schollers; hitherto I haue bespringled them pritilie with the drops of my bountie.

Ingen.: O youre worshippe may be bolde with your selfe, noe other tong will be soe nigarde as to call those dropes, which indeede are plentuous showres, that so often haue refreshed thirstie brains and sun burnt wittes; and might it nowe please the cloude of

>   youre bountie to breake, it neuer founde a drier soile to work
>   vpon or a grounde that will yealde a more plenteous requitall.
>   (Lines 307–17)

Ingenioso had tried to obtain admittance by bribing the patron's serv-
ing-man with the same skills he hoped to sell to the master: "Why
man, I am able to make a pamphlet of thy blew coate and the button
in thy capp, to rime thy bearde of thy face, to make thee a ridiculous
blew sleeud creature, while thou liuest. I have immortalitie in my pen,
and bestowe it on whome I will. Well, helpe mee to the speache of my
maister quicklie, and Ile make that obscure name of thyne, which is
knowne amongst none but hindes and milkmaides, ere longe to
florishe in the press and the printers stall" (lines 249–56).

The comic register of these speeches (and the oblique resentment
of the unemployed college man) should not blind us to the real mar-
ketability of such skills. Stone notes how "Shakespeare reminded his
readers that giving a lift to a great poet could be a more durable
investment than sinking capital in a great tomb: 'Not marble, nor the
gilded monuments / Of princes, shall outlive this powerful rime.'"[51]
Samuel Daniel plays on the commonness (in both senses) of such public applause by praising only his Delia, nominally refusing to soil his
pen by undertaking such mercenary tasks:

>   None other fame myne vnambitious Muse,
>   Affected euer but t'eternize thee:
>   All other honours doe my hopes refuse,
>   Which meaner priz'd and momentarie bee.
>
>   For God forbid I should my papers blot,
>   With mercynary lines, with seruile pen:
>   Praising vertues in them that haue them not,
>   Basely attending on the hopes of men.[52]

Needless to say, this fastidiousness need not be taken at face value. To
claim to praise accurately was obligatory. But such moral rhetoric
reflects on the encomiast too. William Camden's elegy on Roger
Ascham specifies this dual epideictic force: "Ille sed ingenio nomen
quaesivit, et arte / Quo genus et patriam celebrat, celebratur ut ille."
("On the contrary, he sought a name with his natural talent. / And his
skill, through which he honors his family and country; / And by those
means is that famous one himself honored.")[53] The claim to honorable fastidiousness can also affect an author's own political reputation in the competitive regions of social mobility. Richard Mulcas-

ter's dedication of *The First Part of the Elementarie* (1582) to the earl
of Leicester reveals the complexity of the problem. Mulcaster had
dedicated his earlier *Positions* (1581) to the queen. Before he could
begin dedicating *The Elementarie* to Leicester, he had to spend one
and one-half pages justifying his earlier dedication, presumably contra the option of having made the dedication to Leicester.[54] Positive
depictive attention to another, however deserving (and who more deserving than the queen?), can so easily be taken as disparaging of
one's current patron that such a reading must be overtly denied. The
touchiness that occasions such paranoia is captured by Ingenioso's
Maecenas, who agrees to sponsor the graduate, but with a caveat: "It
is fitt, that all suche younge men as you are should knowe that all dutie
is farr inferiour to our desertes, that in great humilitie doe vouchsake
to reade youre labours" (lines 327–30). Daniel's contempt for the servile pen is easy to understand, but both his sneer and the Cambridge
students' satire reveal the university man's resentment of the necessity for such self-debasement.

The other main vicariously depictive commodity is the product of
what we would call ghostwriting: a text offered as the personal epideictic product of the employer or purchaser (the ancestor in fact of
the greeting card). Another modern equivalent, political speech-writ-
ing, comes to mind here, but the purer case is the private emotional
document, putatively heartfelt. It was not uncommon for epistolary
manuals to offer instruction in writing love letters; see, for instance,
Angel Day's *English Secretorie* (1586) and Thomas Gainsford's *Secretaries Studie* (1616). Insofar as these are secretarial manuals, they
address vicarious practice by definition, but more direct examples
can be adduced. When Ingenioso seeks an audience with the patron,
the doorman requires as a gratuity not the print immortality
Ingenioso offers, but "this onlie, that thou wilte make mee a loue
letter in elegant tearmes to our chambermaide" (lines 260–61). Elsewhere Ingenioso obtains like employment from Gullio, a preposter-
ous court hanger-on vaguely related to Don Armado or Parolles. His
task will be to write love poetry for Gullio: "New years day appro-
cheth, and wheras other gallants bestowe Iewells vpon there Mis-
trisses (as I haue done whilome), I now count it base to do as the
common people doe; I will bestowe vpon them the precious stons of
my witt, a diamonde of Inuention, that shall be aboue all value &
esteeme; therfore, sithens I am employed in some weightie affayrs of
the courte, I will haue thee, Ingenioso, to make them, and when thou

hast done, I will pervse, pollish, and correcte them" (lines 1015–23). Here the vicarious element is quite conspicuous: Ingenioso's poems will be presented as Gullio's own.[55] (In fact Gullio instructs Ingenioso to write samples for him in the modes of Chaucer, Gower, Spenser, and Shakespeare, to present a line of goods from which he will make a selection.) Such poetic lieutenancy may have obtained outside the precinct of satire. In the twenty-first sonnet of *Idea* (1619), Drayton describes a love sonnet he wrote for "A witlesse Gallant, a young Wench that woo'd . . . with my Verses he his Mistres wonne, / Who doted on the Dolt beyond all measure."[56] But the tale is, like Daniel's, a setting for the poet's own frustration in love; the vicarious sonnet was written effortlessly and was successful, whereas Drayton's own poems come only with struggle and fail of their goal. Another example is less fictive: Sir Thomas Overbury claimed to be the author of the love letters of Robert Carr, Viscount Rochester, to Lady Frances Howard.[57] (In this famous case the powers of vicarious self-depiction that Overbury deployed for the favorite backfired on the specialist. He won the lady for Carr, and then she had him murdered—also by agent.)

Although it is hard to know how widespread such scribal agency was, these examples show that one might specialize in vicarious poetical seduction, a service rendered not to the lady but to her wooer, with the substitution concealed. The contamination of this private social realm of "authentic emotion" by the commodity of fictive subjectivity should remind us of the social inscriptions of privacy at all times.[58]

The author of vicarious depiction can sometimes claim responsibility for the product (at least while in search of employment, or for rhetorical purposes of comparison); on occasion he may personally suffer the consequences of his own success (as Overbury did). He can on yet other occasions sever himself from personal responsibility for what then becomes the product of alienated labor. The second edition of Gascoigne's *A Hundreth Sundrie Flowres* (1575), which was overtly apologetic regarding the obscure sins of the first (1573), reveals this maneuver. Some have thought that dangerous allegory abounds in *The Adventures of Master F. J.*, though the validity of this reading has been debated.[59] Lasciviousness was also alleged, and Gascoigne replied (perhaps with relief at the generality of the objection) with the familiar argument for selective suction by the wise reader-bee. But Gascoigne also generically disclaimed moral responsibility for the objectionable texts. The eroticism of his poems was not sinful, he said, because it was impersonal piecework, written on order.

> But bicause these Posies growe to a great bundell, and thereof also the number of loving lynes exceedeth in the Superlative, I thought good to advertise thee, that the most part of them were written for other men. And out of all doubt, if ever I wrote lyne for my selfe in causes of love, I have written tenne for other men in layes of lust. . . . In wanton delightes I helped all men, though in sad earnest I never furthered my selfe any kinde of way . . . when I did compile anything at the request of other men, if I had subscribed the same with mine owne usuall mot or devise, it might have bewrayed the same to have beene of my doing. And I was ever curious in that behalfe, as one that was lothe to bewray the follies of other men. (1:16–17)

This last dark remark perhaps means that he concealed his own identity as author in order to camouflage the poem's vicarious status for its eventual recipient. But buying such poems must then be the "follies" of the final phrase. Perhaps Gascoigne is unscrambling *ex nihilo* the fact that his earlier collection contained many poems apparently written by other authors, all of which he now claims for himself. It is upon such obscurities that the possible allegory turns. And it may be that there is a certain psychological truth here, rather than simply a barefaced self-defense. Erving Goffman suggests that in the display of false or insincere deference, "by easily showing a regard that he does not have, the actor can feel that he is preserving a kind of inner autonomy."[60] Whatever Gascoigne's interior state, his defense alleges the vicarious employment of verbal wit in the erotic context, and the moral vacuum that such writing might be claimed to occupy.

Finally, note should briefly be taken of the most tenuous of vicarious depictions, essentially a case of reflected glory. Gilbert's *Queene Elizabethes Achademy* is a familiar example. Gilbert imagines the academy's intellectual productions to be a source of vicarious reputation for the queen who sponsors it. Each reader of "arte and the common lawes" must produce a book, and each language instructor a translation, every six years. By such operations, which publicize the rightful fame of great men of the past, "your maiesty shall not onely haue your share thereof, but also for evermore, once every .3. or 6. yeares at the most, fill the eyes of the world with new and chaunge of matter, wherby all sortes of Studentes shalbe alwaies put in minde of Queene Elizabethes Achademy. And in the mean tyme, the pervsing of the old, and expectacion for the new, shall occupy Continually

euery mannes tounge with Queene Elizabethes fame" (pp. 9, 12).[61]
The queen reaps the fruit normally reserved to those who pay for
another's productions.

All of the strategies thus far considered emphasize that the defining
power of the audience is marked by the quantity of energy invested in
managing it. But we should leave our discussion of these general rhetorical framings with an equally potent denial of audience power, or, it
might be better to say, audience trustworthiness. For what the courtier wants is a sense not only of the rhetorical requirements that confront him but also of his rhetorical success. And it is precisely this
latter sense that the situation ultimately denies him, because of the
corrosive workings of paradiastolic perception. An umbrella statement concerning this indeterminacy can be taken from game theory.
Goffman provides a convenient summary of the famous phenomenon
of the decay of explanation in *Strategic Interaction*. He begins with
"the corruption, or rather the disqualification, of innocence."

> The subject, in realizing that his conduct is likely to be distrustfully exam-
> ined by the observer, will be concerned with the readings that might be
> made of it—with how it might "appear" to the other—even though, in
> fact, the subject is engaged in nothing he might want to conceal or modify.
> He may then be led to style his behavior, to cover his innocent tracks, so
> that likely misrepresentations will not occur. . . . In the same way, the ob-
> server may come to suspect covering actions as being actions designed to
> be seen through. However, just as innocence is disqualified, so is sophisti-
> cation. . . . The most useful information is also the most treacherous. . . . A
> demoralizing oscillation of interpretation can result: the player will feel at
> one moment that he is being oversuspicious and that he should take the
> other at face value or, at the worst, as someone who employs usual covers
> and, at the next, that a trap has been set for him. At one moment he can feel
> that he has finally hit upon indicators that can't be faked, and the next
> moment he can feel that this is exactly how the opponent wants him to
> accept these indications, and that they have been fabricated for this pur-
> pose. Appearances that are obviously innocent are the appearances a
> guilty expert gamesman would give. Appearances that are obviously sus-
> pect can demonstrate innocence, because no competent gamesman would
> allow such circumstances to arise. Yet innocence can reveal innocence and
> suspect appearances guilt.[62]

In such a universe of interpretation, the decision as to where to stop
will be based not on rigorous epistemological concerns but on political affiliations. Interpretive decisions can be made, but they cannot

be made with total confidence. Tyndale's literal sense may be a powerful weapon for mobilizing a public, but as long as power remains fairly securely in the hands of an inward-turned elite, poachings will be accomplished by those who learn the rules, not by those who deny the need for them. And for those who enter this frame, confidence, though continually sought and usually imputed, will seldom be secure and must be reinforced with bullying (of the self as much as of the suspicious audience). Like their courts, courtiers' minds were peopled with crowds of retainers and servants—a doubt police, marginal forebears of Foucault's surveillance orders.[63]

It is only by willfully averting the eye from epistemological murk that the courtier might achieve an awareness anything like the superconductive crystal clarity Wayne Rebhorn attributes to him:

> The most essential ingredient in the courtier's self-consciousness is his constant awareness of the image he presents to others. More important than the reflection he sees in his mirror is the reflection of himself he sees in others' eyes. As he enters a room, he looks cautiously at eyes that smile or frown on him, and as he performs his part, he carefully alters gestures and words at the merest flutter of a lash. Without such complex self-consciousness, this Renaissance star could never manipulate his image successfully and before long would find himself playing to an empty house.[64]

Much more often the courtier must have wondered helplessly about that eye's lash, haunted by the fantasy of the empty house. And the higher one went up the ladder of advancement (and the more one then had to offer), the more obscure the atmosphere became. Even Lord Burghley, of all people the last to need this advice, might be mocked by appearance, or so feared the author of this letter to him:

> Beware whom you trust; for, in your place, it can not be but many will follow you for another end than they pretend; their lucre is not your safety, but their own commodity. Treason is never committed but where there is trust: falsehood is always in friendship and fellowship: every fair beck is not a seal of a faithful heart: poisons are mingled and ministered with honey that they may be the less suspected. The fairer the colours are without, the more suspicious is the ground; and harlots use more painting and decking than sober and honest matrons.[65]

If the action of the eyelash is obscure, how much more so the bath of love laving the great? This is a region not of confidence but of doubt.

Although the now-familiar deconstructionist abyss was only a theoretical possibility for the Elizabethan courtier, it was often a haunting one nonetheless. The sense that perception was grounded in interpretive action usually led, however, not to paralysis (nor to delight) but to efforts to dominate. However far-fetched and insecure the courtier's actions and interpretations might have been, he did have plenty of rhetorical ammunition with which to implement them. In the chapters that follow we shall review three strategic discourses, the first of which concerns the logic of social hierarchy in its most general applications.

3. Tropes of Social Hierarchy: Gentle and Base

The first set of ideological tropes to be considered takes as its goal the founding of an absolute ontological distinction between the ruling class and its subjects. These tropes stipulate the speaker's membership in the class and aim to demonstrate by persuasion the entitlement of the class as a group to supremacy and privilege. The persuasions fall into three categories: arguments by means of total mystery; mystifications of contingent difference as absolute; and arguments from historical origins.

Total Mystery

Guazzo's Annibale resists discussing the conversation of princes: "It pertaines not to us to speake of their dooinges, which are yrreprehensible and incomprehensible" (1:198).[1] The behavior of princes is placed beyond both criticism and comprehension. This gesture of both relative and absolute dismissal suggests the range of effects of mystification. The most complete dismissal denies comprehension by presenting the ruler as fundamentally Other, by definition unavailable to interpretation. Burke's famous note on glamour, suggesting "a hierarchic motive that affects the very nature of perception," helps situate the powers of this kind of mystification.

According to Webster's, the word may be a corruption of "gramarye," which means necromancy, magic. (The relation between grammar and magic doubtless goes back to the days when the knowledge of reading and writing was in itself a strong mark of status, because of the cleric's role in civil and religious administration.) The word is also thought to be connected with an Icelandic word for weakness of sight, while Icelandic *glamr* is a word for the moon, and of a ghost. Four meanings for "glamour" are given: a charm affecting the eye, making objects appear different from what they are; witchcraft, magic, a spell; a kind of haze in the air, causing things to appear different from what they really are; any artificial interest in, or association with, an object, through which it appears delusively magnified or glorified.[2]

This phenomenological notion of glamour links mystery and value. It derives its force from its resistance to assimilation by the familiar world. Objections to the glamourous can be written off as uncomprehending, and Annibale elsewhere argues that such incompetence frequently has an affiliation with "the idle, the ignorant, the unfortunate, and bankerupts, which have no good successe in their own affaires ... [they are] they which seeke to deprave the doinges of other men, and give themselves to speake evill, for that they know not how to doe any thing well" (1:65–66). This dismissal reverses the direction of criticism by making it the badge of jealous meanness "explained" by generic *ad hominem* reference to the critic's character. William, Guazzo's other interlocutor, further notes that no behavior is so good that it cannot be wrongly interpreted. Annibale replies that one should never attend to the censures and reprehensions that come from "the blind communalty, which as ignorant, taketh every thing arsi-versie" (1:45). The fact that criticism originates outside the governing class justifies dismissing it without reference to accuracy. The supposedly total opacity of the governing class to those below is then presented as evidence of a discontinuity in the sociointellectual scale.

Some information of course leaks across this ontological gap—the fact of mystery, signaling the absent presence of transcendent meaning. Burke notes that "in mystery there must be *strangeness*; but the estranged must also be thought of as in some way capable of communion. There is mystery in an animal's eyes at those moments when a man feels that he and the animal understand each other in some inexpressible fashion."[3] Castiglione speaks of a man being "sooner knowne in small matters than in great" (pp. 36/110);[4] *sprezzatura*, when applied to "any deede that a man doth, how litle so ever it be, doth ... by and by open the knowledge of him that doth it" (pp. 48/128). In each case the ostentatiously minor sign, within the reach of the observer, is said to refer to larger realities that transcend the apparent power of reference of the sign. Such "information" refers mysteriously to further meaning, creating transcendence by arousing the observer's inferential urges. Inferiors are encouraged to conceive of their superiors by reference to the thinness of available information as pointing beyond what is seen, to an absolute difference.

The elite may of course be literally absent, pursuing a mysterious life behind closed doors. Puttenham speaks of the "priuate entertainements in Court, or other secret disports in chamber, and such solitary places" (p. 46).[5] The advertisement of "secret" recreations arouses curiosity and fantasy even as it refuses information. The most famous example of such incomprehensible privacy must be Arethusa's frigid rebuke of a "country fellow" who rescues her from death at the hands of her aristocratic lover Philaster: "What ill-bred man art thou, to intrude thyself/Upon our private sports, our recreations?" We share his rude response: "God 'uds me, I understand you not."[6] But such extreme insistence on privacy was more typical of seventeenth-century than of Elizabethan aristocratic life; the queen had a stronger commitment to living in public. Still, the generation of public incomprehension held a place in the Elizabethan elite's strategic repertoire.

There are many specimens of this core strategy. Elyot repeatedly enjoins the governor to inspire *reverence* in his subjects. The religious overtones of the term suggest that the gap between the subject and those he revered was an ontological one and was marked by epistemological obscurity. In order to maintain the mystery, of course, such obscurity had to be elaborately guarded. The author of the *Institucion of a Gentleman* suggests, for instance, the *irrelevance* of information that humanizes the elite: "Although their condicions in al pointes dooe not aunswere to their nobilitie [,] . . . it is to be considered that the more reuerence is done towardes noble men, the more it geueth example of obediens towardes the Rulers and superiours of thys earth. . . . And though sumtyme noble men will forgeat themselues, yet oughte not others therefore to forgeat to dooe their dutyes vnto them" (sig. G7v–8r).[7] Demystification should have no consequences.

Elyot sees such reverence as "pleasant and terrible" (p. 99),[8] which should call to mind the Machiavellian dialectic: the revered is loved and feared at once.[9] The prime site for this kind of reverence is of course the presence of the prince, especially his coronation, which Elyot says must be public, "that by reason of the honourable circumstances then used should be impressed in the hearts of the beholders perpetual reverence, which (as I before said) is fountain of obedience" (p. 163). But the mere presence of royalty will serve at all times as a typical case of mystery. Puttenham devotes much attention to the prickly questions of decorum before princes; in fact, his section on behavioral decorum per se (pp. 261–76) is explicated only by examples from the presence, as if this were the worst case of obscurity for the principles (and practitioners) of decorum to confront.

It might seem that the prince alone is endowed with this incomprehensibility, as God's sole earthly representative, but in fact the concept extended to the governing class. Elyot writes of the governor's right to reverence, not just the prince's; the author of the *Institucion* writes of "rulers and superiours of thys earth"; and Guazzo's prince would in city-state Italy be a local duke, to be subsumed among the nobility in nation-state England. At another level, Arthur Ferguson suggests that "advice-to-princes" texts "were undoubtedly meant for a wider public than that of royalty alone. . . . They could be considered especially valuable as supplementary reading for the local lord, be he squire, knight or magnate, who fulfilled the obligation traditionally incumbent upon a knight to act not only as the sword-arm of the body politic but also as a 'governor.'"[10] Furthermore, Burke suggests that "the conditions for 'mystery' are set by *any* pronounced social distinctions, as between nobility and commoners, courtiers and king, leader and people, rich and poor, judge and prisoner at the bar, 'superior race' and underprivileged 'races' or minorities."[11] All these other categories have analogical relevance to class distinctions, which arouse considerations of mystery at every turn.

Such mystery occurs frequently in ordinary courtly conversation, of course, where different orders of being intersect—where, that is to say, mystery is both aroused and set aside in conversational access. This mixture is by its very existence supposed to induce submission. Guazzo suggests that the gift of blinding light causes the inferior to lower his eyes joyfully: "They are marvellous wel apaid when they see a Gentleman, notwithstanding the inequalitie, which is betweene them, to make him selfe their equall. Wherby they are induced to love him, to honor him, and to doe him service" (1:192). Such delightful condescension is joyful because inexplicable, conferred "notwithstanding the inequalitie, which is between them." The difference in kind is reaffirmed by the submissive response to the offer of abnegation: "Albeit it bee so, that this vertue [courteous affability] bee seemely and commendable in all sortes of people, yet it shineth most brightly in those whiche are our Superiours, either in power or preeminence, when you receive of them curteous speeches, in suche sorte, that what by their gentle woordes, and what by their lively lookes and cheerefull countenaunce, you understande their affections, wheretoo your will doeth easily incline" (1:157).[12] And as the proper answer to this magnanimity is joyful submission, so the proper answer to criticism or intrusion from below is God's hierarchical answer to Job out of the whirlwind: "This is not for you to question—it is beyond you."

Mystification of the Contingent as Absolute

The argument in support of absolute difference has a more particular form: the presentation of difference in degree as difference in kind, of contingent difference as absolute. This makes explicit what was implicit in the *via negativa* of the preceding section, that the commensurate becomes incommensurate—natural rather than positive. The structuration that supports this view is presented in the form of moralized spatial metaphors.

The queen is imagined to occupy the center of a circular social cosmos, acting as the fount of civilization, as in *The Faerie Queene*:

> Then pardon me, most dreaded Soueraine,
>   That from your selfe I doe this vertue [courtesy] bring,
>   And to your selfe doe it returne againe:
> So from the Ocean all riuers spring,
> And tribute backe repay as to their King.
> Right so from you all goodly vertues well
> Into the rest, which round about you ring.
>
> (Book VI, Proem 7)[13]

Elizabeth is sufficiently dreadful, the gap to be crossed is so wide, that apology is necessary even in complimenting her. Puttenham, as we have seen, also relates the queen to "the Roundell": her ideological radiance "makes eche subiect clearly see,/What he is bounden for to be/To God his Prince and common wealth,/His neighbour, kinred and to himselfe" (p. 100). The queen's chastening "rayes" brook no illegitimate intercourse; her central location orients or "places" her subjects where they belong, in appropriate ranks, all humble in relation to her. In a comparable way, her governors, by their justice, bounty, and might—that is, government—seek to place their inferiors below them, similarly humble and joyful.

Along the radius of such a nest of circles a scale can be constructed, which discriminates on the basis of distance from the royal center of social value. Thus the field of human attributes is apportioned along a linear continuum, or axis, marking a singular system of value. The effect is to present a complex space of qualities in a simple quantitative measure. Elyot, for instance, likens the human population to that of the natural world. Each constituent of the latter population has virtues of various sorts, he says, and "where any is found that hath many of the said properties, he is the more set by than all the other, and by that estimation the order of his place and degree evidently appeareth" (p. 3). Similarly, in the human cosmos, "God giveth not to every man like gifts of grace, or of nature, but to some more, some less" (p. 4). In the worlds of both nature and culture a varied field of characteristics is conceived, but its variations are parceled out along a single axis. No notation exists for a rich but stupid man or a poor but talented woman; some simply have more virtue, some less. Romei makes this linearization explicit: "For the preseruation, and liuing wel of a city, it is requisite, there be artificers, mercinaries, husbandmen, marchantes, souldiers, Iudges, Magistrates, Princes, and Priestes: which being (as it is) true; so is it likewise conuenient, that there should be poore, rich, noble, & ignoble" (p. 248).[14] This move smuggles the distinctions of the Pauline functional model into the homogeneous character of the line. Stone characterizes this compression to linearity as a "harmonization" of axes: the dominant ideology, he says, presents "a picture of a fully integrated society in which stratification by title, power, wealth, talent, and culture are all in absolute harmony."[15]

Often this harmony must have been assumed unthinkingly, but some Elizabethans made a conscious translation back and forth between such distinctions of quality and quantity. The records of New Year's gifts given at court (to and by the queen) testify to this fact, as the sample of 1588–89 shows.[16] Although many courtiers simply gave the queen lump sums ("By the Earl of *Darby*, in gold—20 pounds"), many others presented gifts designed to be memorable, that is, to individuate the giver. The earl of Ormond, for instance, gave "part of a petticote of carnation satten embrodered with a broade garde or border of antyques of flowers and fyshes of Venis gold, silver, and silke, and all over with a twist of Venis gold."[17] Hatton, since Leicester's recent death (September 4, 1588) the leading courtier and now lord chancellor as well, felt it necessary to be quite elaborate:

> By Sir *Christopher Hatton*, Knight, Lord Chancellor of England, a coller of gold, conteyninge 11 peeces, whereof four made like scallop shells

garneshed round about with small diamonds and rubyes, one pearle pendaunt and two rubyes pendaunt without foyle, six other longer peeces eche
garnesshed with seven pearles, five rubyes of two sorts, sparks of diamonds
and two rubyes pendaunt without foyle, having a bigger peece in the middest like a scallopp shell, garneshed with diamonds and rubyes of sundry
bignesses, one pearle in the topp, one rock ruby in the middest, having
three fishes pendaunt garneshed on th'one side with sparks of diamonds
and two rubyes pendaunt, without foyle, and with one peece at eche end of
them garneshed with two small rubyes and one pearle, and a paire of
bracelets of gold, conteyninge 12 peeces, six like knotts garnesshed with
sparks of diamonds, and six like knotts garnesshed with sparks of rubyes,
and two pearles in a peece, and two pearles betweene eche peece.[18]

In response to this sort of signal the queen offered quantitative linearity, nearly always in plate. A sample of her gifts reads as follows:

To the Earle of *Shrewsbury*, in guilte plate, K. 30 oz. di. di. qr.

To the Earle of *Darby*, in guilte plate, K. 30 oz. 3 qrs.

To the Earle of *Sussex*, in gilte plate, M. 20 oz. 3 qrs.

To the Earle of *Huntington*, in gilte plate, M. 20 oz. 3 qrs.

To the Earle of *Bath*, in gilte plate, M. 29 oz.[19]

In the records, the return gifts are listed according to the rank of the
recipient, in the following scale: earls, viscounts, marquesses and
countesses, bishops, lords, baronesses, ladies, knights, gentlewomen,
maids of honor, and gentlemen. Last came "free gifts" (unreciprocat-
ed? unearned?) to such servants as grooms. The queen's gifts are described only in quantitative terms, by weight (save for the notation of
maker, such as Keele, Martyn).[20] Hatton received 400 oz., Ormond
140 oz., and others different amounts, presumably allotted according
to rank, favor, the ingenuity of the courtier's gift, and the political
capital to be gained by reward or snub to factions. We do not know
how public this information became. But surely courtiers like Hatton
would have publicized their offerings after presenting them, not to
mention during the act itself, which would have been quite ceremonial.[21] The form of the tabulations (gifts to and from) mirrors the
express function of exchange.

In December 1595 there was a rumor that Elizabeth would "make
both councillors and officers of Household." A courtier had doubts,
"but," he said, "it will increase the Queen's New Year gifts."[22] And in
1591 Sir Julius Caesar archly wrote to Burghley, "It may be that I shall
by the next year be enabled to yield a greater gift."[23] Still, decisions

about return gifts might well have been made in complete disregard of the courtier's gift, or before it was tendered. However these judgments were made, it is hard to imagine Elizabeth being absent from them completely. In any case, she had an institutional functionary compile these records,[24] and his inventory of her gifts almost surely encodes levels of princely sanction in some way. Since the return gifts are itemized only in quantitative terms, it seems that here too, fully consciously, the occupants of a multivalent field fought for rungs on a linear ladder and were given what they came for by a knowing prince. The loads of plate simply materialized the competition.

The next step in mapping the social topography is to punctuate the linear hierarchy with an uncrossable gap, altering it from a continuum to a binary ontological system. As we have already seen, Elizabethans like Bacon divided the social body into "the noblesse and the commonalty";[25] another Elizabethan said that "All sortes of people created from the beginninge are devided into 2: Noble and Ignoble."[26] These terms denote not regions or areas, which could be contiguous, but boxes, literal containers, imposed "from the beginninge" with the Creator's ontological force. They designate social difference as difference in *kind*, not the more usual difference in *degree*, a term admitting of contiguity and perhaps mobility. Castiglione's project to embarrass the malapert assheads betrays the blurring of these regions but aims to reconstitute the traditional binary gap between noble and ignoble. The reading of the difference as qualitative is exemplified by Ferne's distinction between gentle and ungentle lawyers:

> One Lawyer of gentle linage, is more frequented with the Client of *Forma pauperis*, more vigilant, to his clients cause, more easie in his fees, more desirous to make peace at home with his neighbors, then ready to perswade them, to pursuites of actions: more couragious in his faculty, more confident in a good cause, more ashamed in a bad: more liberall in his hospitality: more carelesse of purchase: yea in all his life, more honourable, and well bearing him selfe, then tenne Aduocates, of base and vngentle stocke, though all their vertues, and worthy partes, were collected into one and compared with the other. And of the contrary, one Legist vnnoble in birth, wil be more gredy of his gaines, more inexorable in his office, more giuen to quarels, and suites on foot, then tenne of the other sort. (P. 93)[27]

In this view the ungentle lawyer becomes oxymoronic. Similarly, even the apparently fluid model of Spenser's courteous royal fountain encodes the absolute gap, although between prince and courtiers rather than between governors and governed. Virtues and tributes (such as his poem) flow reciprocally back and forth across the intervening space between upper and lower, but people stay where they are, hesitating even to look across this chasm, much less leap. The biological version of this trope, to speak literally of leaping, grounds most thoroughly the presentation of difference in degree as difference in kind. Ferne argues against cross-class marriage with the following analogy:

> If you suffer your horse of warre, to leape a she Asse, doe you receaue, from his procreation, a steed fit for the armed fielde, or a monstrous mule, desti-mated [*sic*] to the rusticall, and slauish labours, of the countrie pei-saunt? . . . Are we carefull then, from what tree our plant is taken? Of what kind our dogs do come? And of what race our horses are bred? And shall we hold it nothing to the purpose of what parents, a Gentleman is begot-ten? thus you see, how that the law-maker had instruction, euen from na-tures lawe, to forbid such vnegall copling. (Pp. 11–12)

Such marriage is presumably the breeding ground of malapert ass-heads.[28]

The lamination of these concentric circles and of the interrupted continuum of noble and ignoble has several strategic effects. For one thing, the ruling elite is positioned medially between the populace and the prince, ordering communication from either direction. Members of a priestly contingent, they can worship and honor their queen while serving their inferiors with kindly intercession. Indeed, what seemed before to be groups commensurate if not coordinate can be presented as opposites *in need of* the mediation. And the hiatus is portable. It can be shifted to just below the governors, so that they can partake of the utter unlikeness between prince and populace. When the prince is directly addressed, he can be flattered by stationing the hiatus above the elite. All these operations valorize difference; as An-nibale says in another connection, "wee are so much the more es-teemed of, by howe muche our Civilitie differeth from the nature and fashions of the vulgar sorte" (1:123).[29]

Guazzo elsewhere conveys a sense of how this ontological segrega-tion felt from the inside. During the banquet whose description occu-pies Book 4 of *The Civile Conversation*, Lord Vespasian (the ranking guest) speaks of the ambitious man's failure to treasure his own place. "Neither will we looke once backe or downe, to compare or make our selves equal with those, who are in degree inferiour unto us, which if we should doe, in stead of ministring occasions of our owne sadnesse, we should exhilirate our selves [ci rallegreressimo], and thanke God that he hath not placed us in so base and low estate" (2:164/517). The way to avoid the agitation felt by the ambitious is to realize that the crucial elevation has already taken place. The distance from the base estate below is properly exhilarating, a secular shadow of religious transport at election (the purest of such discriminations).[30] The operational benefits of this class self-consciousness are obvious.[31]

There were also pragmatic benefits to be gained from this boundary, at least in theory. Ferne catalogs a set of quasi-legal entitlements accompanying gentility, though he acknowledges to his Inns of Court readers that they are enfeebled by what are "fitly called common lawes . . . tending not only to the disabling of Gentry, but also in some measure derogatory to the regall prerogatiue of a Soueraigne, which other princes, & their Gentry do enioy, by the constitutions of Emperial lawes" (p. 84). Of Ferne's thirty-five privileges I list only portions of a few (from pp. 77–81).

3. The vngentle person, although he haue scraped through niggardlinesse great riches, yet he is not worth a coate-armor, who for the vilenes of his estate (in respect of the excellencie of the other) is bound to yeeld obedience, & the show of honor to a Gentleman in these things following: that if a Gentleman doth speake, he yeeld diligent & attentiue eare. . . .

4. In that a Gentleman of worship being in presence, the vnnoble shall arise from their seates.

5. That none of vngentle degree, presume to take the right hand, or the chiefest seate in the company, or to sit next the Iudge, before a Gentleman. . . .

7. If any person in the publique recapitulation of the names of men, shall purposedly pronounce the name of the vnnoble, before the name of a Gentleman, *Grauiter peccat, pro quo datur iniuriarum actio.* . . .

10. . . . If in common elections of Officers, and the like, voices be of number equall, the voices of most Gentlemen shall preuaile.

19. The promise and word of a Gentleman is construed of the like validitie that his deede, confirmed with the contestation of witnesses and seale, could extend unto. . . .

22. Gentlemen ought to be preferred to offices before the vnnoble. . . .

23. The lawes of the Church haue extended that fauor to the excellent estate of Gentility, that if a Gentleman be a professed Clarke, and entred into the holy orders of the Ministery, he is capable of dispensation to retaine a pluralitie of benefices. . . .

26. There ought more credence to be giuen by the Iudge to the oth of two Gentlemen produced, as witnesses, then to a multitude of vngentle persons. . . .

27. Persons of base and vngentle estate, are no competent witnesses against a Gentleman of bloud, and coate-armor perfect. . . .

The application (or extraction) of these privileges must have varied immensely; where precedent existed, or could be claimed, it was no doubt used as often as possible.

The scale was symbolically reinforced by the application of explicitly moral weights and measures. Elevation was supposed to *stipulate* virtue. Richard Mulcaster observes that "upon whomsoever the prince doth bestow any extraordinary preferment, it is to be thought that there is in them some great singularity, wherewith their princes, which can judge, be so extraordinarily moved."[32] This assumption is based on several arguments. "Vertue is the foundation of gentry," according to Guazzo; "the more good partes bee in a man, the more Gentlemanlike hee is sayde to bee" (1:184). Here virtue is said to be implicit in upper rank. When a prince elevates one to gentle status, Guazzo says, he "doeth approove the vertue and merites of him he rayseth to the state of gentrie" (1:175). This "approval" seems to combine demonstration, appreciation, and recognition, all posterior to the presence of the virtue. Less surely is this true of Puttenham's praise of Queen Elizabeth as "the most excellent Poet" of their time: "by your Princely purse fauours and countenance, making in maner what ye list, the poore man rich, the lewd well learned, the coward couragious, and vile both noble and valiant" (pp. 4–5).[33] Whatever epistemological status these adjectives deserve, they imply the stipulation of virtue by royal fiat. Again, we may note the commonplace *magistratus virum ostendit*, as Guicciardini has it (C163);[34] Castiglione says "promotions declare what men be" (pp. 278/476–77); and Bacon states that "a place sheweth the man."[35] This adage is usually taken to mean that promotion reveals one's true nature, since the stresses of office test weaknesses and strengths. But it seems equally true that promotion immediately declares the man in a stipulative sense; only eventually does it probe his worth. Appointment is revelation, proof of potency if not of desert. It is precisely because of this stipulative factor that face-value acceptance of supposedly denotative definitions of social hierarchy as morally based is unsatisfactory: the presumption of denotation begs the question.

There was a serious danger in the converse of this proposition; virtue could not be allowed to stipulate nobility in practice without
opening doors far too wide.[36] Ferne repudiates the argument from
merit, by means of a plowman, Columell, who is included in his dialogue solely to make this and similar claims that inferiors are loyal to
the nobility of blood and hostile to new gentry. "(Sir Herrat) [says
Columell] let your gentlenesse, wonne by proper merit (for some such
quaint name, you gaue it) be wiped out of your booke: vor poore mens
children may put vp their pipes, vor being made Gentils in these
daies, when as Landlords grow so hard, and places in Schooles beene
so highly sold, and borrell folke han nought to giue" (p. 22). In this
putatively lower-class vision, the word "merit" is poisoned by carnivorous false gentry, who use it to justify a social position that they
exercise solely for their own gain and of which they are ipso facto
undeserving. (The use of dialect to lend naturalistic credence to this
view oddly emphasizes its fictive status.) The argument from virtue
seemed to some a useful guarantee of supremacy, but wholesale endorsement of the notion blurred crucial distinctions; Columell's tone
posits ironic quotation marks useful for Ferne's readers in devaluing
the virtue of the mobile. Still, we can be sure that lip service was, then
as now, a powerful shaper of thought. The lexical coincidence of vocabularies of rank and morality must usually have enhanced the unexamined status of the elite. Princes usually received the uncritical
presumption that they knew their business; seemingly odd appointment would be as likely to arouse doubt of one's own judgment as
doubt of wisdom on high.

In fact, of course, the aristocratic circle of value was theoretically
defined as closed: Annibale holds that "true praise . . . onely proceedeth from praise worthie persons" (1: 95).[37] Two facts support this
view. First, reputations are not only given by one's group-audience,
they are held by it, in an ongoing way; a group fascinated by the
observation and dissection of reputation sustains its promulgation.
Second, only the elite has access to the special media that sustain
reputation in the public eye, beyond personal acquaintance and discussion. The only true glory is that which is immortalized in letters,
according to Castiglione (pp. 70/161). (Since the only "true" letters
are those ratified by high-culture society, balladry can be ignored
when it does not echo the elite perspective.) The members of the aristocracy were the main producers and consumers of immortalizing
writings. They preferred to consider such ratification as the voice of

history, regarding their present as the future's heroic past. The advent
of print complicated this operation, to be sure. Manuscript circulation achieved a new negative cachet when print created a nonaristo-
cratic reading public.[38] But production and consumption in both media were dominated during this period by those who controlled most
other things. A new way to be "in the public eye" had been invented;
attracting the public's attention called for new skills. For the time
being, however, the old skills of the nobility dominated this new
arena as they did existing ones.

The distinguishing virtues stipulated by elevation were arrayed in
the categories of arms and letters (the latter a significant humanist
alteration of the old criteria of arms and piety), which were thought to
organize the modes of significance proper to the ruling elite. Harvey,
for instance, so summarizes Castiglione: "Castilio's Courtier ye right
Gentlemans book, & his only profession Letters or Arms: with continued experience in ye pregnant affaires of the world."[39] And Romei
defines these professions by reference to such affairs: "by armes wee
defende and amplifie kingdomes, and by Letters wee preserue and
gouerne the same" (p. 267).[40] Technological advances had laid to rest
the armed chivalric knight and his plebian successor the archer; small
and large gunnery now dominated warfare, to the detriment of individual feats of socially distinctive heroism.[41] But certain aspects of
chivalric war practice lived on in celebration and recreation,[42] continuing the association of martial prowess with the ruling class. Along-
side this archaic mythology another version of the association had
grown up. By historicizing mythic warfare in the study of great gen-
erals like Caesar, humanism intellectualized it, focusing on strategy
rather than on valor. This might sometimes have been a matter of
compensation. The author of *Institucion of a Gentleman* recommends that if the gentleman "wante[s] stature of body therunto (as
nature to all men hath not geuen great personage,) yet at the least, he
ought to be able to geue hys good counsell or aduyce in matters of
warres" (sig. B7r). But Sidney writes without apology of the value of
the Grand Tour as reconnaissance; it provides "the knowledge of all
leauges, betwixt Prince, and Prince, the topograficall descripcion of
eache Countrie, howe the one lyes by scituacion to hurte or helpe the
other, howe they are to the sea well harbowred or not, howe stored
with shippes, howe with Revenewe, howe with fortificacions and Gar-
risons, howe the People warlicklie trayned or kept under, with manie
other such condicions."[43] Skills such as drawing were justified (and

denied to the subject classes) on the grounds of their strategic util-ity.[44] Courtly recreation might take the form of Philopoemen's game—imagining the strategic implications of whatever geographi-cal formations surrounded the players at the moment.[45] Thus the Renaissance gentleman might, with some mythical, recreational, and intellectual support, claim that "the principall and true profession of a Courtier ought to bee in feates of armes," as Castiglione's Count Lewis argues (pp. 35/109).

The case for assimilating virtues of letters to social elevation was made on different grounds, since the English secular ruling class had not before made this claim, as they had that of military virtue. The link comes from the political vector of the humanist educational ethic. Since it was posited that intellectual skills were to be employed in the functions of governance, the reverse might equally easily be claimed—that government was typically the task of the educated. The relevance of the experience of men long dead was invoked. But the lessons of history (as opposed to tradition) were available only to the literate. As skilled young men from the lower classes brought new pressures to bear on the aristocracy, the revolution in the gentleman's education began. The aristocracy tried to monopolize the new intel-lectualist functions of rule by excluding the lower classes from the education that was becoming obligatory for those who sought politi-cal advancement (and that had been more available to the lower ranks when the intellectual elite was drawn from the church).[46] By its very existence, Gilbert's plan for an aristocratic university emphasizes this monopolistic urge (as, from another angle, does Ascham's treatise *The Scholemaster*, "specially purposed for the priuate bryngyng vp of youth in Ientlemen and Noble mens houses" [p. 171]). Sometimes the motive of dominance was adduced unashamedly. Gilbert plans to have a lawyer teach his elite students not only the basics of the com-mon law, but also to teach "exquisitely the office of a Iustice of peace and Sheriffe. . . . It is necessary that noble men and gentlemen should learne to be able to put their owne Case in law, and to have some Iudgment in the office of a Iustice of peace and Sheriffe; for thorough the want thereof the beste are oftentymes subiecte to the direction of farre their Inferiors" (p. 7).[47] On other occasions a public service function is proposed for such restrictions:

> And when the best shall ordinarily be men of such rare virtue [i.e., when the gentle have received such education as to make possible a monopoly of public officeholding], Then the prince and Realme shall not so much from

> tyme to tyme be Charged, as they haue bene, in rewarding the well deserv-
> ers. ffor honnour is a sufficient paymente for him that hath inoughe.
> Whereas in tymes paste the poorest sorte were best able to deserve at the
> princes handes, which, without great Charges to the prince, could not be
> maintained. So that when theis thinges shalbe performed, ordinarie vertue
> can beare no price. (P. 11)

If Gilbert's plan is adopted, honor will be a sufficient payment for
preferment, since worthy candidates can be drawn from the ranks of
the gentle, who supposedly need no expenditure from the Crown.
(The final sentence in the preceding quotation may also suggest that
the virtuous ungentle ["ordinarie vertue"] can expect no access to the
social reputation that comes with occupational elevation.[48]) Perhaps
best of all, their places in the market might be totally filled by their
inexpensive superiors.[49]

A moralized version of the gap that Gilbert sees as financial derives
from the mind-body distinction—itself a reductive hierarchizing of
the many-functioned Pauline organic body model. The rulers are superior to the ruled as the head is superior to the (remainder of the)
body. Since only the belly and pizzle have "lower" desires, the
"heads" of state can be trusted to be free of them. Guazzo, speaking
of ill speakers (generally the idle, ignorant, unfortunate, and bank-
rupt), charges that "the fault of him which speaketh yll of his
neighbour, to the intent to bring him into hatred, is greater than of
him who pulleth the bread out of the mouth of the poore. For as the
soule is more precious then the body, so it is a greater offence to take
away ones good name, which refresheth the soule, then to defraud
one of food, which sustaineth the body" (1:66). The gentleman cares
more about the reified tangibles of reputation than about material
needs. In fact, the division is double. The gentleman is materially ascetic; any such "pleasures" are merely instrumental to governance.
At the same time, he is as ferocious in defense (and pursuit) of reputation as the starveling is in search of food.

There is also for Elyot a causal relation between material and intellectual dominance. "Such men, having substance in goods by certain
and stable possessions which they may apportionate to their own living and bringing up of their children in learning and virtues, may (if
nature repugn not) cause them to be so instructed and furnished toward the administration of a public weal, that a poor man's son only
by his natural wit, without other adminiculation or aid, never or seldom may attain to the semblable" (p. 14). Elyot's subjunctive here

resonates between a description of the odds and a wish, positing an elegantly self-serving cycle: riches beget education, which begets skill in ruling, to which riches are the logical adjunct (supplied by the subject classes "served" by the rulers). These riches encourage obedience among the lower sort and enable the current governors to prepare their sons for the yoke of office. The family is politically environmental as well as hereditary, coupling the Renaissance achievement model of inheritance with the medieval ascriptive version. (The same doubling underlies Elyot's foundation of the elite's prehistoric elevation on the virtue of "understanding" [p. 4]: he conflates intelligence and education and calls for a reformation to primitive principles analogous to contemporary religious rethinking.)

Such theorized coincidence of aristocratic rank and the virtues of letters required the restriction of educational opportunity. Although such a restriction was never really accomplished, it might have been justified by the retrospective fantasy of the *Institucion*'s author, that "to encrease vertue by way of knowledge, it apperith that universities and places of study wer first founded by nobilitie gentle ancetors oure forefathers . . . for their children to be first broughte up therein" (sigs. A8v–B1r). Gilbert further argued that it should be "no smalle Comodity that the nobility of England shalbe therby in their youthes brought vp in amity and acquintaunce" (p. 11). As was to be true in later centuries, the ruling class was advised to guard its future closure by encouraging the social intimacy of its children from the beginning. Such exclusive efforts were made repeatedly, though never with complete success. James came closest in the period under discussion: in 1604 the new king ordered that "none be from henceforth admitted into the Society of any House of Court that is not a gentleman by descent."[50] The class distinction had finally become theoretically institutionalized, at least for the "third university."

Tension between ideological distinctiveness and the fluid social reality was inevitable, for the struggle brought resemblance rather than distinction. Burke views this resemblance as the deep structure of all competition: "the ways of competition have been . . . zealous ways of *conformity*. . . . What we call 'competition' is better described as men's attempt to *out-imitate* one another."[51] The Renaissance notion of *emulation* precisely captures this coincidence of struggle and assimilation. The *Oxford English Dictionary* defines "emulate" as (1) "to strive to equal or rival . . . to copy or imitate with the object of equalling or excelling"; (2) " . . . to vie with, rival, attain or approach to equality with." R. Pearson's translation (1606) of Giovanni Botero's *A Treatise Concerning the Causes of the Magnificencie and Greatness of Cities* perfectly captures the dual emphasis. "All such as aspire and thirst after offices and honors run thither [to the city] overcome with emulation and disdaine at others."[52] Spenser often uses this binary structure. When Calidore and Crudor fight in *The Faerie Queene*, for instance, moral disparity recedes before martial resemblance:

> . . . both were wondrous practicke in that play,
> And passing well expert in single fight,
> And both inflam'd with furious despight:
> . . . .
> Ne once to breath a while their angers tempest ceast.
> . . . .
> They hew'd their helmes, and plates asunder brake,
> As they had potshares bene; for nought mote slake
> Their greedy vengeaunces, but goary blood. . . .
>
> (VI, i, 36–37)

The poet employs relentless grammatical parallelism to emphasize the problematic status of achievement of peace by such violence.

George Peele uses a similar duality in order to praise, in his *Polyhymnia*,[53] a celebration of the 1590 Accession Day tilt, where Sir Henry Lee transferred to the earl of Cumberland his office of Royal Champion. Peele depicts in loving detail jousts between thirteen pairs of knights, using both classical and chivalric literary resources. He describes each pair and the noble and brave manner in which they run the tilt, but he does not specify a victor.[54] Instead, Peele focuses on the valor of the competitors, or on the honor done the queen, and then moves on to describe the next pair.

> Together went these Champions, horse and man,
> Thundring along the Tylt, that at the shocke
> The hollow gyring vault of heaven resoundes.
> Six courses spent, and speares in shivers split,
> The 2. couple $\begin{cases} \text{The L. Straunge} \\ \text{M. John Gerrarde} \end{cases}$
> The Earle of Darbies valiant sonne and heire. . . .
>
> (Lines 34–38)
>
> And toote they goe, this Lord and lusty Knight
> To doo their roiall mistresse honors right.
>
> (Lines 78–79)

Together goe these friendes as enemies,
As when a Lion in a thicket pent,
Spieng the Boare all bent to combat him,
Makes through the shrubs, and thunders as he goes.

(Lines 123–26)

         ... and on they speed,
And hast they make to meete, and meete they doo,
And doo the thing for which they meete in hast,
Each in his Armour amiable to see
That in their lookes bare love and Chivalrie.

(Lines 140–44)

Peele subtly redeploys the *topoi* of chivalric combat toward effects essentially ritualistic, designed to bond rather than to distinguish.[55] The poem works by the alternation of two modes. First Peele individuates the knights with blazons, recapitulating their appearance on the field in familially distinct armor. At the same time, these furnitures of combat unmistakably identify these men as members of the same exclusive class, clothed in mutual imitation. Peele then further emphasizes parity by selective description of the actual combats. In choosing not to record who vanquishes whom, he deprives us of information conspicuous to the original spectators. Instead, he links the knights by their coparticipation in noble combat, sharing desert and bravery among them without making the tilt the zero-sum game it originally was (most extremely in trial by combat). This had become typical Elizabethan practice. "By the latter half of Elizabeth's reign the tilt had degenerated as a military exercise. The emphasis of the spectacle had shifted to pageantry and its literary superstructure and, from the cheques, it can be seen that it became a matter of routine to break increasingly fragile lances upon the opponent's body—now the only target consistently aimed for."[56] The reporting of scores reflects this deemphasis. The protocol had originally called for prizes to be awarded to the three best knights, thus declaimed: "John hath wele justid, Richard hath justid bettir and Thomas hath justid best of all." Anglo suggests that "from this it was but a step to sparing the feelings of even the most incompetent warrior by announcing that he had done 'well'—though this, in fact, indicated that he had done rather badly."[57] This practice implies that although the tilts did offer a means for expressing (and perhaps catharting) combative energies by aggressive members of the elite, an equally central function was the display of parity through emulation, reaffirming unity in submission to the queen and the consolidating class codes. Spenser, Peele, and late Elizabethan tilting in general reveal how competition can make implicit likeness explicit.

It is just this assimilative effect that makes it necessary for Castiglione to govern the recreative competition of superiors and inferiors with a priori dismissals:

> But who so will wrastle, runne and leape with men of the countrey, ought (in my judgement) to doe it after a sorte: to prove himselfe and (as they are wont to say) for courtisie, not to try maistry with them [*dee . . . farlo in modo di provarsi e, come si suol dir, per gentilezza, non per contender con loro*]: and a man ought (in a manner) to be assured to get the upper hand, else let him not meddle withall, for it is too ill a sight and too foule a matter and without estimation, to see a gentleman overcome by a carter. (Pp. 98/204)[58]

This attitude denies the assimilative force of competition; the manifested parity "does not count." We might similarly employ the dismissive concept of "practicing"—the labor of drill, expended not for competitive self-revelation, but in nominal pursuit of proficiency alone. If the options for invidious comparison are dismissed, then only delightful condescension remains: "practice" with one's inferiors is a gift to them, trimmed of the power to entail real resemblance. Of course the problems of emulation can be more simply dealt with, as Castiglione suggests, by either making sure to win, or avoiding the contest altogether. The author of the *Institucion* states that "noble and gentle men must diligently labour to excell others in vertues, or els there wil rise comparison of worthynes: as why should not Pan aswell as *Apollo?* which thing hath ben the greatest cause of ye ruine wherinto gentry is falne. For the negligence of him which sholde haue ben worthy encouraged ye unworthy to take up y^t which the other let fal" (sigs. *4v–5r). The excelling should take place in advance, lest telling competition allow direct comparison of "worthynes." Allusions to "practice" or "mere courtesy" can be made retroactively when one has misjudged an opponent's abilities.

Threats to absolute social differentiation can also be dealt with by co-optation. Elyot suggests that honor "not only impresseth a reverence, whereof proceedeth due obedience among subjects, but also inflameth men naturally inclined to idleness or sensual appetite to covet like fortune, and for that cause to dispose them to study or occupation" (p. 5). Majesty seems here to keep in their place those who belong there, while stimulating to mobility those who deserve it, those who are fitted for the higher walks of life but who, perhaps for lack of proper energy, have not sought to rise. Occasional "mistakes" can apparently be made in birth and location; the governing class has the duty to rectify such mistakes by summoning the incorrectly born to their proper station and duty. The ontological appearances are saved by identifying and relocating those who "really" belong above. Guazzo similarly argues, dealing with the negative case, that bad princes are not "really" princes, reserving that category for absolute goodness by demoting the exceptions. When William adduces bad princes of the past, Annibale disqualifies them, "for that they were not Princes by nature, but by violence"(*non erano Prencipi per natura, ma per violenza*) (1:203/246). The ontological system subsumes refractory examples. Sometimes ambition can be equated with virtuous activity; to encourage it can be a public service. Elyot argues that "where honest and virtuous personages be advanced, and well rewarded, it stirreth the courages of men, which have any spark of virtue, to increase therein, with all their force and endeavour" (p. 131). The vertical movement of social advancement and the lateral movement of moral improvement can be conflated along either axis: vertical movement can be justified, or the aspirant can be dismissed to the stifling sphere of private moral accomplishment, a mode of elevation proper to any social place, and so a traditional deflection of social movement. These various adjustments allow the ontological purity of gentility to be maintained, allowing or deflecting invasion, making or refusing exceptions, without entailing any thoroughgoing inspection of the absolute underpinnings of the status itself. The benefits of the system's general restrictions are maintained without loss of the possibility of arguments for selective exceptions.

Mystified Origins

The relation of absolute and contingent concepts of virtue and rank can also be projected into the past as a myth of the origins of stratification. Burke calls this maneuver "the temporizing of essence": "Because of the pun whereby the logically prior can be expressed in terms of the temporally prior, and *u.u.*, the ways of transcendence, in aiming at the discovery of *essential* motives, may often take the historicist form of symbolic *regression*."[59] The principal humanist temporizing of essence was historicist, but before turning to this approach we should briefly examine two other common scenarios: biblical derivations focusing on Cain and Abel and Noah's sons, and the argument from force. Ferne summarizes the former: "as *Adam* had sonnes of honor, so had he also *Cayn*, destinated to dishonour . . . vpon restauration of the second world, a notable lesson is left to al ages, to put a difference, between the Noble & vnnoble, euen by that action of *Noah*: whereas God himselfe, in the person of that Patriark and Prophet, adiudgeth the progeny of *Cham* the cursed, to be a servant to his brethren. But *Sem* receiued the benediction of a free estate, and *Iaphet* the blessing of the increase of a famous stocke, and mighty people" (pp. 2–3). Jean Bodin makes the argument from force.

> Before there was either Citie or citisen, or any forme of a Commonweale amongst men, euerie master of a familie was a maister in his owne house, hauing power of life and death ouer his wife and children: but after that force, violence, ambition, couetousnesse, and desire of reuenge had armed one against another, the issues of warres and combats giuing victorie vnto the one side, made the other to become vnto them slaues: and amongst them that ouercame, he that was chosen cheefe and captaine, vnder whose conduct and leading they had obtained the victorie, kept them also in his power and commaund as his faithfull and obedient subiects, and the other as his slaues. Then that full and entire libertie by nature giuen to euery man, to liue as himselfe best pleased, was altogether taken from the vanquished, and in the vanquishers themselues in some measure also diminished, in regard of the conquerour; for that now it concerned euerie man in priuat to yeeld his obedience vnto his cheife soueraigne; and he that would not abate any thing of his libertie, to liue under the lawes and commaundement of another, lost all. So the word of *Lord* and *Seruant*, of *Prince* and *Subiect*, before vnknowne vnto the world, were first brought into vse.[60]

Neither of these mythologies served very fully to support class stratification. The latter model presented the members of the ruling elite negatively, as usurpers of a natural freedom only just becoming visible, and otherwise as strong men hard to assimilate to civil relations (though useful in international contexts, as *Henry V* demonstrates). The scriptural derivation had more uses, especially as it sanctified the forms of material distinction, though it was not sufficiently detailed for application to class issues. But with the fruitful concept of prehistory an account of the origins of stratification could be made that was collective rather than factional and so was theoretically binding for future generations of subjects.

Elyot presents this view in programmatic detail.

> In the beginning, when private possessions and dignity were given by the consent of the people, who then had all things in common, and equality in degree and condition, undoubtedly they gave the one and the other to him

at whose virtue they marvelled, and by whose labour and industry they received a common benefit, as of a common father that with equal affection loved them. And that promptitude or readiness in employing that benefit was then named in English gentleness, as it was in Latin *benignitas* and in other tongues after a semblable signification, and the persons were called gentlemen, more for the remembrance of their virtue and benefit, than for discrepance of estates. Also it fortuned by the providence of God that of those good men were engendered good children, who being brought up in virtue, and perceiving the cause of the advancement of their progenitors, endeavoured themselves by imitation of virtue to be equal to them in honor and authority; by good emulation they retained still the favour and reverence of people. And for the goodness that proceeded of such generation the state of them was called in Greek *Eugenia*, which signifieth good kind or lineage, but in a more brief manner it was after called nobility, and the persons noble, which signifieth excellent, and in the analogy or signification it is more ample than gentle, for it containeth as well all that which is in gentleness, as also the honour or dignity therefore received, which be so annexed the one to the other that they cannot be separate. (Pp. 103–4)

This scheme confers numerous ideological benefits. Social elevation is based on free recognition by willing subjects-to-be of the selfless virtue of their moral superiors. Property is the reward of virtue, hence its sign. And these perquisites conduce to continuing moral elevation, encouraging sons to live up to the example of their forefathers.

To proclaim this "explanation" was of course to reveal it as dormant. Elyot was providing his upper-class readers with a justification for their position; the supply betrays the demand. But he manages to work the need for explanation into his historical myth. "For," he observes, "we be men and not angels," that is, we are fallen creatures, for whom lost perceptions must be recovered. Now "we know nothing but by outward significations. Honour, whereto reverence pertaineth, is (as I have said) the reward of virtue, which honour is but the estimation of people, which estimation is not everywhere perceived, but by some exterior sign, and that is either by laudable report, or excellence in vesture, or other things semblable" (p. 163). Public honor has the same restorative power as rhetoric had for Thomas Wilson in his view of life outside the garden. The originary determinations of virtue have become cloudy and need to be clarified anew through rhetorically conceived projections, including not only material finery but the "laudable reports" of ideologues like Elyot. Humanist training allows such men to see past mere appearances (of luxury or exploitation, for instance) to the selfless and long-standing public motives beneath. These men must obliterate the epistemological decay that has set in since the prehistoric Golden Age when good men, like primitive pastors, did good without expectation of reward, and so were given it.

This inculcation restores the repose of both governors and governed. For the former it supplies a sense of mission and entitlement to privilege; for the latter it affords an explanation that recasts and disinfects the complex of deprivations they inhabit. Elyot's report then comes to have two audience functions. The governors derive peace of mind from it, and they redistribute its nourishment to their inferiors, securing quiescence and acquiescence in return. But the ultimate source of this ontological repose is taken to be the will of the subject classes, who "originally" conferred the status. This mandate is transmitted to the present by means of two complementary formulations. Stephen Greenblatt has noted that the primitive can seem either childlike or ancient.[61] Both terms are at work in Elyot's paradigm. In the primitive childhood of mankind, subjects-to-be chose a governing class on the basis of their nurturing capacities; as God's representatives these rulers worked literally *in loco parentis*, and their descendants became the subjects' political fathers. On the other hand, although the originary imputation of worth was made in the childhood of mankind, the men who subjected themselves to their moral superiors became to their descendants models of ancient wisdom, and such ancient wisdom was not to be questioned. So present subjects could be enjoined to obey both ancient and contemporary fathers: their own ancestors, and a continually self-reincarnating class of governors. Present subjects were doubly children.

This anterior determination can be understood in another way. Raymond Williams suggests that the concept of tradition is not "a relatively inert, historicized segment of a social structure," but "an actively shaping force" expressing the current dominant ideology.

> What we have to see is not just 'a tradition' but a _selective tradition_: an intentionally selective version of a shaping past and pre-shaped present, which is then powerfully operative in the process of social and cultural definition and identification. . . . Any tradition is . . . in this sense an aspect of *contemporary* social and cultural organization, in the interest of the dominance of a specific class. It is a version of the past which is intended to connect with and ratify the present. What it offers in practice is a sense of *predisposed continuity*. . . . [It is] a deliberately selective and connecting

process which offers a historical and cultural ratification of a contemporary order.[62]

Such selection gained new force when humanism reached England and revalorized its history. For instance, Britain came to be said to have been founded by Brutus, the grandson of Aeneas. This genealogy affiliated the dominant order of England with the great orders of Rome and Troy through Geoffrey of Monmouth's fanciful lineage, passing over intermediate history.[63] Similarly, Puttenham speaks to Elizabeth of the long line of poets lavishly supported by their princes (pp. 16–17), conducting her through a list ranging from Euripides, Sophocles, and Homer, through Chaucer to Sternhold and Vargas. (In mentioning the last two he draws in the examples of Henry VIII and his elder daughter, who constituted Elizabeth's most recent personal history.) The queen is implicitly challenged to live up to historical and genealogical precedents for rewarding poets, which otherwise threaten to specify the meanness of the present order.

A segregated tradition of such corroborating props expresses a bias toward continuity in social organization that tends to ontologize the status quo. As Fredric Jameson observes in his critique of bourgeois historiography, this valorization defines change as the exception, as decay or delinquency or deviation. "The truth of social life is [seen as] somehow a deep underlying permanence, a slow and organic continuity whose first image and rhythm is derived from the landowner's fields themselves."[64] The humanist recovery of primordial credentials served different regimes throughout Europe, where different political axes were ground. But all accreditations were based on the analytic capacity to detect instructive parallels between the present and the heroic past, a capacity that suppressed irrelevant or unflattering but real differences in the very process of specifying useful likeness. This, at any rate, was Guicciardini's criticism of Machiavelli: "How wrong it is to cite the Romans at every turn. For any comparison to be valid, it would be necessary to have a city with conditions like theirs, and then to govern it according to their example. In the case of a city with different qualities, the comparison is as much out of order as it would be to expect a jackass to race like a horse" (C110). Where Machiavelli sought (and found) universals, Guicciardini insisted on the exclusive aptness of modern information. But the former's mode was the more common, since it offered a readily accessible fund of adjustable "keys" to current political confusion and employed a class of professional interpreters.

A related employment of mystified origins should briefly be noted. The tools of humanistic thought were literary as well as historical; they were used in the interpretation and promulgation of *texts*. It is then not surprising to find the temporizing of the essence of the literary itself being presented as an original motor of social order. Wilson claimed that rhetorical forces reclaimed man from beastly life. Many others emphasized the mythic origin of civilization in the songs of Orpheus and Amphion, or of poets generally, who remodeled the world of birds, beasts, and stones into the world of human occupation. These tropes complemented the general effort to ontologize the status of the current ruling class, creating yet another form of emphasis on intellectual skills. The values of wisdom and political subtlety might be presented as orders of poetic cognition. This is implicit in Sidney's eicastic imagination,[65] and Puttenham claims that "without it no man could deuise any new or rare thing: and where it is not excellent in his kind, there could be no politique Captaine, nor any witty enginer or cunning artificer, nor yet any law maker or counsellor of deepe discourse" (p. 19). He also specifies it as essential to "Legislators Polititiens & Counsellours of estate" (p. 19). Although Orpheus and Amphion can so figure the governor, they remain poets and so offer a commodity for the literary ideologues themselves. Not only does the poetic gain a new public equivalence with the political, but the poet gains a new importance in public life—ideological celebrant as well as moral guide.

These structures of total mystery, contingent difference as absolute, and mystified origins interrelate and overlap in complex ways in practice. Mystery is the pure form of ontologizing relative distinctions. The move from history to prehistoric time is similarly a move into the absolute, which is then construed and used to order the contemporary world, supposedly contingent upon it. And primordial origins, whether derived from Christian or from pagan scenarios, carry the aura of mystery. (Luther's provision of a vernacular Bible, because it distributed access to the mysteries of God's foundations, was precisely a demystifying act, having political effects quite related to those dealt with here.) In all of these cases the emphasis is placed on the status of groups. In the chapters that follow, my focus shifts to tropes that directly characterize individuals, as noble or base, worthy or depraved, open or devious. First we shall consider the positive half of the paradiastolic system, tropes of praise and flattery.

4. Tropes of Personal Promotion: Praise and Flattery

In turning to the tropes of compliment and promotion we address issues of individual entitlement; the elite's privilege as a class is now stipulated, and the individual uses these tropes to argue his (or another's) membership in the group. Such tropes also constitute the positive half of the paradiastolic matrix—praise and flattery. They allow the manipulation (or effacement) of the notion of desert; they simply impute. And they are perhaps the most numerous as a set, since they lend themselves equally to address of self and of others (unlike the opposed tropes of rivalry, which are generally applied only to others). We shall examine eight varieties, concerned with recreation, *sprezzatura*, clueing, deceit, self-deprecation, the concealment of exploitation, *cosmesis*, and deference.

The Fetish of Recreation

In the ascription of virtues, courtesy enjoins the display of effortlessness. This injunction fetishizes the recreative realm, the unwrought mode of life characterized by leisure, spontaneity, the private, the casual. A life centered here, as the theoretically typical life of the gentleman (who must be able to "live without manual labor," William Harrison tells us[1]), carries some symbolic weight ipso facto. But the recreative realm is also especially suited for the performance of particular actions that, exactly because of their "unserious" character, carry symbolic weight in the world of *negotium*. As a result, the life of *otium* loses much of its playful or unserious aspect. "Urbino knows no leisure at all," says Lanham;[2] and one closer to the scene observes, "If all the year were playing-holidays, to sport would be as tedious as to work" (*Henry IV, Part One*, 1.2. 201–2). Castiglione offers the crucial political (as opposed to structural) definition of this serious function of the recreative. Lord Octavian defines the official utility of courtly grace as follows:

> The ende therefore of a perfect Courtier . . . I believe is to purchase him, by the meane of the [largely private and recreative] qualities which these Lordes have given him, in such wise the good will and favour of the prince [*la benivolenzia e l'animo di quel principe*] he is in service withall, that he may breake his minde to him, and alwaies enforme him franckly of the truth of every matter meete for him to understand, without fear or perill to displease him. . . . And therefore in mine opinion, as musicke, sportes, pastimes, and other pleasant fashions, are (as a man woulde say) the floure of Courtlinesse, even so is the training and helping forwarde of the Prince to goodnesse, and the fearing him from evil, the fruite of it. (Pp. 261/450–51)[3]

This movement from a rhetoric of advantage (cast as a game) to its ideological justification (public service) is itself ideologically presented. The flower (a thing of beauty, to admire and be refreshed by) gives rise to the fruit (the teleological and material end of beauty, to be nourished by). The golden-age courtier offers spring and harvest, blossom and fruit at once and forever. This organic justification legitimates a leisure life of pastimes. It also helps explain the proportions of *The Book of the Courtier*. Some three-quarters of it is devoted to "sportes," and only part of Book 4 is in fact concerned with advising princes. The emphasis on personal charm reveals its central importance, not only for guiding the prince, but for its many other utilities in the scramble for position. However mystifying Castiglione's flower and fruit metaphor may be, personal political success does derive from such private recreations, which then take on the status of work. These activities allow not escape from but entry into the world of negotium.

Sometimes this operation is symbolic, leaping analogically from otium to negotium. "For if [Urbino's] sportes and pastimes (that are used to none other end but to refresh the wearisom mindes after earnest labours) farre passed all such as are commonly used in the other Courts of Italy. . . . What (gesse you) were all the other vertuous practices, whereunto all men had their mindes bent, and were fully and wholy addicted." (Pp. 185/336).[4] But recreation and negotium can be coincidental as well as related inferentially. Elyot suggests this in explaining the progress—not the Elizabethan royal progress but a ruling-class one:

> The governors themselves adorned with virtue, being in such wise an example of living to their inferiors, and making the people judges of them and their domestical servants and adherents, should sundry times during their governance, either purposely or by way of solace, repair unto divers parts of their jurisdiction or province, and making there abode, they shall partly themselves attentively hear what is commonly or privately spoken concerning the estate of the country or persons, partly they shall cause their servants or friends, of whose honesty and truth they have good assurance, to resort in disporting themselves in divers towns and villages; and as they happen to be in company with the inhabitants privily and with some manner of circumstance, inquire what men of haviour [i.e., substance] dwell nigh unto them, what is the form of their living, of what estimation they be in justice, liberality, diligence in executing the laws, and other semblable virtues; contrariwise whether they be oppressors, covetous men, maintainers of offenders, remiss or negligent, if they be officers; and what the examiners do hear the greater number of the people report that they entirely and truly denounce it to the said governor. By the which intimation and their own prudent endeavour, they shall have infallible knowledge who among the inhabitants be men toward the public weal best disposed. (P. 233)[5]

Although such humanistic duties must have occupied relatively little of the time real courtiers spent on progress, such an argument served to rationalize pleasure as public service. This governor is "on the job" even when on vacation.

The cramming of recreative activities with intensely serious political maneuver significantly altered the psychological character of the experience. Such serious recreation with a group imposed continual self-consciousness and caused a corresponding decay in real relaxation. Gabriel Harvey notes in his copy of Castiglione that "the rarest men extend their utterest possibilitie, with a fine (as it were) familiar sleight: & they that do not enforce themselues to display their best, cum ever short of their reckoning."[6] In effect this posture interiorized a social conscience, an internal witness of privacy concerned not with moral injunctions but with social ones. Castiglione remarks early in Book 1 that it is ideal for courtiers to "thinke them selves neither marked, seene, nor knowne, and yet declare a stoute courage, and suffer not the least thing in the world to passe that may burthen them" (pp. 36/110). If unwitnessed behavior is to have such powerful evidentiary force, it clearly cannot be left unwrought. And the arbiter of such manipulation will be a hypothetical internal witness of the sort before whom one would publicly perform—an internal courtly Other. Anything like "really" unwitnessed experience becomes scarce, but the fiction of such behavior remains crucial because of the epistemological privilege it supposedly offers an unseen viewer. Hence there was frequently a consciously manipulative show of falsely unaware or surprised self-revelation.

> I will have our Courtier therefore . . . to allure men to heare or to looke on that hee supposeth himselfe to be excellent in, making semblant alwaies to doe it, not for a bragge and to shewe it for vaine glory, but at a chance, and rather praied by others, than comming of his owne free will.
>
> And in every thing that he hath to doe or to speake, if it be possible, let him come alwaies provided and thinke on it before hand, shewing notwithstanding the whole to be done *ex tempore*, and at the first sight. (Pp. 130/250)

With this scarcity of unwitnessed behavior, the sense of reliable access to others' subjectivity withers, so that plausible evidence is sought ever more energetically. The result here can be the total degeneration of epistemology already noted. But few of us submit to the metaphysical rigor necessary to lose this faith entirely. We simply decide at some point to trust considered appearance, and so a market remains for "evidence." Much ultimately unreliable evidence passes current at the Renaissance court; it is harder than we think to live the totally suspicious life of the stage Machiavel or the detective. We shall in due course consider many such provisional sources of data, one of which will suffice for now: pseudospontaneity proffered as a casual sign of unmanipulated authenticity. Toby Mathew, for instance, wrote to thank Christopher Hatton for his aid to the archbishop of York: "Truly, Sir, I can hardly hold mine idle pen from further enlarging in this behalf your goodness toward him, and his debt to you."[7] The mere spectacle of Hatton's virtue supposedly taxes Mathew's prodigious self-control. Another sign of this kind is the class-specific oath, also peddled as spontaneous. Elyot notes that the mass "is made by custom so simple an oath that it is now almost neglected, and little regarded of the nobility, and is only used among husbandmen and artificers, unless some tailor or barber, as well in his oaths as in the excess of his apparel, will counterfeit and be like a gentleman" (pp. 180–81). When oaths are taken as being typical of status groups, their "spontaneous" production can suggest membership. Elyot also specifies the sign's historical decay: it is no longer spontaneous and no longer a working sign of elevated rank, but neither is it artificial and out of date. Guazzo notes the use of another decayed oath:

> These bee those which straine themselves to sweare at every worde by the fayth of a Gentleman, when there is no oth required of them, by meanes whereof they make them selves suspected, as witnesses which offer themselves before they bee asked for: and they seeme to bee afeard least they should not be taken for Gentlemen, as those who are knowen in lookes, in wordes, and in deedes to bee very clownes. And though they take upon them the name of Courtiers, yet in their behaviour they shewe themselves little better then Carters. (1:176)[8]

The failure is a failure of spontaneity (though even the attempt was risky, as a literal, not symbolic, claim of gentility).

Another employment of the casual rejects studied excellence and excuses nonchalant inadequacy. Castiglione holds military knowledge to be central for the ideal courtier, but not "so perfect a knowledge of things and other qualities that is requisite in a Captaine" (pp. 36/109). Hatton's success in winning Elizabeth's attentions by his dancing could not be undercut by Leicester's competitive provision of a professional dancer: "Pish," the queen is said to have replied, "I will not see your man—it is his *trade*."[9] Count Lewis of Canossa declined the offer of time to prepare his discourse on the ideal courtier. "I will not do as he did, that stripped himselfe into his doublet, and leaped lesse ground than he did before in his Coate. And me thinke my lucke is good that it is late, because the shortnesse of time shall make me use fewe words, and the sodainesse of the matter shall so excuse me, that it shall be lawfull for me to speake without blame, whatsoever commeth first to minde" (31/102). The recreative context might have been sought not only because it offered evidentiary opportunity; as an unserious arena, it also offered a negation of evidence, a view of the performer that excused diminished competence but still credited him with the fact of performance. Action might be fully symbolic without being counted as fully revealing.

For all these reasons the recreative arena might be preferred to the ostensibly serious one. The evidence suggests that courtiers were indeed so serious as to be continually and resolutely purposeful in their pastimes. They played because play was in fact work, play would take them to the top or keep them there; they knew that because their play would be taken seriously, they too must take it so.[10] The scene of play has been eroded; privacy has become public, and productive. In the next section a way of generating these political effects under any circumstances will be examined—the famous *virtu* of *sprezzatura*.

Sprezzatura

With the governing principle of *sprezzatura*, the casual realm of effortlessness expands to encompass all of everyday life. This is the master trope of the courtier, the dynamic mode of the fundamental stylistic category of grace. Hoby presents it as follows.

> I [says Count Lewis], imagining with my selfe often times how this grace commeth, leaving apart such as have it from above, finde one rule that is most generall, which in this part (me thinke) taketh place in all things belonging to a man in word or deede, above all other. And that is to eschue as much as a man may, and as a sharpe and daungerous rocke, too much curiousnesse, and (to speake a new word) to use in everye thing a certaine disgracing [*una certa sprezzatura*] to cover arte withall, and seeme whatsoever he doth and saith, to doe it without paine, as (as it were) not minding it [*quasi senza pensarvi*]. (Pp. 45–46/124)

Here Castiglione wrote: "Trovo una regula universalissima, la qual mi par valer circa questo in tutte le cose umane che si facciano o dicano." ("I find one most universal rule, which seems to me valid in this respect in all human actions and speech.") The exercise of sprezzatura applies to all of human endeavor, rather than just to the private sphere of otium. Eduardo Saccone traces this extension, explaining its development beyond the antecedent classical categories of *venustas* and *gratia*, the direct ancestors of Castiglione's grazia-sprezzatura matrix.[11] He points out that in Pliny, Cicero, and Quintilian the application of the terms is restricted to art, literature, oratory, or female beauty, aesthetic regions mostly marginal to the realm of power (p. 43). In Castiglione the application is not only general ("in all things belonging to a man in word or deede") but explicit; the terms apply to the political zone of power at court, and especially to actions that take place before the eyes of the prince and his court. Roslyn Brogue Henning along with Saccone returns us etymologically to this public realm by deriving gratia from the Greek *charis*; this term suggests "charisma" as a relevant and thoroughly political synonym.[12]

Saccone offers another perspective on the universalizing of effortlessness (discussed in Chapter 2). In considering the coinage of sprezzatura, he suggests translations of "disdain," "misprision," and "depreciation." To this list we might add Hoby's "recklessness" and the modern "nonchalance." These negative terms "apply to (and qualify) *diligentia*, the very art that is put into operation by the practitioner" (p. 44). All these translations stress the concealment of effort. The courtier is enjoined to present a fictional impression of unpreparedness: "let him come alwaies provided and thinke on it before hand, shewing notwithstanding the whole to be done *ex tempore* [*all'improviso*]" (pp. 130/250). And again, "nor yet will I have him to be acknowne that he bestoweth much studie or time about it, although he doe it excellently well" (pp. 98/205). This virtue of sprezzatura, defined as "contrarie to curiositie [*affettazione*]" (pp. 48/128), makes possible the symbolic demonstration of differences in kind between the ruling class and others, in the face of substantive evidence to the contrary. By performing the tasks peculiar to governance (pure negotium, one would have thought) beautifully and effortlessly, the elite reveal the adequate performance of those tasks (or their symbolic equivalents) by others to be mere affectation, *affettazione*, the laborious display of virtues that can be rightly revealed only spontaneously. Substantive competition can be deflected, as letter rather than spirit, if the operations proper to the class are defined in terms of manner rather than matter. It is in this light that the courtier is encouraged to make his mode look easy but be inimitable. The operation amplifies the easy grazia of the courtier and the affettazione, conspicuous and inadequate, of his would-be imitator. The upstart servant, challenged to exhibit the graces of his elite masters, fails at just this imitation:

> His pase it must not be tother Legge tother way, and tother Legge tother-way, as he was wont to throw them, when he turned his Cattle from Plough to Pasture, making Indentures all along the ditches: But his gate and iesture of his body must be direct and vpright, treading as true as though he would tell what paces are in a Furlong. His curtesie with Cappe and Legge must be as his Apparrell of the newest fashion, with all other the rites and ceremonies belonging to this new taken up trade: no small tyme he spendes before he be in this an artist.[13]

The absence of grazia reaffirms ineffable distinction at the level of style even when a substantial imitation is forthcoming. Thus Castiglione can label grazia as the fundamental signifier of value, "a sauce to everie thing, without the which all his other properties and good conditions were litle worth" (pp. 43/121). In the same way the anti-Semite dismisses the Jew's real virtues. "The anti-Semite readily admits that the Jew is intelligent and hardworking; he will even confess himself inferior in these respects. This concession costs him nothing, for he has, as it were, put those qualities in parentheses. Or rather they derive their value from the one who possesses them. . . . To the anti-Semite, intelligence is Jewish; he can thus disdain it in all tranquillity, like all the other virtues which the Jew possesses. They are so many ersatz attributes that the Jew cultivates."[14] Whereas the Jew is viewed as having "mere" intelligence (like the uncourtly "expert"— Leicester's dancing master), the malapert asshead is viewed as having skills that are learned, hence unnatural, hence faked. The irrational dismissal of substance is accomplished magically by the anti-Semite, stylistically by the Renaissance courtier.

The notion of degenerated explanation makes possible the defense of a stylistic elevation accompanied by substantive *inferiority* (as opposed to rough parity);[15] one must exhibit sprezzatura about the exercise of sprezzatura. Planned or subsumed mistakes, inefficient casualness, can demonstrate freedom from the competitive telos of sprezzatura itself; insofar as the principle of grazia distinguishes the elite from those below, one may appear indifferent to the distinction, treating it as a trivial matter not worth attention. Substantive inadequacies can be viewed as insignificant, not worth hiding, indicating a position above concern for the possible disapproval of those present, who are thereby revealed as inferiors whose judgment is immaterial. Indeed, as we have seen, Guazzo presents excessive concern with criticism as a fault growing "for the most part of solitarinesse, and for want of experience in the affaires of the world. Which causeth, that into a base mind, there entreth the distrust of his owne doings, and the feare of other mens judgement" (1:112). Insecurity is defined as base, just as ease signifies belonging.

Needless to say, the infinite regress can lead to diminished returns for sprezzatura. But its flexibility made the display of easy self-confidence nearly canonical. Its power lay in the ease of the leap from "evidence" to conclusions about social ontology. For the evidence might be minimal, a consideration that takes us to the particulars of the symbolic mechanism known as the *clue*.

Clues

Erving Goffman outlines the basic operation of clues in the social construction of identity: "On the basis of a few known attributes, [one] is given the responsibility of possessing a vast number of others. His

coparticipants are not likely to be conscious of the character of many of
these attributes until he acts perceptibly in such a way as to discredit
his possession of them; then everyone becomes conscious of these attributes and assumes that he willfully gave a false impression of possessing them."[16] What Goffman calls virtues of *character* do not specify
the activity in question, but rather how the individual will handle himself in performing the activity; such virtues are conveyed by manner.
"Unlike primary traits [of capacity for substantive activities], those of
character tend to be 'essentializing,' fully coloring our picture of the
person so characterized . . . a single expression tends to be taken as an
adequate basis for judgment."[17] Goffman's list of the major virtues of
character includes courage, gameness, integrity, gallantry, composure,
presence of mind, dignity, and stage confidence. The rhetorical nature
of these virtues tends to characterize, in a way that particular substantive skills do not. In other words, such attributes are actively symbolic;
"essentializing" is a synecdochic process.

Many typically courtly virtues have this kind of force in Castiglione's discussion. High birth, for instance, has an instant effect:
"Where there are two in a noble mans house, which at the first have
given no proofe of themselves with workes good or bad, as soone as it
is knowne that the one is a Gentleman borne, and the other not, the
unnoble shall be much lesse esteemed with everie man, than the Gentleman, and he must with much travell and long time imprint in
mennes heades a good opinion of himselfe, which the other shall get
in a moment, and onely for that he is a Gentleman" (pp. 34–35/108).
Physical beauty has the same ontological force, though it too is socially (and financially) determined. Bembo's debased Platonism postulates that "very seldom an ill soule dwell[s] in a beautifull bodie.
And therefore is the outwarde beautie a true signe of the inwarde
goodnesse, and in bodies this comelines is imprinted more and lesse
(as it were) for a marke of the soule, whereby she is outwardly
knowne" (pp. 309/522). Dress too can have this essentializing force,
according to Fregoso: "Our Courtier . . . ought to determine with him
selfe what he will appeare to be, and in such sort as he desireth to be
esteemed, so to apparrel himselfe, and make his garments helpe him
to bee counted such a one, even of them that heare him not speake,
nor see him doe any manner thing" (pp. 117–18/233). Fregoso later
generalizes these principles to account for the raw power of reputation as a *genus*. I will have, he says,

> our Courtier the best he can (beside his worthinesse [substantive virtues?])
> to helpe himselfe with wit and arte, and when ever he hath to goe where he

is straunge and not knowne, let him procure that there goe first a good opinion of him, before he come in person, and so worke, that they may understand there, how he is in other places with Lordes, Ladies, and gentlemen in good estimation: because that fame, which seemeth to arise of the judgements of many, engendreth a certaine assured confidence of a mans worthinesse, which afterwarde finding mens mindes so setled and prepared, is easily with deedes maintained and encreased, beside that a man is eased of the trouble that I feele, when I am asked the question Who am I, and what is my name. (Pp. 123/241)

This final question reveals the fullness of the lack to which the powers of reputation respond; the answers offered to this question will not be properly questioned until Lear asks, "Who is it that can tell me who I am?" (1.4.231). Lear's question illuminates the fundamental epistemological circularity of virtues of character. The tendency to generalize and essentialize on the basis of a tenuous corpus of "evidence" reveals the precariousness of social identity at court. But whatever the weaknesses of the system, Fregoso's conscious strategy reveals the symbolic operation of the clueing mechanisms of reputation.

Clueing had a further power: its very insignificance could lend it evidentiary force, as we now might expect. "Many times," says Canossa, "men of courage are sooner knowne in small matters than in great" (pp. 36/110). This is especially true of the less spectacular virtues of character, as della Casa points out.

> Though generosity, loyalty, and moral courage are without doubt nobler and more praiseworthy qualities than charm and courtesy, nevertheless polite habits and a correct manner of speech and behavior may benefit those who possess them no less than a noble spirit and a stout heart benefit others. For since each one of us is daily obliged to meet other people and converse with them, we need to use our manners many times each day. But justice, fortitude, and the other virtues of the higher and nobler sort are needed less frequently. . . . Although such qualities are of a higher order and carry greater weight, the points of good behavior are more numerous and more frequently practised.[18]

Bacon endorses this perception with his usual calculation, as well as an awareness of the epistemological problem, in "Of Ceremonies and Respects":

> He that is only real had need have exceeding great parts of virtue; as the stone had need to be rich that is set without foil. But if a man mark it well, it is in praise and commendation of men as it is in gettings and gains: for the proverb is true, *That light gains make heavy purses*; for light gains come thick, whereas great come but now and then. So it is true that small

matters win great commendation, because they are continually in use and in note: whereas the occasion of any great virtue cometh but on festivals. Therefore it doth much add to a man's reputation, and is (as Queen Isabella said) like *perpetual letters commendatory*, to have good forms.[19]

Such achievement is inviting, Bacon thinks, because of the frequency of opportunity. "*The mind of man is more cheered and refreshed by profiting in small things than by standing at a stay in great.*"[20] Such clues conveniently and repeatedly elicit sanction for the self. The cumulative effect, called reputation, has the power not only to generate identity in the eyes of others but to answer the question "Who am I?" Of course, even "he that is only real," as a poor bare forked animal is, may find his identity to be a social fiction, but the answers must be gotten somewhere.

Deceit

In moving from a slim evidentiary link to a false one, one customarily quotes *The Prince*, but Machiavelli is more concerned with concealing vice or weakness or ill intent than with amplifying positive virtues, and in any case he generally emphasizes general strategic attitudes rather than particular tactics. He does say that "having [virtues] and practicing them at all times is harmful; and appearing to have them is useful; for instance, to seem merciful, faithful, humane, forthright, religious, and to be so; but [the prince's] mind should be disposed in such a way that should it become necessary not to be so, he will be able and know how to change to the contrary.... As long as it is possible, he should not stray from the good, but he should know how to enter into evil when necessity commands."[21] Machiavelli advocates a show of good, but he stresses the occasional necessity of departing from the appearance and does not specify how to create or maintain it. For a detailed tactical approach to presenting a deceitful image we must turn to Castiglione, for whom, according to Jonas Barish, detailed image management leads one almost necessarily toward falsity: "The more sharply [a mode of self-presentation] is defined, the more it crystallizes into a distinct code of behavior, the more it tends to become an impersonation, a deception."[22] Count Lewis says that sprezzatura, "accompanying any deede that a man doth ... how litle so ever it be ... many times maketh it to bee esteemed much more in effect than it is, because it imprinteth in the mindes of the lookers on, an opinion, that who can so sleightly doe well, hath a great deale more knowledge than in deede he hath: and if he will apply his studie and diligence to that he doth, he might do it much better" (pp. 48–49/128). Bacon agrees: "if you dissemble sometimes your knowledge of that you are thought to know, you shall be thought another time to know that you know not."[23] In each case modesty arouses inference in excess of the facts. And sheer fabrication can sometimes be effectual, Bacon says: "It often falls out that somewhat is produced of nothing; for lies are sufficient to breed opinion, and opinion brings on substance."[24]

Puttenham argues in considerable detail that the courtier must be deceitful.

> As figures be the instruments of ornament in euery language, so be they also in a sorte abuses or rather trespasses in speach, . . . whereby our talke is the more guilefull & abusing . . . [These figures seek] to inueigle and appassionate the mind: which thing made the graue iudges *Areopagites* (as I find written) to forbid all manner of figuratiue speaches to be vsed before them in their consistorie of Iustice, as meere illusions to the minde, and wresters of vpright iudgement, saying that to allow such manner of forraine and coulored talke to make the iudges affectioned, were all one as if the carpenter before he began to square his timber would make his squire crooked: . . . But in this case because our maker or Poet is appointed not for a iudge, but rather for a pleader, and that of pleasant & louely causes and nothing perillous, such as be those for the triall of life, limme, or liuelyhood; and before iudges neither sower nor seuere, but in the eare of princely dames, yong ladies, gentlewomen and courtiers, beyng all for the most part either meeke of nature, or of pleasant humour, and that all his abuses tende but to dispose the hearers to mirth and sollace by pleasant conueyance and efficacy of speach, they are not in truth to be accompted vices but for vertues in the poetical science very commendable. (Pp. 154–55)[25]

He nominally opposes the royal court to the legal court, but this restriction of the poet's pleading to the recreative realm should by now require no decoding; the ear of the princely dame Elizabeth is an explicitly political chamber. Other passages emphasize this coincidence. Puttenham, as we have noted, defines "*beau* semblant" as the "chiefe profession aswell of Courting as of poesie" (p. 158). He similarly glosses

> the Courtly figure *Allegoria*, which is when we speake one thing and thinke another, and that our wordes and our meanings meete not. The vse of this figure is so large, and his vertue of so great efficacie as it is supposed no man can pleasantly vtter and perswade without it, but in effect is sure neuer or very

seldome to thriue and prosper in the world, that cannot skillfully put in vre, in somuch as not onely euery common Courtier, but also the grauest Counsellour, yea and the most noble and wisest Prince of them all are many times enforced to vse it, by example (say they) of the great Emperour who had it vsually in his mouth to say, *Qui nescit dissimulare nescit regnare....* This figure therefore which for his duplicitie we call the figure of [*false semblant or dissimulation*] [is] the chief ringleader and captaine of all other figures, either in the Poeticall or oratorie science. (P. 186)

In his summary of the art of *cortegiania*, Puttenham definitively centers the notion of deceit.

Wee haue in our humble conceit sufficiently [described] this arte, so alwaies as we leaue him not vnfurnisht of one peece that best beseemes that place of any other . . . which is, that being now lately become a Courtier he shew not himself a crafts man, & merit to be disgraded, & with scorne sent back againe to the shop, or other place of his first facultie and calling, but that so wisely & discreetly he behaue himselfe as he may worthily retaine the credit of his place, and profession of a very Courtier, which is in plaine terms, cunningly to be able to dissemble. (P. 299)

Not for Puttenham Sidney's claim that the poet "nothing affirms, and therefore never lieth."[26] Falsehood is the courtier's charmed medium, the "one peece that best beseemes that place of any other"; the name Courtier governs the trope of allegory, otherwise known as *beau*, fair, and false semblant. This inveigling and abusive practice of figuration, though barred from the law courts, is decisive to courtliness, for courtier, counselor, and "the most noble and wisest Prince" alike. And if the princely "squire," the ultimate model, is crooked, so must courtiers be. Castiglione offers tactical detail, recommending that "for the things [the courtier] hath but a meane skill in, let him touch them (as it were) by the way, without grounding [i.e., dwelling] much upon them, yet in such wise that a man may believe he hath a great deale more cunning therein, than he uttereth" (pp. 130/250). One may in fact be quite actively misleading: "Some there be that knowing themselves to have an excellencie in one thing, make their principall profession in an other, in which notwithstanding they are not ignorant, but when time serveth to shew themselves in that they are most skilfull in, they doe it alwaies very perfectly: and otherwhile it commeth so to passe, that the company perceiving them so cunning in that which is not their profession, they imagine them to bee much better in that they professe in deed" (pp. 131–32/252). This may seem an incredibly roundabout strategy, until we compare it with the battlefield rhetoric of performing brave deeds before the prince's eyes. The difference is that here Fregoso reorients an individual's entire mode of life, if "profession" has the force of specialization or what might be called self-confession. It is worth noting too that this strategem projects substantial skills into a recreational arena, or at least to a realm set aside from one's public profession, thereby suggesting once again that work is play.

Lord Gaspar has moral objections to Fregoso's stage management: "I thinke not this an arte, but a very deceite, and I believe it is not meet for him that will be an honest man to deceive at any time." But Sir Fredericke replies, "This . . . is rather an ornament that accompanieth the thing he doth, than a deceite: and though it be a deceite, yet it is not to be disalowed" (pp. 132/252–53). Deceit is both denied and admitted, redefined and excused; separated from the substance of the action, it becomes, like grazia, a sauce or manner. And though it is savingly aestheticized as an ornament, morally neutral, deceit is a practical essential, if, like grazia, it is that without which all else is of little worth. If the disguised excellence be one's principal profession, then it can only with difficulty be dismissed as a minor deception— an evasion Fregoso does not attempt.

It begins to seem as if deceit and virtue are almost necessarily entangled with one another. Guazzo implies as much in Annibale and William's discussion of elocution. "But for so muche as this parte of action hath force to make men esteemed of above their desertes, I shoulde bee verie glad if you woulde shewe mee wherein consisteth this vertue [*in quale cose consista questa virtu*]," says William. Annibale replies: "Seeing the other good parts, which are in you, are accompanied with this same also, I can not beleeve but you knowe well enough by what meanes you have gotten it" (1:127). Here elocution, like sprezzatura in Castiglione, can amplify beyond substantive reality. But Guazzo goes well beyond Castiglione. William is not only virtuous but eloquent, that is, endowed with the power to make himself attractive beyond his deserts. Since this is the case, says Annibale, William has little need, perhaps even no business, to ask a question to which he must already know the answer. When eloquence has just been defined as a skill conferring the appearance of virtue beyond its reality, Annibale's attribution of both eloquence and virtue to William casts a certain doubt on his possession of the latter. And Annibale's tone carries, it seems, a mild accusation of disingenuousness— "no one with your self-delivery can be so ignorant as you pretend to be, of this of all subjects." William does not, however, acknowledge this marginal irony; he returns Annibale's dry remark as openheartedly as might be wished: "I knowe not howe I may beleeve, that you beleeve so, for I knowe that I never learned any precept of Rethorike." Annibale lets this denial of effort pass, noting only that William is "the more happie to have attained to that without travayle, which others can not come to, with much studie" (1:127). William makes textbook claims for his unlearned knowledge of the principles of eloquence, refusing to allow the special status of their conversation—as being about conversation—to "bare the device." He declines the opportunity for openness that Annibale for the nonce offers, and in so doing he accomplishes the very deceptive amplification he claims ignorance of. By the time such indirect deceptive devices have become conventional, their presence has become indistinguishable from their absence. Claims of innocence carry the suggestion of knowledge, and the self can only be unveiled, it seems, by veils. Revelation is always positive, virtue always contrived.

Self-deprecation

William's denials suggest self-deprecation, a depictive mode closely related to sprezzatura. E. R. Curtius has taught us how to understand modesty *topoi* and gives an extreme example that points up the complexity of the relation between modesty and humility. A Rhenish prelate is said to have exclaimed, "Humility is the rarest of all virtues; God be praised, I have it!"[27] Modesty is the secular equivalent of humility, and as a virtue it is likewise something to be proud of. Bacon puts it succinctly: "Excusations, cessions, modesty itself well governed, are but arts of ostentation."[28]

This formulation grew out of the ubiquitous Renaissance ambivalence about self-praise, resulting from the clash between Christian and classical ideas of virtue. The Christian position is clear enough. Count Ludovico uses it to defend oppressed women whose heroic goodness has not been recorded because they obeyed Christ's injunction to conceal the ravages of fasting (and other suffering), getting reputation with God instead of with man (see pp. 203/362). But for men the more accepted position is the classical one that, as Lord Gaspar has it, men are entitled to "the estimation that belongeth to [fine deeds], which is the true rewarde of vertuous travailes. Therefore among auncient writers, he that much excelleth doth seldome forbeare praysing himselfe" (pp. 37/111–12). Count Ludovico, wanting something more subtle, replies to Pallavicino's rejoinder somewhat testily: "If you have well understood ... I blamed the praysing of a mans selfe impudently, and without respect. And surely (as you say) a man ought not to conceive an ill opinion of a skilfull man that praiseth himself discretely, but rather take it for a more certaine witnes, than if it came out of an other mans mouth" (pp. 37/112). Such wise impudence is a secular version of Christian *pudor*. The dissolution of the double bind lies in "speaking such thinges after a sorte, that it may appeare that they are not rehearsed to that end: but that they come so to purpose, that he can not refraine telling them, and alwaies seeming to flee his owne prayse[s], tell the truth [a mistranslation of "dirle pure," i.e., really to speak them]" (pp. 38/112). Fregoso agrees with this advice, of course, as indicated by his technique of couching self-display in casualness, "making semblant alwaies to doe it, not for a bragge and to shewe it for vaine glory, but at a chance, and rather praied by others, than comming of his owne free will" (pp. 130/250). (The courtier here presents himself as if constituted by the audience.)

Guazzo compares the framing of wealth and beauty by such strategic modesty: "As Goldesmiths sometime cover their ware and jewels with a Glasse, to make them shewe the better, so a mayde under the vayle of modesty, ought to incloase all her other perfections, to increase the brightnesse of them, and the more forcibly to drawe the eyes and the hartes of others, to have her in admiration" (2:80). Such modesty, simultaneously veiling and magnifying the self, is explicitly gainful, whether of reputation or of "hartes." Examples from other zones will clarify this point. Annibale posits two profits for a gentleman who behaves humbly among his inferiors. First, such acts are in accord with "that philosophical and Christian saying, That the more loftie we are placed, the more lowly wee ought to humble our selves: which is in deed, the way to ryse higher" (1:192). Here self-deprecation has spiritual exchange value. Second, as we have seen, inferiors are "marvellous wel apaid" by condescension from a superior, "Wherby they are induced to love him, to honor him, and to doe him service: and whereby they themselves winne credite, and are the better esteemed of by their equals" (1:192). Here condescension is not alienating but bonding. And the yeomen's reciprocal humbling begets credit for them with their betters, and reputation among their equals. Annibale later tells William explicitly that "yeomen ought to know their degree, and by a certaine kinde of humilitie to shew themselves inferiours to Gentlemen in doing them reverence: Assuring themselves, that as by fancy presumption they make themselves hated, so by lowly humilitie, they make themselves loved of Gentlemen" (1: 197). Material gains of service and preferment are prominent, but equally important, for both parties, are gains of ratification, to be gotten from inferior and superior by the same exchange mechanism. Honor, with its power to determine and sanctify identity, is the main coin in circulation here, and it rewards submission.

This paradox of elevation by proper submission is most clearly to be seen in Annibale's discussion of "Gentlemen Courtiers which serve Princes."

> It were good here that wee came to the distinction of servauntes: for that which you say of servantes whiche flie their masters presence [whom they serve only for money], is not generall, and is to be understood of the nature of vile and base servantes, not of the good and suche as are gentlemen: who for the moste parte, are never well, but when they are in their Maysters presence, and serve him lovinglye and willinglye. Whereuppon it is sayd, That the Gentleman loveth, and the slave feareth. . . . The chaynes or Fetters of the baser sorte, are of yron, and those of the Gentlemen, of Golde. . . . [The gentlemen] seeke not intertainement upon constraynt or necessity, as the baser sort do, but are naturally given that way, not pitching their marke at vyle gayne, as the other doe, but at honour and renowne. (2:94)

It is hard at our historical distance to decode this experience of service confidently. Much of the time such language must have conveyed security and order. A *Health to the Gentlemanly Profession of Serving-Men* asks us "what greater loue could almost be found, then betwixt the Maister and the Seruant?" We are told that in the good old days, "it was in maner equall with the Husbandes to the Wife, and the Childes to the Parent."[29] On other occasions the terminology must have carried a more negative weight, implying anxious and transitory service so personal as to resemble infatuation. In a hierarchical society, the received force of rank would often have seemed simply descriptive. On the other hand, this was a society in transition, in which one might begin to wonder, "why bastard? wherefore base?" (*King Lear*, 1.2.6) and to find the old answers unsatisfactory. The perceptions of rigidity (or solidity) and shapelessness (or freedom of opportunity) in courtly literature had prophetic implications for the larger changes in social geology taking place outside the court.

The argument that gentlemen love to serve, whereas the base hate it, has important symbolic by-products. It makes possible yet another reassertion that the gentleman is not like those below; he is more selfless, more public-minded, having fewer of the basic acquisitive urges. (The ideology masks his access to material privilege, which lessens the pressures of need.) What is more, the selfless self may more readily be employed in a near-insolvent world where "the politic and artificial nourishing and entertaining of hopes" governs most preferment, for the employer may think to pay his servant with the perquisites of image, rather than with money or power.[30] There are other mystifying implications in this language of service, to which we will return in due course.

Self-deprecation can take other stylized forms. At the minimal end of such a continuum might be Castiglione's "doubts" of his capacity to write his *Book of the Courtier.*

> I have a long time douted with my self (moste loving M. Alphonsus) whiche of the two were harder for me, either to denie you the thing that you have with such instance many times required of me, or to take it in hand: because on the one side mee thought it a verie hard matter to denie any thing especially the request being honest, to the person whom I love dearely, and of whom I perceive my selfe dearly beloved. Againe, on the other side, to undertake an enterprise which I doe not know my selfe able to bring to an ende, I judged it uncomly for him that weyeth due reproofes so much as they ought to bee weyed.
>
> At length, after much debating, I have determined to proove in this behalfe, what ayde that affection and great desire to please can bring unto my diligence, which in other things is woont to encrease the labour of men. (Pp. 15/79)

Here the clear-eyed objections of the author's perceptive friend force him to set aside his modesty and act on a higher estimate of his powers.[31] He does so, it seems, "not for a bragge and to shewe it for vaine glory, but ... rather praied by others, than comming of his owne free will" (pp. 130/250). He also draws attention to his friend's many requests (many times regretfully declined), the high esteem in which the author is held, and his own diligent affection and great desire to please—not to mention his own modesty, itself a virtue, and his skill in so obliquely deploying it with conspicuous grazia and sprezzatura. Alphonsus helps him to perform all these oblique demonstrations, a service Bacon recognized as one of friendship's great advantages. "How many things are there which a man cannot, with any face or comeliness, say or do himself! A man can scarce allege his own merits with modesty, much less extol them. . . . But all these things are graceful in a friend's mouth, which are blushing in a man's own."[32] Such modest evasion of modesty might even justify the fictional production of friendship for dedications.

The flexibility of the *topos* is very broad. Compare, for instance, the nearly subliminal refusal by Emilia Pia, when the duchess assigns her the governance of the evening's games. "She after a little refusing of that charge" (pp. 22/89) goes on to take it. The formula labels the lady Emilia as properly aware of her place relative to the duchess. Somewhat more elaborate is the hostess's apology for her austere hospitality in Guazzo's Book 4, which begets eight pages of reassurance: "But first L. Caterine, who had invited them, in excuse of her supper, said: Although this meane cheere is not great enough for the highnesse of so noble a Queene [the evening's honorary "ruler"], nor good enough for such honorable personages as you are yet I rely so much on your infinit and accustomed curtesies, that you will hold me excused, and take it in good parte, and to feede your minds chiefly with the meat, of the noblest part of my selfe" (2:133). At the evening's end the queen similarly apologizes for her disappointing royal performance, but she offers in consolation the fact that "since that in high and hardie affaires, the good wil is greatlie esteemed, and often times ought to supplie other defectes, I praie you Lordes and Ladies all, that in steade of those effectes, which neither I was able to declare, and perhappes you looked for at my handes, you would take in good parte these evident and apparaunt signes of my good will, which you have, as it were, reade in my forhead" (2:213–14). These apologies seem strained, but I believe we must conclude that people liked to make them and liked what they got in return—the complimentary denials of their audience.

A more active self-deprecation occurs in Castiglione's oft-quoted tale of the ragged shepherd knight "with an excellent horse and well trimmed for the purpose" (pp. 99/206), whose unlikely appearance undercuts expectation before outdistancing it.[33] This is a peculiarly physical form of amplifying by debasing. We may contrast such active self-deprecation with an exceptionally passive specimen. Annibale lists the guests for the banquet described in Book 4; these "personages, for gentilitie, vertues, and laudable customes, are in most honorable and high degree" (2:119).

At the sight of Lord Vespasian, all the companie rising up [from the table], and offering him the place [of honor], he commaunded them to sitte downe againe, which done, they all kepte such silence for a good space, that they gave Lord Vespasian occasion to saie, that he thought, he was fallen into such a companie, that would have passed the time in some manner of devising, and discourses, but now perceaved himselfe to be rather in a solitarie and silent place.

At which wordes one looking uppon an other, and everie one holding his peace, he rose up to departe, and with a curteous conge, take his leave of the Lordes and Ladies, saying that he would be gone, to leave them an open fielde, and not with his interrupting presence, cease to discontinue their communication. (2:119)

Their strained silence seems, to say the least, rhetorical, designed to extract a response. Lord Vespasian's reaction is strikingly deliberate. He first reproaches their joyless "solitarie" silence, then plays the intruder and apologizes for interrupting their discourse. This statement carries the literal force of a self-debasing compliment; they have extracted a unit of praise. Of course he speaks ironically, and in fact makes offenders of them for failing to welcome him properly. But this is presumably just what their silence was aimed to do—to express a severe self-abasement in his awesome presence. What we seem to have here is the imposition by the ranking guest of a failure of courtesy: he forces the others to acknowledge his distance and to array themselves in relation to it. Instead of accepting the silence as a conspicuous sign of respect, he reads it as insult (literally as a dismissal), for which the group must compensate.

When the hostess tells him to ignore the insult he perceived, he proposes another reason he ought to leave—compelling the group once again to compel him to stay. This time he notes that the number of guests is improperly large. "If I doe not departe, for this reason now alleadged, I must at the least for this that followes, that is, that the persons invited to this Supper, exceed not the number of nine, and now finding the number to be alreadie compleate, it is great reason therefore that my companie maie be well spared, and so departe as a superfluous person, then to remaine as a molestour and breaker of this compacted garland" (2:119). A lesser guest, Lord John, proposes that he leave instead of Lord Vespasian, since he is "the unprofitable Dogge." Lord Vespasian generously allows that there are legitimate uses for "so pleasant, and faithfull a Dogge," but he seeks the opinion of the others. Upon his explicit and repeated demand, they all allow Lord John to stay. But Ladie Fraunces proposes to solve the numerological problem by noting that since two of those present are married, they may by God's law count as one, and the proper number of nine will be kept. "This Christian Arithmatike, was commended of all the companie, but nevertheless, Lorde Vespasian did not rest satisfied, but would heare what Cavallero Bottazzo would saie, concerning the foresaide matter" (2:120). Cavallero argues that though Lord John is a dog worth allowing, and though Lady Frances has rightly defended the number nine, he can show by a third proof that the number ten is also appropriate in this case. "Because if banquets be commonly and wel alluded to the number of the Muses, it is reason to entertaine one guest more, who may in a maner, possesse Apollo his place, and represent his Majestie, and so set downe some good order and fourme of lawes, for the whole assemblie" (2:121). Lord William rises to say that "it were but a wast labour to goe about to create a new Lorde, having alreadie chosen one before, and for mine owne part, I will content mee with the domination of L. Vespasian." "No, no, said L. Vespasian, Imagine that all my titles are left at home, and that amongst you here, Seignior Vespasian is but a private man, like anie other. And therefore let us make triall, to whose Lot it shall befall to beare the swaie and Principalitie amongst us, and so, willed that everie one should cast Lots: And taking up a Petrarq, which lay upon the table, he devised . . ." (2:121).

This chronicle might be continued, but certain aspects of the behavior of these people have become clear enough. Lord Vespasian's precious self-deprecation, however witty (and this we cannot perhaps properly recover), has an unmistakable function. He repeatedly draws the group's attention to his superior rank and to their relative inferiority. All their energies are required to avoid offending him, however jokingly. They respond to his bidding as if choreographed, though quite freely, of course. He actively demands, requests, "would heare" opinions, all politely and in jest, but he gets genuflection every time. He sets the subjects of conversation, controls its duration, and decides singly (and magnanimously) on procedures for the delegation of power for the evening. And he organizes the entire "debate" threateningly around the right of *another* to attend the banquet, though he began by demurring "modestly" (twice) as to his own right. Such "games" have distinction as their explicit goal, however supposedly unserious. Such modesty is indeed an art of ostentation.

From this autocratic example we might turn to a more occasional self-deprecation: the proper response to reward or promotion. This is every courtier's fantasy, and its fulfillment might be expected to arouse rapt gratitude. Although this was indeed to some degree the case, the courtier turns out to have instructions from Castiglione to employ even this occasion for symbolic pressure. Fregoso argues as follows:

> Yet ought a man alwaies to humble him selfe somewhat under his degree [*star sempre un poco più rimesso che non comporta il grado suo*], and not receive favor and promotions so easily as they be offered him, but refuse them modestly, shewing he much esteemeth them, and after such a sort, that he may give him an occasion that offereth them, to offer them with a great deale more instance [*instanzia*].
>
> Because the more resistance a man maketh in such manner to receive them, the more doth he seeme to the prince that giveth them to be esteemed [actually, the more the prince giving them will feel esteemed], and that the benefit which hee bestoweth is so much the more, as he that receiveth it, seemeth to make of it, thinking him selfe much honoured thereby. (Pp. 109/220)

The prescribed response does emphasize the gap between giver and recipient, thus flattering the giver. But at the same time, it extracts repeated offers, reiterations of the recipient's desert. This procedure resembles Castiglione's public reluctance to write his book: refusal arouses wooing and compliment. And like Lord Vespasian's repudiation of the group's silent honor, this mechanism of demur allows one to recycle an occasion of gain for further gain; if such refusal is flattering to the giver, it will be more so to the recipient, if the giver responds properly.

Such reinvestment may help to explain another of Lord Vespasian's predatory self-deprecations. In the midst of the dinner a musician enters, calling the group to silence, and sings this delightfully banal sixteen-stanza song of praise to Lord Vespasian.

> To sing of all your worthie deedes,
>   your honours great and hie,
> My humble voice (thrise noble Lord)
>   cannot it selfe applie.
>
> Orpheus must retourne againe,
>   who with his stile divine,
> Must praise you, and your vertues rare,
>   which like the Sunne doe shine.

For you are he whome Monferrata
   Hills doe still adore,
In cleering of those clowdie daies,
   in which we livde of yore.

In Martiall prowesse from the chiefe,
   you beare the bell awaie,
Both Atlas and Eous seas,
   Your winged fame displaie.
. . . .

Your haughtie and mellifluous stile,
   the Heavens which never fill,
Doth shew that Peleus and Anchises sonnes,
   doe live amongst us still.
. . . .

Your mightie tongue is of such force,
   and workes effects so rare,
That everie soule it can set free,
   that is opprest with care.

And with the passing eloquence,
   wherein it hath great skill,
It drawes the mindes of everie one,
   unto your proper will.

                        (2:156–58)

"Ladie Caterine was not a little commended of the Queene, and of all the companie besides, because in so gentle and curteous maner, she had honoured in her house the noble Lord Vespasian" (2:158) with this poem. In response (who can tell with what tones?), Vespasian reactivates the inversion he used to revise his silent welcome. He first denies the aptness of the praise: "You may entreate, and use mee in your owne house (Ladie Caterine) as it pleaseth you best. But now I remember my selfe, you have not obteined your purpose fullie, because those your guestes will with greater reason, and sooner commend the sweete voyce of your Musition, then be so foolish, as to beleeve anie one thing, that he hath songe, in depainting foorth (as he thought) my praises" (2:158). Lady Caterine and Lady Lelia insist that the musician has spoken less, not more, than the truth; Vespasian accepts this, insofar as speaking less than the truth is lying. This reading is in turn rejected. "Ladie Caterine is a friend to vertue, saide Cavallero, and yet if she would digresse from it in anie point herein, I know not anie one in this companie that would concur with her.

Wherefore Lorde Vespasian, you should doe both her, and us great injurie, if you doe not embrace these praises, and thinke them as due and beseeming your honour, as sincerelie uttered by Ladie Caterine, and not without reason confirmed by us all" (2:159). Vespasian's refusal to "embrace" the praises is taken as an affront first to Lady Caterine, and by extension to the entire group, since all have ratified her perspective. He must set aside his modesty, in order to avoid offending the group by questioning its judgment and sincerity. His response to this courteous pressure is a remarkable chain of indirect self-praise.

> Well, saide Lorde Vespasian, because Ladie Caterine may thinke herselfe in some part satisfied, I wilbe content at this time, that the rest give some small credence to the Musicians wordes, although for my owne part, with safeguard of my honour, I cannot consent to doe the same. But it behoveth rather, saide the Queene, that Ladie Caterine, remaine satisfied in all points, wherefore, by the vertue of my auctoritie in this place, I wil dispence with Lord Vespasian, and enable him, without anie prejudice of his honour, to allow of those louanges [lovings], as most condigne and beseeming his noble person. I will content my selfe, saide Lord Vespasian, at this time, and when so soveraigne a commaunder as you, good Ladie, doth will mee to accept of them, (although contrarie to natural reason, as also to please all parties) I will beleeve that black is white: But I beseech you, gracious Queene, prescribe some definite time, how long these praises shall sojourne and remaine with mee. (2:159)

Lord Vespasian's relentless modesty forces an examination of his right to the praises he has been offered, which results in repeated obtrusions of his worth rather than scrutiny of his qualifications. The denial succeeds for some time (though Cavallero finally deflects Vespasian's call for a time limit by ending the debate with another ploy).

The members of the group actively dance these interactions. They are at home with Vespasian's manipulations. In fact, Cavallero extends the iterations of the debate. The refusal was based, supposedly, on Vespasian's denial of the accuracy of the praise. Cavallero forces him not only to submit but to recant, requiring more steps and repetitions. The letter-over-spirit character of his recantation ("upon compulsion") allows him a further prolonging move, although this last, being deflected by the time limit, is not picked up by the queen. This protracted review of the praise's proper force is a group project, originally proposed by Lord Vespasian as ranking guest and recipient of the praise, but improvised upon by various members of his audience and actively extended by Cavallero. All sides insist upon their right to inferiority, and so amplify their stature as being both polite and clever. Lord Vespasian reaffirms his own rank, and the rest reaffirm their own proper relation to his rank, equally pointedly. All of this stature is achieved by the denial of stature.

This kind of self-revelation raises the question of its opposite: what are the conventional mechanisms for *concealing* the self, defeating interpretive penetration, forestalling disclosure? The trope splits naturally, by object of concealment, into two categories: the concealment of exploitation, and cosmesis, the disguising of vulnerability.

The Concealment of Exploitation

The principal mystification of exploitation is the trope of self-sacrifice. Elyot's version rests upon a question-begging definition of the governor as someone fit by nature to rule:

> Understanding is the most excellent gift that man can receive in his creation, whereby he doth approach most nigh unto the similitude of God, which understanding is the principal part of the soul . . . as one excelleth another in that influence, as thereby being next to the similitude of his maker, so should the estate of his person be advanced in degree or place where understanding may profit; which is also distributed into sundry uses, faculties, and offices, necessary for the living and governance of mankind. (P. 4)

This endowment must receive public employment: "They which excel other in this influence of understanding, and do employ it to the detaining of other within the bounds of reason, and show them how to provide for their necessary living, such ought to be set in a more high place than the residue where they may see and also be seen, that by the beams of their excellent wit, showed through the glass of authority, other of inferior understanding may be directed to the way of virtue and commodious living" (p. 4). The elevation of the governor offers visibility, so to speak—not only for the efficiency of his view, but for the effect of his example on the living habits of the inferior sort.

Material reward properly follows:

> And unto men of such virtue by very equity appertaineth honour, as their just reward and duty, which by other men's labours must also be maintained according to their merits. For as much as the said persons, excelling

in knowledge whereby other be governed, be ministers for the only profit
and commodity of them which have not equal understanding; ... They
that be governors (as I before said) nothing do acquire by the said influence
of knowledge for their own necessities, but do employ all the powers of
their wits and their diligence to the only preservation of other their inferiors. (Pp. 4–5)

The submission of the inferior sort, and their material and reputational maintenance of their superiors, repay the prior selflessness of
their governors, who get "nothing" for their labor. The logic here is
circuitous. Nobles, ontologically grounded in understanding and
public service, are entitled to maintenance and honor. But this statement rationalizes a *present* state of affairs, in which the aristocrat
already receives the maintenance and honor that are supposedly his
due. It is thus only theoretically possible to say "they that be governors ... nothing do acquire," that they "be ministers for the only
profit and commodity of" their inferiors. Elyot's conflation of logical
and historical description makes utterable the falsehood that the aristocracy comes away empty-handed—or would if not properly re-
munerated. My point is not to argue that they are not entitled to such
privilege; it is just such ideological operations as Elyot's that entitle
them to it. I want rather to note that *there never was a time* in which
they were without substantial reward for "public" service; the absence of proper reward is a logical, not a historical, contingency. The
call for reward has the force of a tautology. There is no literal referent
for the indicative assertion that the governors "nothing do acquire."

One may rationalize this claim by saying that governors get nothing comparable to what they give, or that since they serve freely, as a
duty and not for derivative reward, what they get does not motivate
the service and so counts as "nothing." Both of these rereadings lend
Elyot rationality, but they merely sophisticate the more naked reading. For each casts the aristocrat as being unconcerned with material
reward, and hence as a creature of mysterious motives, to be not in-
terrogated but obeyed.

Elyot elsewhere presents rule as a burdensome task having only
cerebral (or soulful) rewards. The selfless governor, like a knight or a
scholar, accepts office from obligation to his fellows and to God, and
not in the interest of preserving his own peace of mind. "Most hard
and grievous judgment shall be on them that have rule over other. To
the poor man mercy is granted, but the great man shall suffer great
torments.... The stronger or of more might is the person, the

stronger pain is to him imminent" (p. 96). Power and privilege were to give no pleasure, being sheerly instrumental to the imposition of reverence and obedience: "Thy dignity or authority wherein thou only differest from other is (as it were) but a weighty or heavy cloak, freshly glittering in the eyes of them that be pur-blind, where unto thee it is painful, if thou wear him in his right fashion, and as it shall best become thee" (p. 165). Not only is the governor unrewarded for his labors, but he must expect harsher eventual judgment from God regarding the exercise of his earthly power. And he will not get pleasure from the things that pleasure other men.

Perhaps these expressions are merely moralizing injunctions from Elyot to a ruling class not fully ready for this ascetic life. But against this view we must consider his fearful self-abnegation at points where he might be thought by his original audience presumptuously to be advising his superiors. Still, his hortatory subjunctives have a "voice in the wilderness" tone: "They shall not think how much honour they receive, but how much care and burden. Ne they shall not much esteem their revenues and treasure. . . . Let them think the greater dominion they have, that thereby they sustain the more care and study. . . . they shall think what reproach were to them to surmount in that which be other men's works" (p. 97). However this may be, Elyot's psychological stance with regard to the elite's material flourishing is finally beside the point.[34] What counts are his written attitudes, henceforth available to the ruling elite as rationalizations, justifications, ways of believing in the public value of private prosperity. These views strategically distanced the governor from personal gratification in his place, and so from culpability for such private pleasures.

Castiglione had already suggested this view when he claimed that the self-indulgent pleasures conned in Books 1–3 "doe many times nothing els but womanish the mindes, corrupt youth, and bring them to a most wanton trade of living [*vita lascivissima*]" (pp. 260–61/ 450) unless they are *used*. This idea has its *locus classicus* in St. Augustine's *De Doctrina Christiana*:

> Some things are to be enjoyed, others to be used. . . . Those things which are to be enjoyed make us blessed. Those things which are to be used help, and, as it were, sustain us as we move toward blessedness in order that we may gain and cling to those things which make us blessed. If we . . . enjoy those things which should be used, our course will be impeded and sometimes deflected, so that we are retarded in obtaining those things which are to be enjoyed, or even prevented altogether, shackled by an inferior love.[35]

For Castiglione the goods of the courtly private life avoid being evil only by being instrumental to the accomplishment of public goals, by purchasing for the courtier the "good will and favor of the Prince." To some degree, of course, it is easy to dismiss the instrumental role of attractiveness in this political project as sheer rationalization, but in fact wills are often managed by such nuances (as any courtier of Elizabeth or James knew). Still, Castiglione and Elyot go to considerable lengths to redefine the pleasures of upper-class life as anxieties, even, if misdirected, as self-waste. The denials aim to insulate the governor from the charge of greed, to make him unenviable and, ultimately, to attest to the singular moral status of one who is indifferent to the allure of power and privilege—and so is to be trusted with them. Such elaborate dismissals of pleasure of course testify to its presence and give the lie to the instrumental vision. The need for prince-pleasing counselors may justify some such governors, but hardly the entire class.[36]

A closely related form of self-concealment disguises the desire for gain by displacing the goal—a reversed temporizing of essence. Material stratification in the present is justified by future, not past, elevation. This temporal model applies to Castiglione: he who is attractive may get to guide the prince, so honing one's attractiveness is a public service. Guazzo offers another variant of this procedure. Annibale and William work through the familiar argument about arms and letters. The latter win since they conduce more to immortality; arms cannot confer immortality without the aid of letters.

> *Guaz.:* I thinke verily, that without some spurre of everlasting praise, fewe men would bee pricked forward to enterprise any thing worthie praise.
>
> *Annib.:* Wee all covet this glory, as the fruite and lawfull reward of our travell: and there is no man but is right glad to consecrate his name to immortalitie. (1:217)

The desire for current praise (along with the grace and favor that accompany it) can be purified into the desire for immortal, future praise. Earthly reward after death cannot constitute material gratification, and so desire for it cannot be seen as ambition or greed.[37] This trope displaces present realities, positive or negative, in the same way King Harry's Crispin Crispian speech does; gratification is delayed so far beyond the orbit of present sacrifices or pleasures that they are eclipsed. To seek eternal fame is to show contempt for local rewards and thereby to be acquitted of the charge of desiring them.

These ways of seeing suppress or explain away the very problem they purportedly account for—aristocratic privilege. The governor is cast as an ascetic but generous masochist. Normal folk cannot hope to achieve this unusual (to say the least) mental state necessary for bearing the privations of privilege. But Castiglione and Guazzo show that for the gentleman, pastime is work, and work, pastime.

Cosmesis

The second mode of self-concealment, a technique needed by both the marginally qualified climber and the insecure aristocrat, camouflages vulnerability. Such concealment might be called *cosmesis*—the use of cosmetic aids to conceal or repair defects. Such manipulation was technically excepted from the general censure of "painting," a practice typically (and strategically) posited in feminine terms. Hamlet makes the prejudice metaphysical, with his "Now get you to my lady's chamber, and tell her, let her paint an inch thick, to this favor she must come"—to the raw stinking skull. But the more usual force of prejudice was moral and social, aimed at the painted woman, who like "any harlot . . . is . . . anxious to hawk her wares and sell them at a good price."[38] Such a woman wears her cosmetics too obviously, contra sprezzatura, as Castiglione's Count Ludovico notes:

> Doe you not marke how much more grace is in a woman, that if she doth trimme her selfe, doth it so scarcely and so litle, that who so beholdeth her, standeth in doubt whether she bee trimmed or no: than in an other so bedawbed, that a man would wene she had a viser on her face, and dareth not laugh for making it chappe: nor at any time changeth her colour, but when she apparaileth her selfe in the morning and all the rest of the day standeth like an image of woode without moving, shewing her selfe onely in torche light, as craftie marchantmen doe their clothes in their darke lights. (Pp. 66/154–55)[39]

It is no accident that antifeminist diatribe is the standard discourse for the blaring condemnation of cosmesis, for this is a case of pots accusing kettles. In terms of the larger struggle with natural weakness—a category including birth as well as beauty—this cheap shooting promulgates a class of female whipping boys. The sarcastic moralism of terms like "bedawbed" diverts attention from the equally frenetic male preoccupation with other evanescent modes of self-creation and repair; livery, like paint, is designed to cover personal inadequacy. Insofar as women were exclusively defined by sexual identity, the impairment of the active erotic status of youthful beauty amounted to the loss of identity per se. To repair such loss was to accomplish ontological rejuvenation. The terms of the injunctions for and against cosmetics for women correspond almost allegorically to many of the male modes of self-management we have examined. Far from counting as a contradiction, this similarity is the point. The mockery of another's self-fashioning disguises the insecure courtier's own predicament and perhaps serves as a catharsis for resentment at his own repulsive self-repair, possibly more slimy than any old woman's new fucus.[40] Anti-cosmetic prejudice is itself cosmetic.

Despite the general nastiness elicited by the trope, the basic motive of cosmesis is theoretically acceptable. In Castiglione's view, "all women generally have a great desire to be, and when they can not be at the least to appear beawtifull. Therefore where nature in some part hath not done her devoir, therein they endevour them selves to supply it with arte" (pp. 66/154). Such supply or repair involves clothing as well as facial cosmetics. "In like manner where she is somewhat fatter or leaner than reasonable [!] sise, or wanner, or browner, [it is appropriate] to helpe it with garments but fainingly as much as she can possible, and keeping her selfe clenly, and handsom, shewing alwaies that she bestoweth no paine nor diligence at all about it" (pp. 194/348). The invocation of sprezzatura cues our assessment of such repair, as legitimate when invisible. But what counts here is that strand of Castiglione's fabric which legitimates cosmesis theoretically: "they that are not by nature so perfectly furnished, with studie and diligence may polish and correct a great part of the defaults of nature" (pp. 33/105). Or as Puttenham puts it, "euery man may decently reforme by arte, the faultes and imperfections that nature hath wrought in them" (p. 287).[41] Della Casa specifies the appropriate response to such repair: others should be "accepted as we accept a coin, not for its intrinsic worth, but at its face-value."[42] This principle at least putatively bounds the field of discourse governing repair.[43]

Elyot provides many examples of the simplest and perhaps the coarsest cosmetic strategy, the overt anticipation of criticism, signaled by warding off.[44] His proem to *The Governor* contains the first of many signs of his fear of audience reprisal. He dedicates his book to Henry VIII, whose personal forebearance and protection from other enemies Elyot seeks, "taking comfort and boldness, partly of your Grace's most benevolent inclination toward the universal weal of your subjects, partly inflamed with zeal" (p. xiii). His aim—to describe a just public weal—itself requires apology, or rather a statement in the form of an apology, in fact a tautology: "Which attempt is not of presumption to teach any person, I myself having most need of teaching, but only to the intent that men which will be studious about the weal public may find the thing thereto expedient compendiously written" (p. xiii). He assures his royal reader that he does not aim to teach those who obviously know better than he. (He cannot seem to find a way to apologize logically for doing what he fully intends to do.) He also disclaims topical references, presuming his reading public to be hostile, in language repeated throughout the century:

> Where I commend herein any one virtue or dispraise any one vice I mean the general description of the one and the other without any other particular meaning to the reproach of any one person. To the which protestation I am now driven through the malignity of this present time all disposed to malicious detraction. Wherefore I most humbly beseech your Highness to deign to be patron and defender of this little work against the assaults of malign interpreters which fail not to rend and deface the renown of writers, they themselves being in nothing to the public weal profitable. (P. xiv)

For personal topical reference he substitutes moral aspersion of those who would misread his advice, who are parasites anyway. Elyot's book thus comes to constitute a litmus test: approval of the book designates the legitimate public servant.

His text proper is filled with similar self-protective aspersions. He plans to deal in a second volume with other matters apt for "the perfection of a just public weal: in the which I shall so endeavour myself, that all men, of what estate or condition soever they be, shall find therein occasion to be alway virtuously occupied; and not without pleasure, if they be not of the schools of Aristippus or Apicius, of whom the one supposed felicity to be only in lechery, the other in delicate feeding and gluttony: from whose sharp talons and cruel teeth, I beseech all gentle readers to defend these works, which for their commodity is only compiled" (p. 12). He tries to coerce the reader to side with him and against the Aristippean and Apician lechers and gluttons, into whom his critics become metamorphosed. Whether or not these hostile readers are the established aristocracy can only be surmised; taken literally, his views certainly legitimate a certain amount of controlled invasion of the ruling class and impose new burdens on those already there. His frequent denials of presumption suggest that he is not trying to elevate himself illegitimately—either intellectually or politically—though of course the book's content casts him as both an authority on elevation and a deserving candidate for it. He has the awkward status of educator to a despotic elite: on the one hand, he speaks from a position of intellectual superiority; on the other, he must play the servant. "Toward the which instruction [of gentle children, in training for rule] I have, with no little study and labours, prepared this work, as Almighty God be my judge, without arrogance or any spark of vainglory; but only to declare the fervent zeal that I have to my country; and that I desire only to employ that poor learning that I have gotten to the benefit thereof and to the recreation of all the readers that be of any noble or gentle courage" (p. 14).

Elyot tosses in gratuitous praise of Henry VIII and follows it with a denial of flattery.

> And of such fair inheritance [of virtuous nobility] his highness may compare with any prince that ever reigned: which he daily augmenteth, adding thereto other sundry virtues, which I forbear now to rehearse, to the intent I will exclude all suspicion of flattery, since I myself in this work do specially reprove it. But that which is presently known and is in experience needeth no monument. And unto so excellent a prince there shall not lack hereafter condign writers to register his acts, with most eloquent style in perpetual remembrance. (P. 85)

As K. J. Wilson observes of Elyot's epistolary prose, his stance "registers a double notation: the conventional song of lavish flattery is accompanied by the self-praise of the second setter-forth of doctrine."[45] Elyot might have avoided the charge of flattery entirely by cutting the reference, but the possible benefits were not to be renounced. A specious *retro me* was appended, followed by a confident suggestion that Henry would not lack for others to fill out the tale. Elyot thus lays the onus for the praise on Henry, who begot it; manfully resists the urge to praise his king, lest he be thought to flatter; dismisses the praise of such self-evident virtue as unnecessary; and imagines many future reiterations of Henry's praise, by men more talented, if less self-controlled, than he.

He even suggests fairly openly on one occasion that his advice should not be taken too seriously. Having praised ascetic vegetarians, he bethinks him of the resentment such apparent advice might arouse. "But here men shall not note me that I write this as who sayeth that noblemen in this realm should live after Socrates' diet, wherein having respect to this time and region, they might perchance find occasion to reprove me. Surely like as the excess of fare is to be justly reproved, so in a nobleman much pinching and niggardship of meat and drink is to be discommended" (p. 215). Such statements have the ambiguous force of Renaissance palinodes, allowing the criticism to stand as long as it is ballasted with denial, quotable at need.

Another way to disguise ambition or presumption is to extend protective self-minimization to actual mockery or trivialization of the self. Puttenham repeatedly alludes to the insignificance of his subject; to its "pleasant & louely causes and nothing perillous"; its lighthearted audience composed of "princely dames, yong ladies, gentlewomen and courtiers, beyng all for the most part either meeke of nature, or of pleasant humour"; and its merely recreative aim "to dispose the hearers to mirth and sollace by pleasant conueyance and efficacy of speach" (pp. 154–55). He completes his treatment of the emblem and the anagram with a metaphysical version of this self-dismissal. Some might say

> that such trifles as these might well haue bene spared, . . . that it is pitie mens heades should be fedde with such vanities as are to none edification nor instruction, either of morall vertue, otherwise behooffull for the common wealth, to whose seruice (say they) we are all borne, and not to fill and replenish a whole world full of idle toyes. . . . To these I will giue none other aunswere then referre them to the many trifling poemes of *Homer, Ouid, Virgill, Catullus* and other notable writers of former ages, which . . . haue bene in all ages permitted as the conuenient solaces and recreations of mans wit. And as I can not denie but these conceits of mine be trifles: no lesse in very deede be all the most serious studies of man, if we shall measure grauitie and lightnesse by the wise mans ballance who after he had considered of all the profoundest artes and studies among men, in th'ende cryed out with this Epyphoneme, *Vanitas vanitatum et omnia vanitas.* (Pp. 111–12)

Elyot, as we have seen, admits to aiming for "discourses of estate" but claims to need instruction more than anyone he might teach, thus presenting a diminished image free from the stigma of presumption. Puttenham argues that aiming at *any* high goal would be presumptuous for a mere man. By leveling all performances to one stratum, that of toys, he defends his own trifling along the way as being no more trivial than anything else. Ascham argues that a lowly argument is really easier to defend than one highly billed: "A meane Argument, may easelie beare, the light burden of a small faute, and haue alwaise at hand, a ready excuse for ill handling" (pp. 217–18).[46] Gascoigne defends his *Posies* by a sneer, or rather a mock-sneer, at their youthful misguidedness. From the more mature perspective that two years of experience have afforded him, Gascoigne can twit his readers for having failed to read the poems as cautionary. Although the author readily admits the perceived immature lustfulness of his earlier writings, he feels his audience has failed him in not taking them as aversive examples. He deflects his self-condemnation onto them, but the success of this strategy depends on a prior trivializing of the younger author.

Reminiscing about the revisions of his "Declination of Monarchie," Fulke Greville tells of his sense of the danger of advising princes: "When I had in mine own case well weigh'd the tendernesse of that great subject, and consequently, the nice path I was to walke in between two extreames; but especially the danger, by treading aside, to cast scandall upon the sacred foundations of Monarchy; together with the fate of many metaphoricall Phormio's before me, who had lost themselves in teaching kings and princes, how to governe their people: then did this new prospect dazzle mine eyes, and suspend my travell for a time."[47] (Cicero reports the derision that met Phormio the philosopher when he delivered a lengthy lecture to Hannibal on the arts of war, having "never seen an enemy or a camp, or had the least concern in any public employment."[48]) Greville had thought to promote his project by using a richer style, "but while these clothes were in making, I perceived that cost would but draw more curious eyes to observe deformities. So that from these checks a new counsell rose up in me, to take away all opinion of seriousnesse from these perplexed pedegrees; and to this end carelessly cast them into that hypocriticall figure Ironia, wherein commonly men—to keep above their workes—seeme to make toies of the uttermost they can doe."[49] Javitch quotes this passage to link irony and *sprezzatura*.[50] I suggest instead that Greville uses irony not to display self-deprecation (a tactic that would amplify his image), but rather to undercut himself truly, to trivialize the action in order to avoid the dangers of serious questioning. It is the difference between making the major minor in a conspicuously false way (archness) and doing so in an inconspicuously false way (hypocrisy). The former tactic amplifies the self; the latter conceals it. We may verify Greville's desire for self-dismissal with the tale of burning his *Antony and Cleopatra*, "lest while he seemed to looke over-much upward, hee might stumble into the astronomer's pit. Many members in that creature—by the opinion of those few eyes, which saw it—having some childish wantonnesse in them, apt enough to be construed or strained to a personating of vices in the present governors and government."[51]

The more explicit danger drove him from Ironia to the flames—a total minimization.

Finally let us turn to the self-concealment strategy that works through a fictional frame. Critical matter is presented in the form of a fictional report, hence dissociating the historical author from historical responsibility for his affirmations. Puttenham is the prime exemplar here. He links the generic origins of satire, comedy, and pastoral to the social experiences of authors in an environment of audience reprisal.

> [The] most bitter inuectiue against vice and vicious men, was the *Satyre*: which to th'intent their bitternesse should breede none ill will, either to the Poets, or to the recitours, (which could not haue bene chosen if they had bene openly knowen) and besides to make their admonitions and reproofs seeme grauer and of more efficacie, they made wise as if the gods of the woods, whom they called *Satyres* or *Siluanes*, should appeare and recite those verses of rebuke, whereas in deede they were but disguised persons vnder the shape of *Satyres*. (P. 31)

Comedy, like satire a sharp and critical form, was likewise founded on self-defending moral guidance. The authors "were enforced for feare of quarell & blame to disguise their players with strange apparell, and by colouring their faces and carying hatts & capps of diuerse fashions to make them selues lesse knowen" (p. 32). And pastoral turns out not to be a primitive form at all, but to have developed much later, in order "vnder the vaile of homely persons, and in rude speeches to insinuate and glaunce at greater matters, and such as perchance had not bene safe to haue beene disclosed in any other sort, which may be perceiued by the Eglogues of *Virgill*, in which are treated by figure matters of greater importance then the loues of *Titirus* and *Corydon*. These Eglogues came after to containe and enforme morall discipline, for the amendment of mans behauiour, as be those of *Mantuan* and other moderne Poets" (pp. 38–39). These expositions defictionalize fictional forms, designating the fictiveness as a historical strategy of evasion. Puttenham implies a hostile environment of immoral and powerful men and women, in which moral poets comment on the elite (and so, in fact, serve them) despite the risks. He seems, in other words, to have projected a self-flattering version of the Elizabethan scene into a prehistoric time. Here we find a temporizing of the essence of his place in his own paranoid age, similar to Elyot's anthropological grounding of *nobilitas*. But Puttenham retrojects this formation to criticize rather than to ratify the present. And in resorting to this stratagem he utilizes the very strategy that he imputes to early satirists; by making a fictional displacement he comments deniably on contemporary corruption.

With Puttenham's archaeological evasions we may compare Guazzo's use of the dialogue form, in the discussion of princes, where discretion is indispensable.[52] Annibale has said that princes' doings are "yrreprehensible and incomprehensible" (1:198). By giving this position to his normative speaker, Guazzo arranges to have a voice within his fiction that he can name as his own at need. The possessor of this voice senses something sacrilegious in even broaching the subject: "To reason of and call into question their dooinges, is nothing else, but with the Gyants, to lay seige to heaven" (1:198). William (also obliquely authorial, of course) reads this reticence as self-protective, as concealing a critical stance: "I perceive well, that according to the Proverb you love to stand farre of from Jupiter, and lightning, being assured that no man shall accuse you for that you shall not say, and me thinkes you have regarde to that which is sayde by one, That to reprehend princes it is dangerous, and to commend them, plaine lying" (1:198–99).[53] Annibale replies indignantly (or ironically; we cannot prove the latter):

> It is so farre of, that I meant to signifie any such thing, that I did not so much as think it. For being perswaded that they holde of the divinitie, I thinke they cannot easily erre or commit acte woorthie reprehension. Neyther can I choose but laugh at certaine curious fellowes, who discoursing of the affaires of the worlde, and not knowing the hidden secretes of the deepe devises of the Pope, the Emperour, the king or great Turke make of their doings a thousande wrong and fond interpretations, being farre wide of their thoughts. (1:199)

By distributing the ideological lines in this way, Guazzo arranges for William to be able to voice any antiprincely sentiments he may choose without the creator being responsible for them. For the dominant Annibale labels just such thinking "farre wide" and laughable, thus satirizing William, whose statements have become negative exemplars. Furthermore, it may be that by assigning the criticized criticism to his brother William, Stefano Guazzo claims to demonstrate his own devotion to the truth, despite personal loyalty. The dominant interlocutor is, after all, a physician, occupied with curative action.

Still, it suits Guazzo's intellectual purposes to discuss princes' conversation. And so, through William's sarcasms, Guazzo insists that Annibale absolutize his position before making an exception to it.

William then speaks of one who chose, in self-defense, not to argue with his prince, though he was probably in the right. "That fellowe coulde not bee without a reply to beate backe the nayle againe: but perchaunce he liked better to yeelde with his tongue, then with his heart, by the example of the Peacocke, who saide the Eagle was a fayrer byrde then hee, not in respect of his feathers, but of his beake and talents, which caused that no other birde durst stand in contention with him." Annibale replies (or rather, does not reply) as follows: "Well, I say to you againe, that the dooings of Princes are blamelesse, altogether without the compasse of our judgement, and alwaies mistaken of us" (1:203). Not to be misled by avian analogies, Annibale reiterates the purity of his resistance to discussing princes' actions. Then, when William points out cases of bad princes, Annibale avers, "they were not Princes by nature, but by violence" (1:203), giving away his whole argument, in fact, while maintaining it hypothetically. He can now discuss princely depravity as he likes, always able to aim his negative remarks at bad (that is, false) princes, or non-princes; criticism of them cannot be said to relate to any princes who might be offended—who are presumably "good" (though to be offended might brand them as "bad").

One more narrative displacement of criticism of princes may be noted, again in *The Civile Conversation*. At the outset of Book 4, Annibale asks William his opinion of the view of a learned Greek who argued that a man might wish to be reincarnated as a lower animal rather than as a man, because "it availeth not for man to be vertuous, noble, or valiant, because the flatterer possesseth the first place, the second the Calumniator, and the traytour and trecherous person the third, and so consequentlie the vile persons and naughtie livers, have also their places appointed for them" (2:117–18). William judges this view to derive from "a will to reproove those Princes, who having altered their appetite, goe about to make the wicked mightie, and throw the good downe headlong into bitter disgrace" (2:118) but wonders why Annibale has alleged this opinion. "To no other ende," he replies, "then to honour and extoll the most renowned Lorde Vespasian Gonzaga, whose vertues both singuler and rare, if they were common to all other Princes, the foresaide inconveniences should not now take place amongst us" (2:118). First the saturnine William (already discredited) reads the negative view, imputed by Annibale to an ancient and unnamed philosopher, as being critical of princes; then Annibale reveals his purpose in raising the issue to be simply a desire to laud Lord Vespasian, who is first introduced at this point in the narrative. The criticism of princely corruption, bitterly stated, operates as a rhetorical foil for the advent of Lord Vespasian, whose goodness is revealed in his alienation from his evil peers. Resentment at evil princes receives expression but is generalized and then bypassed as a result of its employment as a framing mechanism. Catharsis and flattery combine.

Such narrative embedding of critical postures resembles Puttenham's synthesis of poetry and courting in dissembling, to give both solace and "serious aduise" (p. 299). Javitch, however, distinguishes poet from courtier (or at least good poet from bad courtier) by establishing strictly moral categories, purifying Puttenham's courtly ethic of deception for the poet.[54] He bases this separation on Puttenham's explicit "we doe allow our Courtly Poet to be a dissembler only in the subtilties of his arte" (p. 302). But Guazzo's narrative procedure and Puttenham's own practice and theory all directly relate the subtlety of art to extraliterary social comment. Javitch fails to consider the way Puttenham situates his selective legitimation of poetic dissembling.

> These and many such like disguisings do we find in mans behauiour, & specially in the Courtiers of forraine Countreyes, where in my youth I was brought vp, and very well obserued their maner of life and conuersation, for of mine owne Countrey I haue not made so great experience. Which parts, neuerthelesse, we allow not now in our English maker, because we haue geuen him the name of an honest man, and not of an hypocrite: and therefore leauing these manner of dissimulations to all base-minded men, & of vile nature or misterie, we doe allow our Courtly Poet to be a dissembler only in the subtilties of his arte. (P. 302)

The application of Puttenham's criticism to "forraine Countreyes" is not just "chauvinism,"[55] but a strategic displacement (similar to setting scurrilous plays in Renaissance Italy or Tiberian Rome, when Jacobean court life could not be safely touched yet was irresistible as a dramatic subject). Such disguises, like overt denials, usually *signal* topical reference. To comply with a careful distinction of "poetic dissimulation from the fraud and falsehood which justifiably provoke moral outrage"[56] is to accept Puttenham's stratagem instead of analyzing it. (I find it difficult in any case to imagine the iron-age Puttenham provoked to "justifiable moral outrage" so easily.) And in fact Javitch marginally registers this awareness: "Of course the *Arte* hardly permits this distinction [between poet and courtier] since the poet is shown finally to fulfill his vocation by doing precisely what is expected of the proper courtier."[57]

The *Arte* is indeed a manual of courtly conduct, as Javitch was perhaps the first to say,[58] but one that was itself subject to the censoring pressures it so eloquently describes. Puttenham aimed to anatomize the techniques of artful courting: both strictly poetic ones (a distinction I think he would have thought only artful) and sociopolitical ones necessary for the daily purposes of the courtier, both poetic and oratorical—that is, political. But such candid wisdom was not for open publication; the ingredients of this art had to be deniably encoded in a scrambled form. The regular collocation of moralistic and Machiavellian postures simply accomplishes the deceptive circumspection enjoined throughout the book. An analysis of these injunctions will make Puttenham's studied rhetorical mode clearer.

Poetry is frequently described in the *Arte* in terms of otium and solace, even of entertainment or recreation. This last term, by a modern critical rewriting, can also refer to a higher contemplation, a form equally severed from worldly practice. Puttenham presents both these views of poetry "proper." But the many remarks that insulate the realities of poetry from "real life," by either transcendentalizing or trivializing poetry, are interspersed with as many quite contradictory arguments that fuse the two realms, making poetry a political tool. I think such incoherence is in fact duplicity, marking a conscious evasion of envy and the censor. Puttenham inserts capsules of banal propriety into strongly critical or subversive texts, for citation as needed. Javitch's grid of organic form imposes an inappropriate continuity on contradictory material; it is controlled by the very strategy under scrutiny, for the sententious utterances are designedly quotable. Javitch's reading misses, indeed conceals, the proper wholeness of this palimpsest. These dissonant postures are truly contradictory—as both offensive and defensive structures. The tonal variations of evasive sarcasm and boring orthodoxy are quite conventional, seen one at a time. They coexist perfectly well in Puttenham, with the loss of only a falsely Olympian model of the author—distant, contemplative, undisturbed by, even unaware of, the very stresses of court life that saturate this remarkable text. We must ask what dangerous readings his denials disenfranchise; if the subversions are set forth, even by being dismissed or undercut, then we must infer the presence of such camouflage as Puttenham finds at the heart of the literature of reprehension.[59]

We have noted Puttenham's displacements to prehistory and to non-English courts, and Guazzo's to the dialogue form; it remains only to consider the pastoral evasion. Much has been written of late on the literary pastoral proper; I shall attend here to some less literary usages of the pastoral structure at court.[60] Perhaps the minimal rustic form is always implicitly revealed by the self-important proffer of humility. Elyot makes this clear in his affection for pastoral fables of baseness rewarded. K. J. Wilson notes the use in the proem to *The Governor* of "the disingenuous exempla from Plutarch of the 'pore husbondman' whose offering was not rejected by the Persian king, Artaxerxes, and from Horace of Choerilus, whom Alexander honorably retained 'all though that the poet was but of a small estimation.'" Henry's applause for this work (reported by Elyot in the preface to *Of the Knowledge Which Maketh a Wise Man*) reminds Wilson of "the philosopher-emperor Antoninus, who asked to have his faults recounted by 'a playne and rude persone / whiche alwaye spake in the rebuke of all men,' and who afterward, incidentally, not only retained this plain speaker but also gave him 'dowble wages.'"[61] Here the *topos* of meanness combines self-trivialization with the virtuous desert of total humility (which also confers the clear-sightedness of the ultimately poor), while disguising audacity as ignorant bluntness. In the same preface, Elyot broaches another kind of pastoral trope, increasingly important to him, for another sort of self-protection. He asks whether wisdom is to be found in authority or in experience: "One sayeth it is in moche lernynge and knowledge. An other affirmeth / that they whiche do conducte the affayres of greatte princis of countrayes, be onely wyse men. Nay saythe the thyrde, he is wysest that leste dothe meddle, and can sytte quietly at home and tourne a crabbe, and looke onely unto his owne busynesse."[62] Here the defense is not active, conducted in the pursuit of employment, but rather a resigned retreat from both modes of greatness to an unstylishly humble life. At such distance from court a noble can also screen the independent exercise of power in the provinces, as Raleigh's second "state mystery" implies: "that the nobility may be accustomed to bear the government of the prince, especially such as have their dwelling in remote places from the prince's eye, it is expedient to call them up at certain times to the prince's court, under pretence of doing them honour, or being desirous to see and enjoy their presence."[63] The manipulated noble might well reply to such a call with praise of the humble virtues of country life.

Sir John Harington uses pastoral *topoi* for self-defense more explicitly, when he dares to mention the Essex expedition to Ireland (during which he was knighted). Writing to Sir Anthony Standen in 1600, he says: "You wonder I write nothing of *one*:—believe me I hear nothing; but *he* is where he was, and I think must be, till these great businesses be concluded. Let this suffice from a private country knight, that lives among clouted shoes, in his frize jacket and galloshes, and who envies not the great commanders of Ireland, but hereby commends himself to them."[64] Harington makes no secret of the ironic tone here, yet he takes advantage of its insulating effect. He does likewise in another letter on the same subject: "but hereof enowe, as it becomethe not a poore countrye knyghte to looke from the plow-handle into policie and pryvacie."[65]

Essex himself used these *topoi*. Perhaps Ireland, the land that for Spenser was the wilderness of self-definition, and for Essex was reputation's grave, somehow demanded these terms. In any case, Essex used them to express his unhappiness with (and away from) the queen:

> Happy were Hee could finish foorth his Fate
> In some unhaunted Desert, most Obscure;
> From all Society, from Love, from Hate
> Of Worldly Folke! Then should Hee Sleepe Secure;
> Then Wake againe, and yield God ever Praise,
> Content with Hipps, and Hawes, and Brambleberry,
> In Contemplation passing still his Daies,
> And Change of Holy Thoughts to make him Merry;
> > Who when Hee dies, his Tombe may bee a Bush,
> > Where Harmeles Robin dwells with Gentle Thrush.[66]

Here the hapless lord manages very smoothly to combine the wish to trade his pastoral wilderness for a pastoral meadow with the wish to trade it for a cozy nest at court, where he might harmlessly sing as he does now. To buy this nest he offers the melancholy thought of a sweet-sad life and death away from his beloved queen. And all the sympathy and remorse he hopes to arouse derive from the rhetorical interchanges possible in the topoi of the lowly life.

To find a ground for Essex's use of the pastoral structure to argue for a return to court, we should turn to Puttenham's remarkable catalog of paradiastolic evasions of courtly attendance. For we must always credit the motive of fear as well as that of ambition, as a letter from Heneage to Hatton in 1582 suggests. Heneage writes from a country retreat, but even there uneasily:

> My dear and most honourable knight, Your letters declaring your noble kindness and remembrance of me, together with the notice of her Majesty's but once thinking graciously of so poor a man as myself, doth bring especial comfort unto me, that otherwise, in this unthankful and forgetful age, should be very little displeased to be both forgotten and contemned, which the high and great minds of the world so much scorn and hate. Yet this same base contempt and withdrawn life is found full oft to be no unsafe shadow from very great displeasures, which the pride and disdain that accompanieth praise, and the business of much action and greatness of place, doth bring unto men.[67]

Such courtly threats gave rise to an endless repertoire of evasions, as Puttenham makes clear.

> Is it not perchance more requisite our courtly Poet do dissemble not onely his countenances & conceits, but also all his ordinary actions of behauiour, or the most part of them, whereby the better to winne his purposes & good aduantages, as ... when a man is whole to faine himselfe sicke to shunne the businesse in Court, to entertaine time and ease at home, to salue offences without discredite, to win purposes by mediation in absence, which their presence would eyther impeach or not greatly preferre, to harken after the popular opinions and speech, to entend to their more priuate solaces, to practize more deepely both at leasure and libertie, and when any publique affaire or other attempt & counsaile of theirs hath not receaued good successe, to auoid thereby the Princes present reproofe, to coole their chollers by absence, to winne remorse by lamentable reports, and reconciliation by friends intreatie. Finally by sequestring themselues for a time fro the Court, to be able the freelier & cleerer to discerne the factions and state of the Court and of al the world besides, no lesse then doth the looker on or beholder of a game better see into all points of auauntage, then the player himselfe? ... Or as I haue seene in diuers places where many make themselues hart whole, when in deede they are full sicke, bearing it stoutly out to the hazard of their health, rather then they would be suspected of any lothsome infirmity, which might inhibit them from the Princes presence, or enterteinment of the ladies. Or as some other do to beare a port of state and plentie when they haue neither penny nor possession, that they may not seeme to droope, and be reiected as vnworthy or insufficient for the greater seruices, or to be pitied for their pouertie. ... Or as others do to make wise they be poore when they be riche, to shunne thereby the publicke charges and vocations, for men are not now a dayes (specially in states of *Oligarchie* as the most of our age)

called so much for their wisedome as for their wealth, also to auoyde enuie
of neighbours or bountie in conuersation, for whosoeuer is reputed rich
cannot without reproch, but be either a lender or a spender. Or as others
do to seeme very busie when they haue nothing to doo, and yet will make
themselues so occupied and ouerladen in the Princes affaires, as it is a great
matter to haue a couple of wordes with them, when notwithstanding they
lye sleeping on their beds all an after noone, or sit solemnly at cardes in
their chambers, or enterteyning of the Dames, or laughing and gibing with
their familiars foure houres by the clocke, whiles the poore suter desirous
of his dispatch is aunswered by some Secretarie or page *il fault attendre,
Monsieur* is dispatching the kings businesse into Languedock, Prouence,
Piemont, a common phrase with the Secretaries of France. Or as I haue
obserued in many of the Princes Courts of Italie, to seeme idle when they
be earnestly occupied & entend to nothing but mischieuous practizes, and
do busily negotiat by coulor of otiation. . . .

  These and many such like disguisings do we find in mans behauiour,
and specially in the Courtiers of forraine Countreyes. (Pp. 299–302)

At this point we return with a yet richer context for Puttenham's dismissal of pragmatic deception from the English court. His numbing
catalog of deceits suggests that the smallest daily acts of courtly life
have an infinitely varied symbolic weight (and hence are vulnerable to
differing interpretations). In such an epistemological arena the ascription of these actions to foreign courts is embedded in the selfsame
list of evasions of responsibility.[68] By deftly eluding the dangerous
aspects of both wealth and poverty, illness and health, busyness and
idleness, Puttenham's wise courtier reveals the essentially formal
structure of evasion beneath these various strategies. Protean self-depiction here makes possible not only "freedom to," but finally "freedom from"—through protective coloration. Who would not pity and
fear this our chameleon?

Deference

  The final trope of promotion to be discussed, deference, is the one
most actively concerned with the depiction of others as well as of the
self, but its reflexive force is always significant, for such offerings of
respect (called *prestation* by Marcel Mauss[69]) extract a similar sign of
recognition. Both sides of this transaction are apparent in Guazzo's
discussion of ceremonies, which emphasizes the fundamental sanctity of social grace. Burke emphasizes this sanctity in *A Rhetoric of
Motives,* calling it "the hierarchic mystery (the principle of secular

divinity, with its range of embarrassment, courtship, modified insult, standoffishness, . . . its scenic embodiment in the worldly equivalent of temples, ritual vestments, rare charismatic vessels, and the like)."[70] Annibale emphasizes this link: "As the sacred Ceremonies, which are voide of superstition, are not displeasant in Gods sight, and stirre up to devotion the mindes of the ignorant people, whiche are not come to the perfect knoweledge of Gods worde: so these worldly ceremonies purchase us the good will of our friendes and superiours, to whom they are addressed, and make us knowne for civile people, and from rude countrie loutes" (1:166). Both sacred and secular ceremonies identify and characterize the relevant stratifications. Such effects can reconstrue the act as instrumental rather than absolute, as Annibale implicitly recognizes: "Who ought not to bee glad to honour another, for so muche as (according to the saying of the Philosopher) hee whiche honoureth, receiveth more honour, then hee whiche is honoured, for like unto the Sunne, the beames of honour by reflexion, as it were, doe shine backe againe uppon him. And as hee whiche is ceremonious may bee thought to bee a dissembler, so hee whiche is not so, may bee taken to bee a clowne, a rudesby, or a contemner of others" (1:165). Courtly deference benefits its author twice over: by gaining his superiors' goodwill, and by distinguishing him from the rudesby who knows no better. Submission to a superior elevates one above the rudesby.

Elyot observes that promoting good men benefits their betters, for it stimulates such men to "endeavour themselves with all their power to increase that opinion of goodness, whereby they were brought to that advancement which needs must be to the honour and benefit of those by whom they were so promoted" (p. 192). In part this is a way of increasing employee production, but it is also clear that the superior's own reputed identity derives from the character of his dependents so that preferment of others will indirectly depict the self. Seen in this light, promotion constitutes a reflexive deference to the promoted: Castiglione's project was aimed at creating "such a Courtier, as the Prince that shall be worthie to have him in his service, although his state be but small, may notwithstanding be called a mighty Lord" (pp. 16/80). Such a courtier can so transform his prince that the prince "shall attaine unto that heroicall and noble vertue, that shall make him passe the boundes of the nature of man, and shall rather be called a demy God, than a man mortall" (pp. 276/474). Such deferential service to a discerning prince both marks the courtier and deifies the prince. Who would not hire such a man?

Guazzo also deals with the depictive force of deferential followers, though more skeptically: "Commonly the greater are flattered by the lesser, and the more they are in prosperitie, the more they are beset with flatterers: who alwaies make their repaire thither where profite is to be reaped" (1:88). The gathering of flatterers can signify arrival in the zone of prosperity, hence can be a burden borne, even sought, for its symbolic value. The anonymous author of the *Institucion of a Gentleman* similarly cites Tully's conversion of another negative, envy, into a positive value: "I haue been alwayes of theys opinion (sayth he) y^t enuy got throughe vertue I holde it righte honour, and no enuye at all" (sig. C5v).[71] And Guazzo's parasitic flatterers can be somewhat cleansed, by his distinction between "fauning" and flattering. "It is permitted," Annibale says, "(neither can it bee saide to bee a faulte) to dissemble without harme, and without intent to hurt another" (1:87). There is no prohibition against benefiting from the act. And in any case, one must "doe them honour for the reverence due to their estate, if not for affection" (1:87).

Having considered the self-depicting power of vertical deference, we may now note the utility (and risk) of lateral deference, in the gift of intimacy in friendship. Castiglione sees this as

> an other thing that giveth and diminisheth much reputation: namely, the choise of friends, with whom a man must have inwarde conversation [*intrinseca pratica*]. For undoubtedly reason willeth, that such as are coupled in strayte amitie, and unspeakable company, should be also alike in will, in minde, in judgement, and inclination.... Therefore I believe that a man ought to have respect in the first beginning of these friendships, for of two neare friendes, who ever knoweth the one, by and by he imagineth the other to bee of the same condition. (Pp. 119/235)

This effect obliges one to screen potential friends for their symbolic effect on his reputation. As Peacham has it, one must consider "how they haue beene reckoned of others."[72] Raleigh proposes numerous criteria for screening out unworthy associates: "Let them therefore be wise and virtuous, and none of those that follow thee for gain ... make election rather of thy betters than thy inferiors, shunning always such as are poor and needy.... If thy friends be of better quality than thyself, thou mayest be sure of two things; the first, that they will be more careful to keep thy counsel, because they have more to lose than thou hast; the second, they will esteem thee for thyself, and not for that which thou dost possess."[73] The reflexive force of such relations is made clearer in Castiglione's hierarchical framing of the proper execution of less intimate friendships:

> I would have our Courtier therefore to finde him out an especiall and hartie friend, if it were possible, of that sorte wee have spoken off [trustworthy, etc., i.e., appropriate to be identified with and by]. Then according to their deserts and honestie, love, honour and observe all other men, and alwaies doe his best to fellowshippe himselfe with men of estimation that are noble and knowne to bee good, more than with the unnoble and of small reputation, so he bee also beloved and honoured of them. And this shall come to passe, if he be gentle, lowly, freeharted, easie to bee spoken to, and sweete in companie, humble [*officioso*, i.e., conscious of his duties or office] and diligent to serve, and to have an eye to his friendes profit and estimation, as wel absent as present, bearing with their naturall defaults that are to be borne withall, without breaking with them upon a small ground, and correcting in himselfe such as lovingly shall bee tolde him, never preferring himselfe before other men in seeking the highest and chiefe roomes of estimation. (Pp. 120–21/237–38)

These gracefully submissive attitudes superintend reflexive friendly relations with "men of estimation."

Guazzo shows how coordinate friendship may derive value from a comparative sense of the choice among various friends. William welcomes Annibale for another day of conversation, especially grateful because the latter has chosen to return rather than go to a wedding to which he has been bidden by a "speciall friend" (2:2). William takes "marveilous pleasure . . . to see that you make more account of me then of him . . . [I hope] that you may have just cause to continue your good opinion of me, and I may be made worthy of the prayse you give me, in esteeming me more than all the magnificence of Genes [Genoa]." Well-chosen friends confer depiction derived from their own worthiness and from their active reciprocal choice (in William's case) or acceptance (if we attend to Castiglione's tone) of oneself. In fact, a third motive for choice might be added. Bacon says that "there is but one case wherein a man may commend himself with good grace, and that is in commending virtue in another, especially if it be such a virtue whereunto himself pretendeth."[74]

Certain other deferential moves can be noted here. The first occurs in Hoby's dedicatory epistle, addressed to Henry Hastings, "Sonne and Heire Apparant to the Noble Earle of Huntington." Hoby desires that Castiglione, his new courtier, be properly welcomed, "well entertained and much honored. And for somuch as none, but onely a young Gentleman, and trayned up all his life time in Court, and of worthy qualities, is meete to receive and entertaine so worthie a Courtier, that like may felowship and get estimation with his like, I do dedicate him unto your good Lordship" (p. 2). It is not clear who has passed the test here, Castiglione or Hastings. Is the former to "get estimation" from associating with Hastings, or vice versa? Hoby offers to Hastings the opportunity to bestow ratification, and to Castiglione preferment to an appropriate reception. And each of these offers compliments Hoby's discrimination.

The banquet in Book 4 of *The Civile Conversation* includes a good deal of strategic deference. For instance, Cavallero Bottazzo makes the error of making "a signe" to one of the waiters for more wine; "without anie more wordes" he drinks it down. For this he is roundly reproached by the company, since "not having respect to this companie, [he] hath called for his Wine with a privie becke in this place, priviledged for everie one to speake freelie what he thinketh, and to call for francklie what he lacketh" (2:150). In fact Lord Vespasian (the ranking guest) rather than the hostess, initiates the reproach, since a rebuke from her might threaten her reputation for generosity. Lord Vespasian speaks for the group, it seems, to whom the house belongs for the evening; Cavallero is forced to "make himself at home." He replies with alacrity, endorsing the sentiment by telling of one who, for the same offense, got an even more intense "punishment": The servant to whom this "privie becke" was addressed put on his cloak and went to the sideboard; he there poured a glass of wine and brought it under his cloak to the gentleman, saying, "I imagining it was your pleasure, that the rest should not see it, I brought it therefore as closelie as I could possiblie doe" (2:150). Here the pusillanimous guest is corrected by a servant, whose job is to know how a guest should demand and receive deferential service; the correction is to the credit of the household.[75] Cavallero recovers from his own lapse by appropriating the servant's ironic perception.

Two discussions of overt presentation of deferential praise are also informative. First, when Lord Vespasian modestly refuses to accept his hostess's song of praise, Cavallero judges the adequacy of his rejection. "It is reported that Caesar caused Pompeius statutes [statues], which were broken downe, to be raysed, and set up againe, whereupon one saide: Caesar doth fortifie his owne statutes, in erecting Pompeius his. And therefore Ladie Caterine, imitating Caesar herein, hath extolled Lord Vespasian, the more to magnifie herselfe, and her owne judgement: wherefore it shall thus rest, That Lord Vespasian accept halfe of these praises, and leave the other halfe to Ladie Caterine" (2:159–60). The reflexiveness of Lady Caterine's praise is publicly recognized; indeed, the lady's skill in praising earns an explicit social reward from the group.

In the second instance Lady Jane, the nominal "queen" of the evening, is the recipient of similar praise and similarly refuses it. Cavallero has held forth at length on her beauties of mind and body, in response to another game-challenge. She replies:

> You might (Seignior Cavallero) have added to the number of these praises which you have published in my behalfe, the great patience which I have endured to the ende, in suffering your tongue to burst out with this ardent desire, which you hadde, in going about to praise mee, which I would not interrupt, not because I did presume that these praises were due unto mee, but to permit you to get that commendation and glorie, your selfe, to the which you did aspire, in that you did labour tooth and nayle, to make that apparent, which in deede is not, which having brought to passe, I cannot for my owne part, but greatly commend you. (2:190)

Again the effort of praise is presumed to be primarily reflexive, though this example is from the performative context of a game, encouraging variations upon a theme. A limited sample from Cavallero's speech suggests this.

> You most honorable ladie, even you I saie, may be esteemed and called the most glorious creature in the world, since nature hath enriched your person with those treasures of beautie, for want of which, those which are commonlie called amongst us faire, are verie poore. This beautifull nature hath placed the seate of Majestie in your high forehead. In your eyes it hath kindled so sweete and temperate fire, which holdeth all mennes hearts bound betweene hope and feare. In your cheekes [etc.]. (2:188–89)

After Cavallero's display Lord Bernardine, fearing, he says, that the other ladies might feel neglected, brings out poems to each of them (and—of course—to Lord Vespasian) in praise of their virtues. The poems were obviously prepared in advance, and Bernardine held off on delivery until the proper occasion for the presentation.

All these utterances seem to us far from "sincere," but we err, I think, for they were fully authentic in their reflexive aims, and the group was happy to reward such inventors repeatedly with the coin of recognition. Insofar as such operations must be seen to have aimed at collective ratification, we should properly speak of the evening as filled with ritual instead of games. Despite the competitive forms employed, the differentiation brought about by the various games was, in the course of the evening, thoroughly distributed. The usual procedure was to disqualify intermediate winners, so that others might then win too. In fact *everyone* was specified as exceptionally clever or beautiful or exalted, in one way or another. The group reaffirmed its view of itself, through a fluid mixture of self-flattering deference and refused praise.

Having reviewed in this chapter the cooperative conventions of praise and flattery that created and maintained the sense of self of the Elizabethan courtier and of his actual and potential allies, we can now turn to the competitive counterparts of blame and slander. With these tropes the courtier fended off rivals and critics of all sorts, and perhaps in darker moments also lacerated himself for what he feared were his own inadequacies.

5. Tropes of Personal Rivalry: Blame and Slander

In this chapter we consider those tools of the courtier's trade that function as weapons. The combative maneuvers of slander and detraction, the limiting definitions of obedience and sumptuary legislation, and the devaluations of newfangled ideas and skills, all aim to dismiss substantial competition. In the process many gestures of support now familiar from Chapter 4 are reformulated for purposes of denial, in accordance with the paradiastolic matrix.

Combative Modes

It is useful to conceive hostility by first considering courtly attitudes toward amiability and affection. Elyot's narrative of Titus and Gesippus, exemplary friends, concludes with the following description of human relations at court:

> Undoubtedly it is wonderfully difficult to find a man very ambitious or covetous to be assured in friendship. For where findest thou him (saith Tully) that will not prefer honours, great offices, rule, authority, and riches before friendship? Therefore (saith he) it is very hard to find friendship in them that be occupied in acquiring honour or about the affairs of the public weal. Which saying is proved true by daily experience. For disdain and contempt be companions with ambition, like as envy and hatred be also her followers. (P. 151)[1]

Elyot situates Cicero's moral criticism in the daily context of the court. Here the frequent allusions made during the Renaissance to the infinite value of friendship begin to seem wishful, and so emphasize the pressures militating against it, pressures specific to the values of honor and ambition. Castiglione reports Bembo's similar argument as to the problematic character of intimate court friendship.

> To be bound in friendship with such agreement of minde as you speak of, me thinke in deede a man ought to have great respect, not onely for getting or loosing reputation, but because now adayes ye finde verie few true friendes.
>
> Neither doe I believe that there are any more in the world, those Pylades and Orestes [and other such], but rather it happeneth dayly, I wote not by what destinie, that two friendes, which many yeares have lived together with most hartie love, yet at the ende beguile one an other, in one manner or other, either of malice or envy, or for lightness, or some other ill cause: and each one imputeth the fault to his fellow, of that which perhaps both the one and the other deserveth.
>
> Therefore . . . I have thought with my selfe alone to bee well done, never to put a mans trust in any person in the worlde, nor give him selfe so for a pray to friende how deare and loving soever he were, that without stoppe a man should make him partaker of all his thoughts, as he would his owne selfe: because there are in our minds so many dennes and corners, that it is unpossible for the wit of man to know the dissimulations that lye lurking in them.
>
> I believe therefore that it is well done to love and beare with one more than an other, according to their deserts and honestie: but not for all that so to assure a mans selfe, with this sweet baite of friendship, that afterward it should bee too late for us to repent. (Pp. 119–20/236)[2]

Bembo does not argue that others or evil men are untrustworthy but that we are *all* so: it is in *our* minds that the "dennes and corners" of dissimulation are to be found, generated by the "destinie" of the courtly environment. The telos of "acquiring honour" mandates this when honor "gained and broken upon another hath the quickest reflection," as Bacon notes.[3] Friends must continually resist the temptation to spend one another in return for the coin of image.

Annibale suggests the distressing sensitivity this situation encourages, by his controlled and impersonal rejection of unlimited friendship.

> Where at this day are those true friendes to bee found? Know you not that according to the Philosopher, Perfecte friendshippe extendeth not towardes divers persons, but is restrained to the love of one alone? I knowe not who is your assured friende, but I am sure that I have not yet founde mine, with whom I might use suche open, simple, and free behaviour as you meane. . . . And though in token of true friendship, you call your companion brother, perchaunce hee shall have no minde to tearme you so: and to take that custome from you, hee wyll call you Maister Guazzo. And that

you may not use too familiar speeche to him, hee will speake to your worship in suche sorte, that you shall bee faine to retyre one steppe backe, and
use him rather Ceremoniously then lovingly. Of this common course of the
world I gather, that those with whom wee are conversaunt, being rather
well willers, then true friendes, it is our partes to take heede of too broade
and to familiar behaviour with them, whereby wee may hazzarde to loose
their good will: and to followe the example of Flies, which will not become
tame amongst us, though they dayly dwell with us, and eate of our cates
when wee doe. (1:167)[4]

Annibale not only advises uncontaminated stuffiness but enacts it
too, overtly reminding William that they are not friends, however
well willing they may be. The act of openness required to initiate
friendship must often have seemed more likely to endanger reputation than to enhance it. Even the goodwill of neutral peers falls before
the inertial force of an inevitable self-concern.

Such an environment was conducive to a thoroughly developed
rhetoric of combat. Early in the *Arte*, for instance, Puttenham divides
his poetic taxonomy into inclusive genres of praise and genres of reprehension. And in his lengthy treatment of rhetorical devices many
stand out as verbal weapons. The members of the set of "dissembling" devices are "souldiers to the figure *allegoria* and fight vnder
the banner of dissimulation" (p. 191).[5] (Does any other device in the
Arte have as many aliases as its leader?) "Ye doe likewise dissemble,
when ye speake in derision or mockerie, & that may be many waies:
as sometime in sport, sometime in earnest, and priuily, and apertly,
and pleasantly, and bitterly" (p. 189). The set includes *ironia*, or the
dry mock; *sarcasmus*, the bitter taunt; *asteismus*, the merry scoff or
civil jest; *micterismus*, the fleering frump; *antiphrasis*, the broad
flout; and *charientismus*, the privy nip. Each of these devices dissem-
bles, Puttenham suggests, by departing from the bare and proper
statement of fact; and each is conceived in the spirit of combat,
though such a spirit may convey various types of force. Seriousness
and game, cleverness and muttering, all seem implied by Puttenham's
list. In addition,

ye haue yet two or three other figures that smatch a spice of the same *false
semblant*, but in another sort and maner of phrase, whereof one is when
we speake in the superlatiue and beyond the limites of credit, that is by the
figure which the Greeks call *Hiperbole*, the Latines *Dementiens* or the
lying figure. I for his immoderate excesse cal him the ouer reacher right
with his originall or [*lowd lyar*] & me thinks not amisse: now when I

speake that which neither I my selfe thinke to be true, nor would haue any other body beleeue, it must needs be a great dissimulation, because I meane nothing lesse then that I speake, and this maner of speach is vsed, when either we would greatly aduance or greatly abase the reputation of any thing or person, and must be vsed very discreetly, or els it will seeme odious. (Pp. 191–92)

These tools may operate in either vector of blame or praise, and, as in dueling, the choice of weapons may affect one's own reputation.

Other weapons are listed throughout this section. *Antitheton*, the quarreler, is named after "al such persons as delight in taking the contrary part of whatsoeuer shalbe spoken" (p. 210). These folk are also called gainsayers, of whom more will be said later. *Metanoia*, the penitent, is used when "we speake and be sorry for it, as if we had not wel spoken, so that we seeme to call in our word againe, and to put in another fitter for the purpose" (p. 215). Puttenham employed this device to minimize offense, in a poem about Elizabeth:

Meaning to praise her for her greatnesse of courage [and] ouershooting my selfe, [I] called it first by the name of pride: then fearing least fault might be found with that terme, by & by turned this word pride to praise. . . .

Your pride serues you to seaze them all alone:
Not pride madame, but praise of the lion.

(P. 215)

Although compliment is the stated goal in this case, metanoia would also allow the poet to smuggle criticism into comment and then deny it. Elsewhere Puttenham describes poets as "being in deede the trumpetters of all praise and also of slaunder (not slaunder, but well deserued reproche)" (p. 35). These examples might have served in Chapter 4 to explain self-concealment; Puttenham is speaking here of apology. But I want to emphasize that the negative element does get voiced; only then is it disavowed. Metanoia can function as a critical device, with a defensive component—resembling *occupatio* or *praeteritio*, wherein something is emphasized by conspicuously claiming to pass it by.

Meiosis, the disabler, has numerous eristic purposes. It may be used "for despite to bring our aduersaries in contempt," or "to excuse a fault, & to make an offense seeme lesse then it is," or "by way of pleasant familiaritie, and as it were for a Courtly maner of speach with our egalls or inferiours," or "to be giuen in derision and for a kind of contempt" (pp. 219–21) when insult by diminutives is wanted. *Parisia*, or the licentious, resembles metanoia in its bipartite structure:

The fine and subtill perswader when his intent is to sting his aduersary, or els to declare his mind in broad and liberal speeches, which might breede offence or scandall, he will seeme to bespeake pardon before hand, whereby his licentiousnes may be the better borne withall, as he that said:

If my speech hap t'offend you any vvay,
Thinke it their fault, that force me so to say.

(P. 227)

Paramologia, the figure of admittance, allows the enemy's argument to be admitted and then avoided in some way afterward. The converse is *dichologia*, or the figure of excuse, wherein one's own weaknesses can be acknowledged and then set aside.

Two sorts of comparative figures may also be mentioned. Puttenham offers this example of *orismus*, the definer of difference: "Is this wisedome? no it is a certaine subtill knauish craftie wit, it is no industrie as ye call it, but a certaine busie brainsicknesse, for industrie is a liuely and unweried search and occupation in honest things, egernesse is an appetite in base and small matters" (p. 231). Another device Puttenham would call the *paragon*, if the term were not taken as appropriate for dealing with the queen. This "figure of comparison" is used "as when a man wil seeme to make things appeare good or bad, or better or worse, or more or lesse excellent, either vpon spite or for pleasure, or any other good affection, then he sets the lesse by the greater, or the greater to the lesse, the equall to his equall, and by such confronting of them together, driues out the true ods that is betwixt them, and makes it better appeare" (p. 234).[6] These paradiastolic tropes are designed to enable reinterpretation in accord with the speaker's political affiliations and aims.

Finally we may note *paralepsis*, or the passager,

very many times vsed for a good pollicie in pleading or perswasion to make wise as if we set but light of the matter, and that therefore we do passe it ouer slightly when in deede we do then intend most effectually and despightfully if it be inuective to remember it: it is also when we will not seeme to know a thing, and yet we know it well inough, and may be likened to the maner of women, who as the common saying is, will say nay and take it.

I hold my peace and will not say for shame,
The much vntruth of that unciuill dame:
For if I should her coullours kindly blaze,
It would so make the chast eares amaze. &c.

(P. 232)

These examples might be supplemented with examples from other rhetorics, but enough has been said to make certain summary statements possible. First we may note that although such terms are generally familiar from classical writings, Puttenham self-consciously roots them historically in his own time. This procedure is of course part of the project of annexing classical virtues by providing modern examples. But it is equally clear that these strokes and parries are specific to the courtly experience per se, that Puttenham includes them not only for their poetic utility but also for their value in the cut-and-thrust of ambition. The residue of violence is made conspicuous by the emphasis on self-defense against aroused anger and enmity. The intention of some uses may be "mere" banter (though this formulation probably just renames the problem), but many others deal in contempt and invective, natural conditions of the world in which Puttenham's would-be courtier-poet must seek his place of unquiet rest. In such a world, talk is not cheap; it is therefore to be managed with great care. For this purpose Puttenham proposes his courtly adaptations of the more metropolitan and forensic battalions of classical rhetoric.

We should recall that such tools have epideictic as well as instrumental force. Many such devices generate *quotable* actions that can be repeated anecdotally to the credit or disgrace of the original speaker or butt. Thus they serve two purposes at once. In the short view they enable one to score against a current antagonist; in the longer view, they add to the investment capital of one's reputation—as a wit, a stout verbal adversary, or even just a man or woman to be invited back, sheerly for entertainment's sake (like Benedick or Beatrice). Such investments often seem trivial at first, but they still may have long-term expediency for the maintenance of self; that is to say, immediate reputational gain is not always essential.

Like Puttenham, Guazzo treats the rhetoric of combat, in a detailed examination of slander. He believes that "those which aspire to the degree of vertue, and which will shewe themselves woorthie to bee admitted into civile conversation, ought above all things to have regarde that they offende no man with their tongue" (1:122). Nonetheless, slanderers are "tolerable," because whatever damage they do is done secretly. In any case, "that fault is at this day common throughout the worlde, and therefore wee must spite of our teeth beare with ill tongues" (1:65). Guazzo thus tolerates concealed slander, while sneering, as we have seen, at revealed slander as the product of "the idle, the ignorant, the unfortunate, and bankerupts" (1:65). This bias favoring concealment should discount at least part of the moral animus directed in the following catalog toward "ill speaking." For if the would-be is the have-not, resentful at being kept out of the charmed circle, Annibale's charges of slander seem to be the product of a class prejudice. Criticism criticized becomes a lie, its speaker a liar who can be dismissed without further attention. But not all courtly criticisms are illegitimate blame; verbal assaults on faultfinders are frequently social rather than moral and should be seen as functions of struggle, not of contemplation.

Annibale sees numerous kinds of "those Curre dogges, which without barking bite us privily. . . . Some of them I call Maskers, some Rethoricians [*sic*], some Poets, some Hypocrites, some Scorpions, some Traitours, some Forgers, some Biters, some Mockers, and some unknowne" (1:67). The maskers are "certaine naughty tongued fellowes [who] under the maske of modestie, say they will not name him whom they reprehende, and yet they set him out so evidently, that all the hearers knowe whom hee meaneth" (1:67). The rhetoricians "are those who with a certaine figure, called by the Maisters of Eloquence Occupatio, make as though they would not speake evill, and yet doe it" (1:68), like Puttenham's users of metanoia and parisia. The poets employ antiphrasis and, "speaking by contraries, will give in mockage, the name of faire to a woman that is foule, and of honest, to one that is an harlot" (1:68). The hypocrites "under the colour of griefe and compassion, to be the better beleeved, lamentably rehearse the ill haps of other" (1:68). The scorpions use Puttenham's trick of paramologia, allowing and discounting virtue in this way: "[']I thinke not possible to finde a more curteous and honorable Gentleman then Maister Guazzo, whom I should farre more account of, if he had not one great fault.['] You knowe howe afterwarde he beginneth in manner of a Scorpion to sting you with his tayle, in speaking yll of you" (1:69–70). The traitors fail to honor confidences.

> *Annib.:* If perchaunce you have received some hard intreatment at your Princes hande, and as it were to ease your stomake you make complaint thereof to some one, uppon trust that you repose in him, and hee goe and discover it to your Prince, wil you not judge him to bee an ill tongued traytour, and one that seeketh your spoile?
>
> *Guaz.:* Yes truly, and yet that fault is rife in Courts, and oftentimes Princes, being desirous to try out the truth, have graunted their servants the combate one against the other. (1:70)

This no doubt refers to a duel, but Elizabeth's encouragement of faction must often have aroused just such "treason," if not the more Mediterranean physical combat to follow. Annibale also includes in this group "all talebearers, and al spies, all coyners and sowers of discord, and al those which bewray other mens secrets" (1:70). William suggests mutilating such men, but he understands them: "I marvaile nothing though many fal into this falt, for that we naturally run upon things which are forbidden us. . . . Wherefore I hold him for a very foole, which discovereth his secrets to another, if necessitie force him not" (1:70–71). This statement is in effect another argument against trust and friendship.

The forgers are those who

> wil accuse you to have done or saide that which you never thought. Wherein you oftentimes receive injury of two persons: to wit, of the false accuser, who according to the proverb, speketh reprochful words to one that is deafe, which is, to backbite the absent: and of him who before he understand the matter, giveth credite to those false surmises. This questionlesse is an over great fault, and in the number of these forgers I put those, who if you shall speake any thing unto them soberly and sagely, make a false and perverse interpretation of it, and wrest it to some evill meaning. (1:71–72)

The biters follow, "out of whose mouth proceede certaine short nips, which pearce our hearts more then sharpe arrowes: And though they quippe and scoffe often times according to the trueth, yet they are not cleare from gilt, for that they doe it with a spyteful minde: whereby they incur blame and ill will: Yea they are so indiscreet and insolent, that they had rather foregoe a faythfull friende, then a scoffing speeche" (1:72).[7] The mockers (and flouters—apparently a synonym) "without any comely grace, deride every man" (1:72). The unknown types are two: those who "by slaunderous Lybels impaire the honour of others" (1:73) (these libels are aimed mostly at "Princes and great Lordes"); and pornographers or blackmailers, who "with tablets and pictures use to represent men and women in some infamous and dishonest act" (1:73).

Annibale generally objects to harmful speech rather than to lying. (Sixteenth-century law by no means identified slander with falsity, as we tend to do.[8]) This stance constitutes a political objection to voiced hostility that situates the entire discussion of slander. Several categories simply bypass the issue of accuracy. The hypocrites, for instance, pass along gossip of events that are unfortunately true; the traitors convey the truth with ill will; the biters make remarks that are frequently true, sheerly for the sake of expressing a witticism. In each case the slander derives from the public harm done to reputation. Maskers and rhetoricians, who leave out names or employ occupatio, are in another category. They are condemned for evil speech, but they may seem to us more obviously guilty of self-defense; their deceit is essentially formal and suggests fear of reprisal rather than moral depravity.

In these cases the accusation of slander either ignores the issue of accuracy or points to what may be a merely instrumental falsehood allowing the critical speech to be voiced. And, if we recall Annibale's earlier assumption as to the likely class origin of slanderers, we may suspect that his vocabulary of combat is being used even as it is being defined. If so, then this vocabulary operates in a social region of conflict, rather than in the moral and epistemological realm of truth and falsehood that our modern view stresses.

The depiction of Forgers completely socializes the moral referent of slander. The speaker can label the forger's interpretations of his words as slander if his own speech is turned against him despite his denial (that is, if culpability is revealed in his words). This culpability must often be present when the speaker characterizes interpretations as "false and perverse" and full of "evill meaning," for the label itself is expressed in the reactive language of combat. Many interpretations that "slanderously" argue "evill meaning" do in fact convict the speaker rather than the interpreter: think of references to topical meaning in the drama. Authorial denials anticipate just this danger. Critical meanings often lie waiting in texts, in danger of interpretive exposure. In fact, penetration by the reader is desired at one level, feared at another; the skillful dramatist wants his comment to be simultaneously visible and deniable. The evasive tactics of Puttenham's comedy, satire, and pastoral are similar specimens of Borges's dictum that "oppression is the mother of metaphor."

Although some interpretations were truly slanderous in intent, surely the putatively slandered author was often disingenuous, denying as slander those readings which carried real threat. For that matter, Guazzo's own maskers and rhetoricians evince this strategy in avoiding condemnation. Similarly, the condemnation of forgers is also at least potentially devious, since it is based on the assumption that only the obvious is true, and the true always obvious. So Guazzo's anatomy of slander is immersed in its own contradictions. He criticizes the obscured meanings of "ill speakers" and denies having any of his own. And he assumes the right to make penetrating state-

ments such as they make, while insisting that others take his own as
della Casa recommends—at face value. In passing judgment on such
critics, whom he specifies in advance as have-nots, Guazzo aims to
deny them not only the right but the capacity to criticize their rivals
and betters.

Finally, though Annibale recommends a disenfranchising silence as
the best response to such slander, he cannot resist making at least
some critical (or slanderous) shots in return. Wise and proper silence
will "represse their unbridled tongues, and get great honour and credite with the wise" (1:74), he says, but so too will an elegant, Olympian, contemplative treatise of riposte. Silence is enjoined, but a stab-
bing reply is enacted. Guazzo is no stranger, it seems, to these frays.
This section of his taxonomy of civil conversation is a primer for the
application of paradiastolic dismissal, one in which the question of
truth never comes to the center. Such morality is politically referential, shaped by the very tools through the depiction of which Annibale
dismisses criticism of the gentle. His catalog is an acute specimen of
"slaunder (not slaunder, but well deserued reproche)," a principal
duty of Puttenham's reprehensive poet.

We may close this review of slander with a consideration of Elyot's
related dismissal of "detraction" as apparently—for this is presented
as a paradigm—irrelevant and inherently disorderly. Although his
example does not account for all criticism, it suggests a formal disposal of *ad hominem* argument.

> If a man, being determined to equity, having the eyes and ears of his mind
> set only on the truth and the public weal of his country, will have no regard
> to any request or desire, but proceedeth directly in the administration of
> justice, then either he which by justice is offended, or some his favourers,
> abettors, or adherents, if himself or any of them be in service or famili-
> arity with him that is in authority, as soon as by any occasion mention
> happeneth to be made of him who hath executed justice exactly, forthwith
> they imagine some vice or default, be it never so little, whereby they may
> minish his credence, and craftily omitting to speak anything of his rigour
> in justice, they will note and touch something of his manners, wherein
> shall either seem to be lightness or lack of gravity, or too much sourness, or
> lack of civility, or that he is not benevolent to him in authority, or that he is
> not sufficient to receive any dignity, or to despatch matters of weighty im-
> portance, or that he is superfluous in words or els too scarce. . . . And this
> do they covertly and with a more gravity than any other thing that they
> enterprise. (Pp. 234–35)

Elyot's detractor undercuts the governor's virtues by aiming at his *private* character, criticizing his style in terms of seriousness and wit, appropriate submissiveness (benevolence to authority?), verbal felicity, and generosity. Such criticism seems to be feared in part because it carries the weight of the "inside view," the privileged behind-the-scenes reading that claims to depend on the hermeneutics of style, those capacities typified by subtlety of image. This fear reveals that private activities are vulnerable in ways public acts are not. The critic can attack them obliquely, with the knowledge that the attack will also impugn public virtue. This attack, at any rate, is the specialty of the detractor, and so Elyot's formula opens up another paradiastolic dismissal: "this criticism is merely detraction." Such a rejoinder implies that the critic dares not address the central issues and that, in resorting to aiming at private virtues, he reveals his malice. Attention is again deflected from the substance of the claim to the character of the critic. And so by accusing a critic of detraction, one detracts; like the supposed detractor, one assaults character rather than the criticism. The issue is no longer accuracy, but morality and decency. If the critic should reply that his target's mind is subdued to what it works in, he begets the familiar infinite regress typical of paradiastolic warfare.

A final combative strategy may be called *ontological criticism.* A rival can be stifled by calling him an upstart, accusing him (truly or falsely) of falsifying his status. This is Castiglione's attack on the malapert asshead: comparison with the "real thing" reveals the upstart's real falsity. Such a critique presumes the existence of an underlying falsehood. But this reality beneath can also be stipulated by imputing the act of climbing. We have already seen how Puttenham fears that his courtly poet may be "disgraded, & with scorne sent back againe to the shop, or other place of his first facultie and calling" (p. 299). Elsewhere Puttenham depicts another such exposure, in discussing failures of decorum of the high style:

> Generally the high stile is disgraced and made foolish and ridiculous by all wordes affected, counterfait, and puffed vp, as it were a windball carrying more countenance then matter, and can not be better resembled then to these midsommer pageants in London, where to make the people wonder are set forth great and vglie Gyants marching as if they were aliue, and armed at all points, but within they are stuffed full of browne paper and tow, which the shrewd boyes vnderpeering, do guilefully discouer and turne to a great derision. (P. 153)

This kind of forcible revelation supposedly uncovers the truth; what is underneath is presumed to be true when what covers it can be specified as false. Such an extrapolation is by no means always correct. But in an age where not only disguise but the sage penetration of disguise is fetishized, a strategy that markets such flattery to a third party while managing what that party "sees through to" has a major motivational bait working for it. An enemy may be usefully repressed or embarrassed, and others reinforced in common identity, simply by the exemplary exposure of a posturing scapegoat.

The main attack is the accusation of affectation. This assault denies *sprezzatura*, which Castiglione specifically defines by contrasting it to *affettazione* ("this vertue...contrarie to curiositie" [pp. 48/ 128]). The courtier must at all times avoid affectation because it is a sign of labor. Two forms of attack on affectation can be distinguished. One sort of affectation is deceitful: the familiar false claim to a virtue or capacity one does not have. Exposure of this real absence devastates the claim. But another kind of attack reveals a knowledge or skill as being exercised only with strain; this is a matter of trying too hard. Here the issue is not overt deceit but the stylistic virtue of self-management. The problem is not the substantive skill but the "social character" of the person. (Goffman's virtues of composure, dignity, presence of mind, and stage confidence are modern equivalents.) Castiglione recognizes this problem as a matter of taking chances unwisely.

> And in that hee knoweth himselfe altogether ignorant in, I will never have him make any profession at all, nor seeke to purchase him any fame by it. . . . If necessitie compel him, let him rather confesse plainely his lacke of understanding in it, than hazarde himselfe, and so shall he avoid a blame that many deserve now adayes, which I wote not through what corrupt inwarde motion or judgment out of reason, doe alwaies take upon them to practise the thing they know not, and lay aside that they are skilfull in. (Pp. 130–31/250–52)

Many of these individuals presumably reveal themselves as fumblers; their failure of performance constitutes a failure of style. But the urge to take risks is easy to understand. The courtier must conceal his weaknesses (the emphasis on confession in the passage just quoted is unusual), yet he must also frequently endeavor to suggest more skill than he has. And he must never fail. He may well have difficulty deciding which of these injunctions applies at a given moment. The pressure to join in often presents itself as an opportunity rather than as a test.

But one may do something poorly, rather than fail at doing it. This relative inadequacy can provide either relative or absolute information, depending on what (and who) is at issue. One may dance poorly and be thought a less than ideal dancer, or one may dance poorly and be thought a liar or a fraud. In other words, ineptness may be taken to suggest relative as opposed to definitive social inadequacy. In such cases the judgment is often arrived at in advance, so that the clue is taken to speak to an issue already decided upon and therefore obvious. But the substantive behavior as such of two poor performers might be essentially identical. Annibale's discussion of presumptuous yeomen is an example of this reasoning.

> Many of them have an infirmitie more greevous and pernicious then any before rehearsed: which is, that they will not acknowledge and confesse themselves inferiour to Gentlemen, both by nature, fortune, and vertue: not knowing that amongst the seven degrees of superioritie, this is particularly set downe of Gentlemen over the baser sorte, who by all reason ought to submitte themselves to their will and pleasure. . . . Some of them falle into suche blinde arrogancie, and so foolish a vaine, that they wil not sticke to vaunt themselves to be that which they are not, and both in their talke and in their apparel brave it out like Gentlemen. (1:195)

The vaunting and braving are presumably not blind and foolish because ill-done in some technical sense (though this as it were substantive failure of style might often have occurred; think of Parolles). But in making a judgment one had in general to recognize the fact that many superiors often talked or dressed less skillfully than the upwardly mobile, given variations in both native and learned abilities. A distinction then had to be made between a misstep by an established courtier and a blunder by a would-be, in the *absence* of substantive difference in misperformance. This distinction must often have been achieved by the application of prior judgment or information on status. With the necessary advance knowledge, one could read both similarity and difference in style as evidence of ontological difference. The skillful would-be was a scheming trickster; the clumsy one, an oaf. More inclusively we might say that the missteps of a less skillful peer were likely to be read as relative, contingent, dismissable; those of an impostor as decisive, or at least presumptive, identification of a clever or clumsy fraud.

Attention must also be given to the basis for the concept of excess, since the concept is often used to account for judgments of affectation. Insofar as sprezzatura is equivalent to making a fetish of effortlessness, its opposite implies laboriousness. The idea of the normative quantity of effort, beyond which lies excessive affectedness, is difficult to define. Ideas of a "mean" are not useful here. What is in fact at issue is success, for excessive effort is usually construed from evidence of failure. William Guazzo notes two examples to this effect: the proverb "By too much spurring, the horse is made dull" (1:134), and the behavior of some "who the more they strived to shewe themselves, the more did they overthrowe themselves" (1:135). In each case excess is signaled by a failure of performance. When the horse runs well, it is presumably getting the right amount of spurring; the former demonstrates the latter. Likewise, he who "shows himself" maximally well will not be taunted with trying too hard. And of course quite often the failure was specified as such by reference to class sign; it is easy to fault enemies for acts that friends perform with impunity. So even the substantive failure would often be politically grounded.[9]

We may generally conclude that the accusation of affectation is likely for several reasons to be a derivative device—either the recipient of the slur has probably already been judged an inferior, or he has already revealed his excessive effort by failing and so merits the charge of laboring in excess of results. In each case the charge is derived from a prior or substantive fact: either identity is "known" in advance, or the climber slips (or is said to slip). If the subject has been prejudged as inferior, then one who makes a judgment of affectation construes his "false" resemblance to his "real" betters. If the subject has already failed at the activity in question, then one who charges affectation can construe his ambitious mental state, his motivation. When applied to would-bes, the device imputes fraud and denies merely contingent difference. Finally, both success and failure of self-projection can be construed by the charge of affectation as evidence of inferiority.

Limiting Definitions

Instead of exploiting after the fact the implications of attempts at emulation, as the ontological critic does, the combatant can formulate a priori definitions of his enemy or inferior that disallow emulations in advance. The first such limiting definition is based on the concept of *obedience*, a structure of asymmetrical public responsibility derived from the organic metaphor of the body politic. One of the governor's chief duties is the prescription of duties for the ignoble. This division of labor generates a one-way flow of power: the governor's job is to give orders, the subject's is to take them. The governor's public service simultaneously liberates him from constraints, as Castiglione makes clear. The prince should so govern that

> each man woulde willingly obey the lawes, when they should see him to obey them himselfe, and be (as it were) an uncorrupted keeper and minister of them.
>
> And so shall he make all men to conceive such an assured confidence of him, that if he should happen otherwhile to goe beyond them in anie point, every one woulde know it were done for a good intent: the selfe same respect and reverence they woulde have to his will, as they have to the lawes. And thus should the Citizens mindes bee tempered in such sorte, that the good would not seeke for more than is requisite, and the bad shoulde not bee able. (Pp. 285–86/489)

The prince is to govern so trustworthily that if he breaks the law his subjects will, on the basis of their preestablished trust, absolve him from any ill intent (that is, any intent the law was meant to harness). His wisdom and rectitude liberate him (and often his representatives, the governors) from laws ideally reified beyond the bounds of his own will; the inferior sort are restricted to "what is requisite." These restrictions will be gradated, of course, but the passage emphasizes the relative freedom of the governor and the relative restriction of the governed.

The fable of the unselfish king bee and the drone helps illuminate this issue. Elyot's version of the public weal of bees is "a perpetual figure of a just governance or rule." His bees have "among them one principal bee for their governor, who excelleth all other in greatness, yet hath he no prick or sting, but in him is more knowledge than in the residue. . . . The captain himself laboureth not for his sustenance, but all the other for him; he only seeth that if any drone or other unprofitable bee entereth into the hive, and consumeth the honey gathered by other, that he be immediately expelled from that company" (p. 7). In Shakespeare's *Henry V* the king's lackey, the archbishop of Canterbury, echoes Elyot's description of a rather puritanical model commonwealth, placing similar stress on productivity and correction. His bees

> . . . have a king, and officers of sorts
> Where some like magistrates correct at home,

Others like merchants venture trade abroad,
Others like soldiers armed in their stings
Make boot upon the summer's velvet buds,
Which pillage they with merry march bring home
To the tent-royal of their emperor—
Who, busied in his majesty surveys
The singing masons building roofs of gold,
The civil citizens kneading up the honey,
The poor mechanic porters crowding in
Their heavy burdens at the narrow gate,
The sad-eyed justice, with his surly hum,
Delivering o'er to executors pale
The lazy yawning drone.

(1.2.190–204)

Shakespeare is probably drawing on three classical sources here, most obviously Aeneas' first view of Dido's Carthage.

Eagerly the Tyrians press on, some to build walls, to rear the citadel, and roll up stones by hand; some to choose the site for a dwelling and enclose it with a furrow. Laws and magistrates they ordain, and a holy senate. Here some are digging harbours, here others lay the deep foundations of their theatre and hew out of the cliffs vast columns, lofty adornments for the stage to be! Even as bees in early summer, amid flowery fields, ply their tasks in sunshine, when they lead forth the full-grown young of their race, or pack the fluid honey and strain their cells to bursting with sweet nectar, or receive the burdens of incomers, or in martial array drive from their folds the drones, a lazy herd; all aglow is the work and the fragrant honey is sweet with thyme. "Happy they whose walls already rise!" cries Aeneas.[10]

The ironic relations between the two speeches are multifold. In both the "natural" bee activity is taken to explain and legitimate the human urge to shape or control. But Aeneas's goals differ from Henry's ("we'll bend it to our awe, / Or break it all to pieces" [1.2.224–25]), and from that of his father (to "busy giddy minds / With foreign quarrels" [*Henry IV, Part Two*, 4.5.213–14]). Virgil's description unfolds civil and ritual dreams of Aeneas. Canterbury's fantasy is designed to legitimate what he casts as "merry pillage," mobilize national harmonies for war, and justify such persecution of dissidents as is suffered by Cambridge, Scroop, and Grey (2.2) and Bardolph (3.6).

Shakespeare's police action is more severe than Virgil's. Whereas Virgil's drones are either banished (the harsher reading) or driven out of the hives to work, Shakespeare's are put to death. (The *Oxford English Dictionary* adduces this passage to define "executor" in the sense of "executioner"—sb. 2.) But Shakespeare has further loaded the dice by locating the police force inside the social cosmos in the king bee and his agents. This decision was influenced by Virgil's *Georgics* and Pliny's *Natural History*. Virgil emphasizes, by introducing a human beekeeper, the external function of expelling lazy drones: "But when you [the farmer-reader] have called both captains back from the field [of battle], give up to death the meaner of look, that he prove no wasteful burden; let the nobler reign in the palace alone. . . . For there are two sorts: one is better, noble of mien and bright with gleaming scales; the second squalid from sloth, and trailing ignobly a broad paunch. . . . [The former sort] is the nobler breed; from this, in the sky's due season, you will strain sweet honey."[11] This purging benefits the human, not the bees that remain. Further, the bee king does not deliver his own kind up to death, nor does he benefit from their expulsion. Pliny's bees, however, conduct their own purges. "They mark the idleness of any who are slack and chastise them, and later even punish them with death. . . . [They] make a practice of driving away wasteful and greedy bees just the same as lazy and slothful ones."[12] When Shakespeare casts Canterbury's fable as an allegory of human society, he retains the death-dealing rigor of Virgil and locates it as Pliny does within the frame. This decision politicizes the conflict, by imputing its violence to the species-peers of the victims. The effect is muted fratricide, the very issue with which Williams and Bates tax Henry in his nocturnal disguise as their peer.[13] A shadow of the Georgic beekeeper outside the frame may survive in Henry's "God so graciously hath brought to light / This dangerous treason" (2.2.185–86). Henry's habitual invocation conceals his own elaborate stage-managing of the traitors' exposure and amounts to an ideological reextension of the depradation, because it is credited to a divine beekeeper.

The metaphor of the bee society suggests the following limiting definition. The Pauline body politic model is a multidimensional paradigm of mutual service that Elyot's bee society replicates. But the contributory function of rule is a special case, for it imposes a vertical binary structure that is one-dimensional: those at each end still reciprocate, but what they exchange is dominance for submission. Canterbury stresses this function of dominance, dividing his state into those who serve the prince and those who enforce the obligation to serve (with the possible exceptions of the traders and those who "knead up the honey"). Henry needs a scenario of unitary obedience, not of multiple function, to legitimate his invasion of France and so to distract giddy English minds. The reduction of loyal service to obedience, to what Castiglione calls "respect and reverence . . . to [the prince's] will" (pp. 286/489), casts as criminal those who do not actively assent to Henry's plans. The various particular services of the subject classes are subsumed under the notion of obedience, of sheer instrumentality to the prince's will. The subjects' constriction liberates him. Their fullness is to obey.

But this exploitation is presented as an even exchange, of service for service. The subject must match his superior's service (ruling) with his own (obedience). This equation is determined by just such eloquence as Wilson's preface specifies for the segregation of sweat. "Who would trauaile and toyle with ye sweat of his browes? Yea, who would for his Kings pleasure aduenture and hassarde his life,"[14] had he not been persuaded to accept this sense of his role by the eloquent reason of his humanist governors? If we then recall that Adam was condemned with *all* his seed to earn his bread by the sweat of his brow, Wilson's division of labor is revealed to have a radical force. Instead of a factional good mystified as universal, we have a universal condemnation mystified as factional. Bee commonwealths like Canterbury's stress such subjected labor and obedience; conversely, equations of law with the will of the prince imply his personal superiority to legal constraint. These tropes work together to legitimate absolutist authority.

The reduction of the complexities of the subject's duties to mere obedience achieves a simplification similar to that of the cash nexus with its ad hoc contractual force. The false equality of the nexus of obedience rests on the idea that equal quantities of service are contributed to the social totality by rulers and ruled alike. Canterbury conflates these contributions, saying that "many things, having full reference / To one consent, may work contrariously" (1.2.205–6). But the single focus is the governor's will, not the harmony of the whole. Or rather, his will is taken as symbolic of the total harmony; then disobedience counts as a cosmic disruption of order. This model turns the subject into a mere function of the ruler's will, casting this asymmetry as symmetry by equating rule and obedience under the rubric of service. Such a paternalistic model hides exploitation under the mantle of mutual service; what seems sacramental hire and salary is in fact a confidence game.

Like the asymmetrical construct of obedience, *sumptuary legislation* was designed to maintain the received hierarchy by restrictive definitions of rank. By the mid-sixteenth century gaudy dress had become a common rhetorical code for registering elite status. Elizabeth led the way in developing the arts of symbolic fashion, carrying cost and intricacy to new extremes.[15] The court soon followed suit; indeed, as early as the *Institucion* (1555), this system of signs had become intellectually self-conscious. The anonymous author laments the passing of the old days, when gentlemen were "conquerers, and not scollers, applying oure myndes to learne euery new tryfell in weryng our apparel" (sig. J7r).[16] Tailors were quick to exploit the material benefits of planned obsolescence.[17] Their productions dialectically aroused new hungers and pleasures in their customers, especially the well-to-do. So accepted became this pattern that even the *Homilie against Excesse of Apparrell* had to recognize the legitimacy of a desire for "an honest comelinesse" going beyond the needs of shelter, to "refresh our senses with an honest and moderate recreation."[18] Some sartorial creativity was even endorsed in the sumptuary proclamations themselves: "If any person shall be disposed for his ability to cut and garnish the outside of his hose with anything that he may lawfully wear, for the plucking out betwixt the panes and the cuts, he shall be so suffered to do according to his ability, not using anything therein excessively, nor anything that he may not wear by the laws of the realm."[19] But such creativity easily became infringement and had to be suppressed in order to maintain the hierarchy.[20] Sometimes private response was sufficient; Camden records the resourcefulness (essentially financial, in fact) of Sir Philip Calthrop in this regard. This knight was having a rich gown made by a tailor when he discovered that a shoemaker, John Drakes, had bought an identical length of cloth and was having the same tailor duplicate Sir Philip's gown exactly. "I will (said [Sir Philip]) have mine made as full of cuts as thy sheers can make it." When Drakes came to pick up his noble gown and found it, like its model, in shreds, he swore "by my latchet . . . I will never wear Gentleman's fashion again."[21]

More often, however, the ruling elite felt collective restriction to be called for, and so, along with the rapid developments in fashion in the

Elizabethan period, sumptuary prohibitions proliferated. Actively negative imposition may have been considered; Spenser, at any rate, had Eudoxus, his normative speaker in his *View of the Present State of Ireland*, argue that

> men's apparel is commonly made according to their conditions, and their conditions are oftentimes governed by their garments. . . . Therefore it is written by Aristotle "Then when Cyrus had overcome the Lydians that were a warlike nation, and devised to bring them to a more peacable life, he changed their apparel . . . and instead of their short warlike coats, clothed them in long garments like wives . . . by which in short space their minds were so mollified and abated that they forgot their former fierceness and became most tender and effeminate."[22]

Usually, however, contemporary sanctions sought to deny positive rather than to impose negative self-fashioning, especially since mobile new money often went at once to purchase inordinate clothing. It was even claimed (predictably) that such illicit dressing might subvert not just the ruling elite's peace of mind, but the stability of the state. Romei argues that by means of sumptuary prohibition, "richesse . . . is not onely preserued (the props of Nobilitie) but also pride is abated, all occasion of enuie taken away, of hatred, disdaine, and consequently of all seditions: In that those men, equall in Nobilitie, but in riches inferior to others, not being able to tollerate, the pompe and pride of them more opulent, in apparel, & other exterior apparances, excelled by these discontented with their own estate, they would easily labour after innouation of state in the common-wealth" (pp. 207–8).[23]

In order to suppress unwanted ambition and forestall noble resentment, then, an elaborate legal structure was established in this period, specifying in remarkable detail various ranks' entitlement to the symbolic privileges of life-style. These canons were organized (very confusingly) both by region of imposition and by responsibility for enforcement—that is, by who was to obey and who to command. Both of these frames roughly followed the structure of concentric circles we have already noted as organizing the class structure generally. The regions were the court (divided into the chamber and the household), the city of London, the Inns of Court and Chancery, the suburbs, and all cities, towns, and villages throughout the realm.[24] The proclamation of 1574 conveniently summarized those who were to enforce these distinctions:

> For the execution of which orders her majesty first giveth special charge to all such as do bear office within her most honorable house to look unto it,

each person in his degree and office, that the said articles and orders be duly observed, and the contrary reformed in her majesty's court by all those who are under their office, thereby to give example to the rest of the realm; and further generally to all noblemen, of what estate or degree soever they be, and all and every person of her Privy Council, to all archbishops, and bishops, and to the rest of the clergy according to their degrees, that they do see the same speedily and duly executed in their private households and families; and to all mayors and other head officers of cities, towns, and corporations, to the chancellors of the universities, to governors of colleges, to the ancients and benchers in every the Inns-of-Court and Chancery, and generally to all that hath any superiority or government over and upon any multitude, and each man in his own household for their children and servants, that they likewise do cause the said orders to be kept by all lawful means that they can.[25]

In light of this dispersion of responsibility throughout all regions of cultural authority, it is surely significant that by 1580 the queen's displeasure was expressed as follows, that "there hath appeared no less contempt in the offenders than lack of dutiful care in those to whom the authority to see due execution of the laws and orders provided in that behalf was committed."[26] We may wonder whether this implicit indictment of offenders and officers alike does not in effect identify the two, given the regularity of elaborate and sometimes inordinate dress at court and among the dominant.[27] But before considering this ambivalence, we should examine the nature and development of the prohibitions themselves, discussed in detail in Frances Baldwin's classic study, "Sumptuary Legislation and Personal Regulation in England."[28]

Most sumptuary restrictions had to do with apparel, especially with luxury in material, decoration, or construction. For instance, the first important Tudor act (in 1533) specified that servants, yeomen, and all persons with incomes under 40 shillings per year could not wear hose made of cloth costing more than 2 shillings per yard, or made of more than one kind of cloth, or decorated with any fur except grey coney and black-and-white lamb, all of which had to be British in origin.[29] However, symbolic consumption of food was also restricted. In 1517 it had been decreed that the number of courses served at feasts was to be in direct proportion to the rank (variously defined) of the highest person present. If a cardinal were guest or host, nine courses might be served; if a lord of Parliament, six; if a citizen with £500 per annum, three.[30] And as late as 1573 overelaborate feasts of livery companies had to be suppressed.[31]

The clothing ordinances originally served economic motives; they supported home industries by restricting imports of such luxury

items as silks and furs. It was also feared that English workers out of
work due to such competition, as well as those impoverished by the
cost of luxuries, might turn to a life of crime. But the wearing of inordinate apparel soon began to carry symbolic weight, as some members of the lower classes strove to imitate their betters, and Cromwell's innovative act of 1533 (24 Henry VIII, c. 13) "departed from
the traditional emphasis on the excessive cost of conspicuous consumption in order to stress the preservation of an organic hierarchical
order in society."[32] These principles were restated and further detailed in statutes of 1554–55 (1 and 2 Philip and Mary, c. 2, the last
actual laws passed)[33] and were variously reiterated throughout Elizabeth's reign. In 1559 she objected to "the wearing of such excessive
and inordinate apparel as in no age hath been seen the like."[34] Her
proclamation of 1574 specified two evils flowing from inordinate
dress: the alienation of English capital to foreign manufacturers, and
the "wasting and undoing" of young gentlemen obliged to squander
their fortunes to maintain their dress.[35] The proclamation of 1597,
the last of her reign, named three results: the decay of hospitality
owing to financial drain for dress; the "confusion also of degrees . . . ,
where the meanest are as richly appareled as their betters"; and the
increase of crime, specified earlier.[36]

The pursuits that these proclamations were designed to govern
could not have been viewed as Elyot suggested they be; he said when
the governors

> behold their [own] garments and other ornaments, rich and precious, they
> shall think what reproach were to them to surmount in that which be
> other men's works, and not theirs, and to be vanquished of a poor subject
> in sundry virtues, whereof they themselves be the artificers [p. 97]. . . . In
> semblable manner the inferior person or subject ought to consider that
> albeit (as I have spoken) he in the substance of soul and body be equal with
> his superior, yet for else much as the powers and qualities of the soul and
> body, with the disposition of reason, be not in every man equal, therefore
> God ordained a diversity or pre-eminence in degrees to be among men for
> the necessary direction and preservation of them in conformity of living.
> (P. 166)

The laws and proclamations seem to suggest not an aversion to sensuality and ambition, but rather a continuing desire for sumptuary
indulgence in many sectors of society. The frequent iteration by proclamation suggests that the project of suppression continued to be un-
successful and the unremitting pressure created an enforcement

problem. The bill of 1533 began by noting that "before this tyme dyvers lawes ordynances and statutes have ben with greate deliberacion and advyse provided establisshed and devised, for the necessarie repressing avoyding and expelling of the inordynate excesse dailye more and more used in the sumptuous and costly araye and apparell accustomablye worne in this Realme . . . which good Lawes notwithstanding, the oulteragious excesse therin is rather frome tyme to tyme increased than diminysshed."[37] This frustration helps explain the numerous reaffirmations of earlier acts and proclamations during the sixteenth century (most frequently of 24 Henry VIII and 1 and 2 Philip and Mary). During her reign Elizabeth issued nine royal proclamations reaffirming earlier sumptuary laws.[38] The continuing variation in enforcement procedures in these restatements is also suggestive; such innovation implies a search for a solution to perceived ineffectiveness.[39]

Most of the pressure for enforcement came from the queen and her agents at court, where the problem was most intense. Baldwin says that the English cities were "seemingly content to leave the regulation of many of the smaller details in the lives of their citizens to the control of the central government."[40] But more modern students find the evidence to be obscure, especially that pertaining to events occurring later in the reign, and feel that the response of the populace was mixed. Some local enforcement efforts must have been in harmony with the government's goals, but the situation in melting-pot London was more tense in every way.[41] What is clear is that there was substantial opposition to the proclamations. Thirteen sumptuary bills were introduced in at least five sessions of Parliament; none passed.[42] Some of this opposition was constitutional, since many feared that the extension of the power of rule by proclamation would encroach upon the power of Parliament to make law.[43] (Such de facto legislation dates from 1539, when Henry VIII was so empowered with the advice of his council.) And Elizabeth issued more such orders during her reign than were ever issued before, or have been since.[44] However, in addition to constitutional fears, the proclamations also aroused economic and social objections. London hosiers, for instance, objected to the leniency with which Middlesex hosiers were treated, which allowed them to pander to the London market for flashy clothing without the repression their London counterparts experienced. To the City men, this amounted to interference with a major market.[45] For the purposes of this study the most interesting possibility is that opposition from Parliament mirrored the aspirations and resentments of the socially mobile, who saw themselves being denied the very tools they were becoming conscious of needing. In other words, perhaps the changing social climate helped make it harder for the queen to get statutory reiteration of earlier sumptuary laws through Parliament.[46] Concerning the regulation of personal conduct in general during this period, Joan Kent has concluded that "if any one concern dominated the attitudes of the members of the Elizabethan and early Stuart House of Commons to the regulation of social conduct, it was the fear that they would be deprived of the authority and privileges commensurate with their social position and that their own conduct might thus be subject to regulation."[47]

Despite the queen's personal investment in such legislation, there was an inconsistency in her own public behavior that corresponded with the pressure fronts of social mobility in the culture as a whole. Although she desired restriction, she was also entitled to license exceptions to the laws in particular cases (a privilege exercised as early as 1566).[48] She must regularly have used such licensing to fine-tune the power balances she lived by, for her own awareness of the powers of image would have gone far beyond her own wardrobe. She seems to have been wary of the power for change implicit in such performing—power she preferred to dominate. Both her own indulgence in elaborate dress and her restriction of her subjects' sumptuary rights were parts of the same project of controlling the forces of control, adjusting them to the uses of the established order, and making exceptions only when they might enhance its power.

Such a reading of her motives rests on a relation argued by Guazzo between the power and well-being of the prince and the clarification of social distinctions among his subjects:

> *Guaz.:* ... this abuse [extravagant apparel] is so in use at this day in Italy, that as well in men as women, a man can discern no difference in estates. And you shal see the Clownes will be as brave as the Artificers, the Artificers as the Merchantes, and the Merchants as the Gentlemen. In so muche that a Taylour using to weare weapons, and to be appareled like a Gentleman, is not knowne what hee is, untill he be seene sowing in his shop. But you shall not see this disorder and confusion in Fraunce, where, by aunciente custome severall apparell is worne, according to everie ones calling. So that by the garments only, you may know whether a woman be the wife of an Artificer, a Merchaunt, or Gentleman: And which is more, by the apparel, you shall knowe

> a difference betweene Gentlewomen them selves, for some attire
> is proper to Ladies, and those that attende in the Court uppon
> some Queene or Princesse, likewise to the wives of Presidentes,
> Counsellours, and principal Magistrates, which neverthelesse is
> not allowed to everie Gentlewoman.

Annib.: Our abuse herein is in deede insupportable, and requireth that
> Princes should put their handes hereto, and cut the combes of
> these clownish cockscombes, and make them come downe from
> their degree of gentrie, by forcing them to weare suche apparell
> as may bee at least different from Gentlemen, if they will needes
> have it as costly, for besides, that under such a maske there may
> ⌐ be much falshood wrought, it is reasonable also, that as princes
> woulde finde themselves greeved with gentlemen if they would
> preferre themselves before them any way, so they ought not to
> suffer the honour and degree of gentrie to be disgraced by the
> ⌞ presumption of malapert clownes. (1:196–97)

The distinction of the prince produced similar distinction of the ruling elite from its inferiors. For the prince to guard the privilege of this
class was to guard his own preeminence. But the system became
problematic when there was a good deal of change in sumptuary
habits of persons moving within and into the elite. And the queen
herself crucially set the pace with her own excesses of apparel, as
Burghley circumspectly acknowledged to his son in 1597: "I doubt
much that the length of all these commandments and provisions will
hardly be executed abroad until there be some good example in the
Court and the city."[49] The members of the elite of course behaved
similarly. They may have wished to deprive those below of this tool,
but they wanted it for their own use, whereas their ambitious inferiors were quite unwilling to relinquish so valuable a tool for the nominal sake of the community as a whole (in which phrase they could
easily hear their betters closing the door). Efforts were made to place
particular pressure on the meaner sort; the 1562 proclamation stated
at the outset that "no sort of people have so much exceeded, or do
daily more exceed in the excess of apparel . . . than such as be of the
meaner sort and be least able with their livings to maintain the
same."[50] In 1574 Burghley took special pains to blame the lower
classes.[51] And sometimes special punishments were meted out: the
Court of Aldermen in London arranged for a mean man's "monsterous hose to be treshured for a time in some open place in the nether
hall where they maye aptly be seen and consideryd of the people as an
example of extreme folye."[52] Efforts were also made to spread the

responsibility for the offenses of meaner men. In 1562 it was stipulated that the masters of offending mean men were to be examined for knowledge of their men's offenses and bonded for 200 marks if they had such knowledge.[53]

All this suggests that most of the discriminatory enforcement was aimed at denying and punishing pretensions to gentry status. Baldwin gives a suggestive example from a 1577 indictment for sumptuary offense.

> Item, we present that concerning the statute of apparell we fynde walter earle to ware gardes of velvat on his hosse, John delylls wyffe a peticot gardid with vellat, martyne howes a gowne of norwyg [Norwegian] worsted with a brode byllyment [habiliment] Lace of sylke and his wyffe a hatte of taffitie lyned with vellat, ... broughton a hatt Lynid with vellat, John goddardes wyffe a hatt of taffitie lynid with vellat, John mylls wyffe a cape of vellat and gardes in her gowne, John hoptons wyffe a taffytie hatt, Roger mylls wyffe a hatt of vellat, Andro harris a cloke Lynid with tufte taffitie, John markes a cloke with cape of vellat with divers others as we suppose offendeth the statutes in that behalfe providid.[54]

By examining the schedules for 1577 (Figs. 1 and 2), we can establish the approximate rank of these offenders. Since they were perceived as violating these schedules, it seems they were not knights or knights' wives or children, nor holders of high office; nor were they worth much yearly (£20 to £200 in lands or fees, depending on the exact offense, or £100 to £500 in goods), nor attendants of a superior of significant rank, nor maintainers of great war-horses. This ranking of legitimacies suggests that these folk were seen by the examiners as usurping the signatures of the gentry, as defined by their privileges and responsibilities. Indeed, as early as 1574 a proclamation had precisely described the offense as "seeking by show of apparel to be esteemed as gentlemen."[55]

The absence of criteria for the lower classes in the published schedules is itself a significant aspect of the administration of the law. In the 1580 proclamation, for instance, the lower orders are enjoined simply to obey the provisions of 24 Henry VIII and 1 and 2 Philip and Mary; no detailed restrictions are made for them. The schedules lend considerable definition to a very small segment of the populace and little if any to the remainder. The principle is a sort of *occupatio* in reverse; instead of not stating what someone is, the proclamations specify what someone is not. The elaboration of such exotic details also aids in the glamorous mystification of degree as kind.[56] Although the explicit point of the schedules was to differentiate among the segments of the ruling elite (and so perhaps to govern its internal competition), the segments of the elite would have seemed to their inferiors to be more alike in terms of their shared wealth than differentiated by the particular forms to which they were restricted. The simple cataloging of these luxuries at the top of the mineral and sartorial chains of being would have made concrete the accumulative magnitude that status was supposed to represent. Rank and wealth were not absolutely coincident, but in these schedules they were placed side by side; criteria of ascriptive rank (the status of earl, baron, or knight) and criteria of achieved property and income ("persons that are assessed in the last subsidy books at £200, lands or fees"; those "that may dispend 300 marks"; those "valued at £100 in goods") counted alike as bases for discrimination. And in fact we do sometimes find express coincidence of ascribed and achieved criteria, as with "the son of a knight, or of any man that may dispend 300 marks." By such congruences old and new governors were bonded together in a single category, and the lower orders disenfranchised; the list of luxury items specified what none but exceptional persons should wear. The rule simultaneously legitimated and deprived by restricting access to the traditional signs of rank, but it also reveals the failure of this deprivation, since it was posed contra the regular poaching by the unentitled upon the realm of power signifiers.

Ascham describes the total ambivalence of ruling-class attitudes toward such restrictions.

If three or foure great ones in Courte, will nedes outrage in apparell, in huge hose, in monstrous hattes, in gaurishe colers, let the Prince Proclame, make Lawes, order, punishe, commaunde euerie gate in London dailie to be watched, let all good men beside do euerie where what they can, surelie the misorder of apparell in mean men abrode, shall neuer be amended, except the greatest in Courte will order and mend them selues first. I know, som great and good ones in Courte, were authors, that honest Citizens of London, shoulde watche at eurie gate, to take misordered persones in apparell. I know, that honest Londoners did so: And I sawe which I sawe than, & reporte now with some greife, that som Courtlie men were offended with these good men of London. And that, which greued me most of all, I saw the verie same tyme, for all theis good orders, commaunded from the Courte and executed in London, I sawe I say, cum out of London, euen vnto the presence of the Prince, a great rable of meane and light persons, in apparell, for matter, against lawe, for making, against order, for facion, namelie hose, so without all order, as he thought himselfe most braue, that durst do most in breaking order and was most monsterous in

Figure 1. Men's Apparel

None shall wear in his apparel

{ Silk of the color purple, cloth of gold, or silver tissued, nor fur of sables } — under the degree of an earl.

{ Cloth of gold, silver, or tinsel satin

Silk, cloth, canvas or any stuff in any apparel, that shall be mixed or embroidered with any gold or silver } — under the degree of a baron.

{ Woolen cloth made out of the realm, saving in caps only

Velvet { crimson, carnation, or blue }

Scarlet cloth

Furs of { black genets, or lucerns }

Embroidery, or tailor's work, having gold, or silver, or pearl therein, nor any enamel, musk, ambergris, agate, or any other precious stone, in chain, button, or aglet. Nor any doublet, jerkin, or other apparel of any stuff perfumed } — under the degree of { A knight of the Order, one of the Privy Council, or a gentleman of the privy chamber. }

{ Gowns, cloaks, capes, or other uppermost garments } of velvet

Furs of leopards

Embroidery, or tailor's work like to embroidery, with silk, bugle, or any other like thing

Nor any caps, hats, hatbands, capbands, garters, boothose, trimmed with } gold or silver

Or silk nether stocks

Shirts, shirtbands { garnished, mixed or wrought with gold }

Ruffs made or wrought out of England, commonly called cutwork } — under the degree of { A baron's son, a knight, a gentleman in ordinary office, attending upon her majesty's person, or persons that are assessed in the last subsidy books at £200 lands, or fees. }

None shall wear

{ Spurs, Swords, Rapiers, Skeans, Woodknives, or hangers, Buckles of girdles }

{ damasked, } — under the degree of { a knight of the order, one of the Privy Council, or a gentleman of the privy chamber. }

{ gilt, } — under the degree of a knight.

{ silvered, } — under the degrees and persons above mentioned.

None shall wear { in trappings, or harness for any their horses }

{ studs, buckles, or other garniture, being { gilt, silvered, or damasked, }

nor stirrups gilt, silvered, or damasked,

nor any velvet in saddles, or horse trappings, } except { the degrees before mentioned, and all other gentlemen only in the furniture of their great horses meet for service. }

Figure 1. (Continued)

None shall wear

Velvet in { any kind of hose, or in garding of any garment, or in slippers, shoes, or pantofles, }

Gown or hose of { satin, damask, silk camlet, taffeta, or tufted taffeta, or hose made of silk lace, }

Fur, whereof the like kind groweth not within the Queen's dominions, except foins, gray genets, calaber, badger, outlandish hare, or fox,

except men that be of the degree and persons above mentioned; and men that may dispend 100 marks in land or fees by the year, and so valued in the subsidy books; or valued at £ 500 in goods; or such person as shall continually keep a great horse furnished for service in war.

any { bonnet, hat, girdle, or scabbard of swords, or rapiers } of velvet,

any { satin, damask, taffeta, or camlet } in { jackets, coats, jerkins, doublets, or any silk of any kind, in linings of hose, }

any fur of { foins, gray genets, or other, whereof the kind groweth not within the Queen's dominions, }

except the persons and degrees above mentioned, the son of a knight, or of any man that may dispend 300 marks, or the eldest son of him that may dispend £100 by the year and is so assessed, *ut supra*; and men that may dispend £20 lands and fees by the year, *ut supra*; or valued at £100 in goods; or a gentleman attending in ordinary office upon any peer of the realm or lord of the parliament, or upon the widow of any peer, or upon a knight of the order, or upon any of the Privy Council.

Note that the Lord { Chancellor, Treasurer, President of the Council, Privy Seal, and other like great offices of the realm } may wear in their apparel, and upon their horses, mules, and geldings, as they might have done before by the provision of former statutes of this realm.

Note that the { Bishops, and other of the clergy, justices of either bench, Barons of the Exchequer, Master of the Rolls, sergeants at law, the Queen's learned counsel, and the Queen's physicians and all other graduates in the two universities, masters of the Chancery, apprentices of the law, mayors, aldermen, sheriffs, and all other head officers of cities and towns corporate, and wardens of occupations, during the continuance of their offices, Barons of the Five Ports } may wear in their apparel, and upon their mules and horses as they have done before by the provisions of former statutes.

Figure 2. Women's Apparel

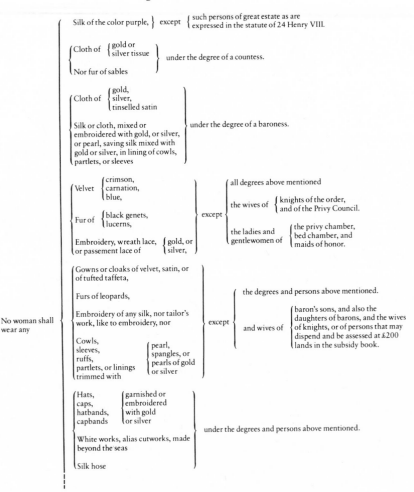

No woman shall wear any

Silk of the color purple, } except { such persons of great estate as are expressed in the statute of 24 Henry VIII.

Cloth of { gold or silver tissue } Nor fur of sables } under the degree of a countess.

Cloth of { gold, silver, tinselled satin } Silk or cloth, mixed or embroidered with gold, or silver, or pearl, saving silk mixed with gold or silver, in lining of cowls, partlets, or sleeves } under the degree of a baroness.

Velvet { crimson, carnation, blue, } Fur of { black genets, lucerns, } Embroidery, wreath lace, or passement lace of { gold, or silver, } except { all degrees above mentioned — the wives of { knights of the order, and of the Privy Council. } the ladies and gentlewomen of { the privy chamber, bed chamber, and maids of honor. }

Gowns or cloaks of velvet, satin, or of tufted taffeta, — Furs of leopards, — Embroidery of any silk, nor tailor's work, like to embroidery, nor — Cowls, sleeves, ruffs, partlets, or linings trimmed with { pearl, spangles, or pearls of gold or silver } except { the degrees and persons above mentioned. — and wives of { baron's sons, and also the daughters of barons, and the wives of knights, or of persons that may dispend and be assessed at £200 lands in the subsidy book. }

Hats, caps, hatbands, capbands { garnished or embroidered with gold or silver } White works, alias cutworks, made beyond the seas — Silk hose } under the degrees and persons above mentioned.

Figure 2. (Continued)

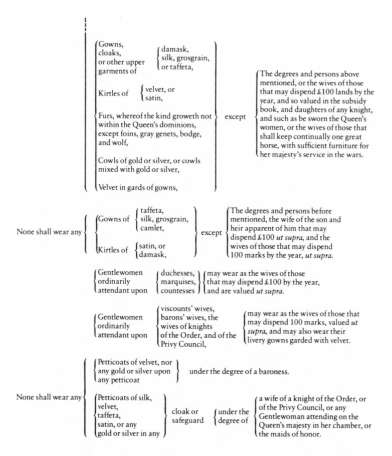

Gowns, cloaks, or other upper garments of { damask, silk, grosgrain, or taffeta,

Kirtles of { velvet, or satin,

Furs, whereof the kind groweth not within the Queen's dominions, except foins, gray genets, bodge, and wolf,

Cowls of gold or silver, or cowls mixed with gold or silver,

Velvet in gards of gowns,

except

The degrees and persons above mentioned, or the wives of those that may dispend £100 lands by the year, and so valued in the subsidy book, and daughters of any knight, and such as be sworn the Queen's women, or the wives of those that shall keep continually one great horse, with sufficient furniture for her majesty's service in the wars.

None shall wear any

Gowns of { taffeta, silk, grosgrain, camlet,

Kirtles of { satin, or damask,

except

The degrees and persons before mentioned, the wife of the son and heir apparent of him that may dispend £100 *ut supra*, and the wives of those that may dispend 100 marks by the year, *ut supra*.

Gentlewomen ordinarily attendant upon { duchesses, marquises, countesses } may wear as the wives of those that may dispend £100 by the year, and are valued *ut supra*.

Gentlewomen ordinarily attendant upon { viscounts' wives, barons' wives, the wives of knights of the Order, and of the Privy Council, } may wear as the wives of those that may dispend 100 marks, valued *ut supra*, and may also wear their livery gowns garded with velvet.

None shall wear any

Petticoats of velvet, nor any gold or silver upon any petticoat } under the degree of a baroness.

Petticoats of silk, velvet, taffeta, satin, or any gold or silver in any } cloak or safeguard { under the degree of } a wife of a knight of the Order, or of the Privy Council, or any Gentlewoman attending on the Queen's majesty in her chamber, or the maids of honor.

No person under the degrees above specified shall wear any gard or welt of silk upon any cloak or safeguard.

The modernized text for figures 1 and 2 is taken from Hughes and Larkin, *Tudor Royal Proclamations*, Proclamation 646 (1580), 2:458–61, which is identical to Proclamation 623 (1577), not printed (see 2:417). The format is taken from the original, STC 8092, from University Microfilms 564/ *12,850 (from a copy in the Bodleian Library: Arch. Bodl. G.C.6, pp. 180–85).

misorder. And for all the great commaudementes, that came out of the Courte, yet this bold misorder, was winked at, and borne withall, in the Courte. I thought, it was not well, that som great ones of the Court, durst declare themselues offended, with good men of London, for doinge their dewtie, & the good ones of the Courte, would not shew themselues offended, with ill men of London, for breaking good order. (Pp. 220–21)[57]

The spirals of extreme fashion and planned obsolescence emanated from the same center where the sumptuary prohibitions originated. The tools that made possible the conservative manifestation of status also allowed its fluid manipulation. Those who sought to restrict this fluidity used the tools for themselves and thus flouted the sumptuary prescription they established for others. What is more, they often found intolerable the additional stress of overt correction by those whom they sought to restrict:[58] "Who almost are not grieved at the luxuriant authority of Justices of Peace?" complained one member of Parliament.[59] This anger must have derived in part from what many presumed were the inferior origins of the justices.[60] Some of the provisions for enforcement also suggest that such efforts must often have seemed like invasions by the unentitled. A letter from the Privy Council to the City Corporation in 1559 "contained the novel suggestion that two watchers should be appointed for every parish, armed with a schedule of all persons assessed to the late subsidy at £20 per annum, or £200 in goods and upwards, in order to see that the prohibition against silk trimmings was being obeyed."[61] These watchers would surely have often been of a status inferior to that of the offenders; in 1576 the gentry-dominated Commons addressed this possibility directly, objecting to a bill from the Lords because "authority was given to any officer 'were he never so inferior' to arrest offenders and take from their backs the unlawful garment."[62] Such orders might originate at the pinnacle of government, but at the point of execution they would easily seem presumptuous to anyone possessing (or affecting) high rank. The court was the center for both attitudes, but the confusion was never cleared up.

The aims and effects of sumptuary legislation may be summarized as follows. "False" ostentation had always existed, but legal efforts at repression by the central government reached an all-time high under Elizabeth, who was both personally instrumental in this effort and a selfish beneficiary of the same powers of image the laws sought to restrict. The transgressions that seemed most offensive to her government were those which counterfeited the images of the governing elite. The queen retained license to make useful exceptions, in order to get the maximum benefit from both the problem and its solutions. The repressive actions met with resistance from all ranks; the problems of enforcement elicited repeated articulations of the same principle, in varying forms and with varying devices for implementation. But none of it worked too well, perhaps because the very texts used to disenfranchise also clearly advertised the elaborate pleasures of luxurious apparel, and because many at court were unwilling to cooperate. By the time James came to the throne, self-bolstering through dress had become so commonplace that "both the government and the Commons claimed [the earlier acts] had become burdensome and unenforceable."[63] It now seemed fruitless to waste further time and effort, and the Parliament of 1604 wiped out all earlier sumptuary regulations in one blow (in 1 James I, c. 25).[64] No further sumptuary acts were passed, though occasional lesser regulations were issued.[65] The individual self-determination that such laws sought to restrict had become normative, and what many had wished to retain as differences in kind had finally become differences in degree only. At least in the realm of symbolic clothing, the chasm between ruling elite and subject classes had become permanently bridgeable.

Devaluations

It is fitting to bring our taxonomy to a close with a crucial kind of combative dismissal that aims at devaluing the entire set of potencies this study has been concerned with: the rejection of successful courtliness as corrupt. This courteous attitude is found among both established courtiers who have been displaced by newcomers, and would-be courtiers who have fallen in the competition. The clearest statement of the attitude is made by Castiglione's Vincent Calmeta, who claims that "now adaies very few are in favour with princes, but such as be malapert [*prosuntuosi*]" (pp. 110/222). The project originally aimed at containing the malapert assheads has become their own. Indeed, the presence of this sneer in *The Book of the Courtier* shows, as we are now able to see, that it was necessary and available as a self-protective attitude from the beginning, rather than that bad courtesy eventually drove out good all across Europe, in some linear way. But the combative tropes with which courtesy treats its own corruption stand properly at the end of our survey, for they contain a reflexive contemplation of the motives courtesy ultimately aroused and served—compulsions that led finally to the corruptions of felicity occupying Shakespeare's Claudius, Edmund, Macbeth, Webster's Flamineo and Bosola, Middleton's De-Flores, and James's Buckingham.

Bacon pinpoints the conceptual raw material for the accusation of courteous corruption when he observes that "in base times active men are of more use than virtuous."[66] He speaks, in effect, as an employer of such men, and he approves their hungry activity as desirable *virtu*. But the members of the established group displaced by such active men were likely to regard their "virtues" with anger and vocal scorn. The author of the *Institucion* records the inception of this attitude in England by noting the rise of the term "upstart," a verbal tool for insulting successful new men (with whom his own sympathies lie). There are many new gentlemen these days, he says, who have risen by their own virtue to gentle rank, "wherby it should appeare that vertue florisheth among us. These gentlemen are nowe called vpstartes, a terme lately inuented by such as pondered not ye groundes of honest meanes of rising or commyng to promocion . . . which name though it were geuen to them in disdeigne, yet it importeth & bryngeth with it righte glory" (sig. C4r–v). It seems likely that the means of rising had been pondered all too well by the users of this term, who sought to devalue the powers that had displaced them.

For the governor who finds or fears himself displaced, promotions no longer declare the man positively; in a world now enviously reconceived as corrupt, they declare only negative or false virtues. In the example of Calmeta this betrays Castiglione's prejudice against the princes of his age (a common attitude in Italy, harder to voice in England): such elevation of evil men must be laid at the door of those who appointed them. But another constituent of this plaint is a basic resentment of the new competitive forms of political advancement. To the established aristocrat these forms were, in Bacon's term, not virtues but "activity." Political accomplishments based on new kinds of ability were now read as subversive of the old order. But the members of that order had long recognized the role of ability (those raised as humanists could do no less); the powers manifested by the promotions therefore had to be denied *qua* virtues. Political success was redefined as failure, that is, as moral ugliness; political failure was redefined as a moral purity in one who chooses to turn aside from public life rather than to occupy its roles at the expense of integrity.

This attitude has long been familiar as a way of mystifying the di-

rect engagement of a leisure class in political dominance by denying
its engagement in the most obvious manifestations of power. Bembo's
speech at the close of *The Courtier* shows the emergence of such an
attitude. A functional reading of his Neoplatonic aria reveals the
courtier retaining secluded privileges while turning ostentatiously
away from the foundation of dominance upon which they rest. This
disconnection is also employed in the first chorus of Tasso's *Aminta*,
in a speech criticizing the code of sexual "honor." When the speaker
rejects this courtly code in favor of a primitivist sexual liberty, he dis-
sociates himself from those in power, who live by this code, and affiliates himself with the meaner (and morally purer) sort.

> But thou [Honour] (of Nature and of Love
> The Lord, and scourge of mighty Kings,)
> Why do'st thou shrowde thy greatnesse thus
> In our poore cells? hence, and remoove
> Thy powre; and it display above.
>   Disturbing great ones in their sleepe;
> And let us meaner men alone. . . .[67]

Honour is enjoined to cease annoying the speaker and to go haunt the
political world of the great. But the speaker has just described this
same Honour as an idol first raised by the "madd vulgar,"[68] to whom
he feels clearly superior. By rejecting the intrigue and frivolity of the
courtly institution of honor, the speaker masks his relations to that
world; at the same time, by imputing responsibility for this corrupt
code improbably to the vulgar, he is able to cast himself as socially
superior to those below. It is from this double evasion that some of the
appeal of pastoral tragicomedy derives.

Tasso's mask hides exploitative rank not behind a show of implicitly powerful self-sacrifice (as we saw earlier in Elyot), but behind one
of powerless disconnection. But a third and very different version
must be emphasized here, where the trope is used to comment on the
Other's achieved power—to devalue it—rather than on the only
nominally powerless self. The general form of such aspersion is the
reference to malapertness; what is suggestive with regard to the displaced governor is the critical emphasis on the negative agency of wit.
Barnabe Googe's "Egloga Tertia" makes this explicit. The erstwhile
traveling shepherd Coridon, now a town dweller, is asked, apparently

by old country friends, to speak of "the Townes estate," a conventionally vicious realm. He speaks of social decay:

> Wyt is not ioynde with Symplenes,
>   as she was wont to be,
> But sekes the ayde of Arrogance,
>   and craftye Polycie.
> Nobylitie begyns to fade,
>   and Carters vp do sprynge,
> Then whiche, no greater plague can hap,
>   nor more pernicious thynge.
>
>   . . . .
>
> The chiefest man, in all our towne,
>   that beares the greatest swaye,
> Is *Coridon* no kynne to me,
>   a Neteherd th[e]other daye.
> This *Coridon* come from the Carte,
>   In honour chiefe doth sytte,
> And gouernes vs: because he hath
>   a Crabbed, Clownish wytte.[69]

Googe imagines a primordial bond between intelligence and openness, historically prior to the simultaneous advent of mystification and social mobility. What was "understanding" for Elyot (who allowed generous interstitial room for mobility) has become "craftye Polycie"; the shift from the moral to the political is explicit. But this openly political mode is judged from a traditional, moralistic stance: no rationalist political science for Googe.

Given this moralistic stance, it is curious that the sinfully elevated neatherd shares a name with our commentator.[70] The speaker denies kinship with his namesake the governor, but he too has chosen to dwell in town, has heard the call of opportunity and heeded it. By the end of this poem he opts to return to the leveled and communal shepherd's life, clearly rejecting the other Coridon's path. But one wonders whether this rejection is a case of sour grapes, for our Coridon condemns the other for having a "clownish" wit. This is no "city mouse and country mouse" scenario; both Coridons come from the cart, neatherd and shepherd alike. And our Coridon, like his counterpart, has urban sympathies; in fact, his characterization of the other Coridon as "clownish" clearly registers an urban condescension. The term *shepherd* in this context signifies a positive identification with the lowly status (however fanciful), but only a relatively citified shepherd could sneer at a neatherd-governor as a clown.

So the speaker's attitude is confused, suggestively so for us. On the one hand, he adopts a standard pastoral attitude toward the corruptions of city life and those who succeed in cities; their intelligence is cankered and twisted, suited for arras work and destructive of the natural system of rank and order. On the other, his name indicates, however obliquely, an identity with his supposedly opposite number, Coridon the governor, though he denies this metanoiacally. He scoffs at the neatherd's wit as clownish, a term from their shared glossary of values, suggesting an aspiring mind that, once thwarted, has failed to recover fully the normative viewpoint of the uncorrupted shepherd. For Googe, then, the governor is new, fresh from the cart; he rules with his wit, which is clever and devious but also somehow clownish and crabbed. This last adjective indicates that the city wit is unsympathetic as well as contemptible, if "crabbed" here means crossgrained and obstinate, as the *Oxford English Dictionary* suggests. (We might compare Castiglione's "crabbed" court lady, who denies sexual favor and settles her lover in despair [pp. 241/421].)

The combination of our Coridon's rejected kinship and similarity of name suggests both ambition and disappointment; when he expresses his contempt using the other Coridon's term from the lexicon of those newly arrived in power, scornful (and secretly ashamed) of their origins, the contradictions begin to crystallize. It is after all a familiar scenario when the disappointed intellectual sneers contemplatively at an active life he would be happy to lead if given the chance. Bacon sees this as a natural part of ambition.

> Ambition is like choler; which is an humour that maketh men active, earnest, full of alacrity, and stirring, if it be not stopped. But if it be stopped, and cannot have his way, it becometh adust, and thereby malign and venomous. So ambitious men, if they find the way open for their rising, and still get forward, they are rather busy than dangerous; but if they be checked in their desires, they become secretly discontent, and look upon men and matters with an evil eye, and are best pleased when things go backward.[71]

The country Coridon's resentment is all too close to envy, an attitude usually voiced through detraction, as Bacon's view might imply. The frequent pairing of envy and detraction, in Spenser for instance (see *Faerie Queene* 5.12.28ff.), formalizes the proverbial notion of sour grapes by a dialectical conversion of the desired to the rejected. Or, as the earl of Oxford put it, ". . . desire can have no greater payne,

/ Then for to see an other man, that he desirethe to obtayne, / Nor greater Joy Can be than this, / Than to enjoy that others mysse."[72] Bacon further unfolds this complex. He might be speaking of Googe's eclogue when he notes that "near kinfolks, and fellows in office, and those that have been bred together, are more apt to envy their equals when they are raised. For it doth upbraid unto them their own fortunes, and pointeth at them, and cometh oftener into their remembrance, and incurreth likewise more into the note of others; and envy ever redoubleth from speech and fame."[73] Bacon also emphasizes the personal character of envy, which "is ever joined with the comparing of a man's self; and where there is no comparison, no envy; and therefore kings are not envied but by kings."[74] This idea goes far to link the envious attitude of the country Coridon and the fact of his sharing a name with what looks more and more like his alter ego. Country criticism of urban corruption was a common literary *topos* in this period. Bacon writes about this poetic recurrence, referring not so much to the country Coridon as to such writers as Googe himself and his greater partners in pastoral critique of the court. Bacon explains the attraction of the subject in terms of abundance of objects: "Of all other affections [envy] is the most importune and continual. For of other affections there is occasion given but now and then. And therefore it was well said, *Invidia festos dies non agit* [Envy keeps no holidays]. For it is ever working upon some or other."[75] Much Renaissance literary activity did sublimate the direct political activity enjoined by humanist ideology. But we must also posit envious detraction as the content of much moral criticism of court life. In fact, as the lives of both Renaissance satirists and their Roman forebears suggest, a literary career can be founded on such a stance, however authentic the emotion underlying it. Bacon offers a logic for this extension to the creative realm. "A man that is busy and inquisitive is commonly envious. For to know much of other men's matters cannot be because all that ado may concern his own estate; therefore it must needs be that he taketh a kind of play-pleasure in looking upon the fortunes of others. Neither can he that mindeth but his own business find much matter for envy. For envy is a gadding passion, and walketh the streets, and doth not keep home: *Non est curiosus, quin idem sit malevolus* [An inquisitive man is sure to be malevolent too]."[76] As the minds of those retired (or expelled) from the core continue to range upon the corruptions left behind, they gad with just this painful "play-pleasure," returning compulsively to the arena of failure. Even the more important retrospectives, such as Spenser's in *Colin Clout's*

Come Home Again, still allow both the catharsis of envy and the contemplation of an alternative past, perhaps not yet utterly beyond recapture. For the country Coridon's enamored rejection of civic life is to be understood in light of Guicciardini's caution: "Do not believe those who say they have voluntarily relinquished power and position for love of peace and quiet. Nearly always, their reason was either levity or necessity. Experience shows that, as soon as they are offered a chance to return to the former life, they leave behind their much vaunted peace and quiet, and seize it with the same fury that fire seizes dry or oily things (C17)."[77] What is missing from this formulation is the option of disappointed retirement—without, rather than after, advancement. Guicciardini is less concerned with upward mobility than we must be in regard to Tudor England. With this proviso, we may judge that Googe's deflected portrayal of his own resentment underlies the two Coridons. When another's success is derived from wit, then the assimilation of wit to corruption is explained.

Roger Ascham, writing at nearly the same time as Googe, presented an unusually rich version of this assimilation. As an educator, Ascham confronted the practical fallout from the invitation delineated by Elyot a generation earlier, in which the "augmentation of honour and substance ... inflameth men naturally inclined to idleness or sensual appetite to covet like fortune, and for that cause to dispose them to study or occupation" (p. 5). The ambiguous character of those aroused can be seen in Puttenham's claim that Elizabeth makes "the poore man rich, the lewd well learned, the coward couragious, and vile both noble and valiant" (pp. 4–5). Those elevated by their own efforts or the queen's are here cleansed of their earlier moral status: idleness, sensuality, lewdness, cowardice, vileness—all are lost in the translation. But Ascham fears that this stipulation is a confidence game, that the governing class is indeed populated by the lewd, the vile, and the malapert, precisely because of the policies regarding study and occupation that were central to advancement at court. It is against these policies that his new schoolmastery is projected, against the monopoly of what the university Recorder of *II Return from Parnassus* calls "your proud uniuersity princox [who] thinkes he is a man of such merit the world cannot sufficiently endow him with preferment ... an vnthankefull Viper that will sting the man that reuiued him" (lines 1155–59).[78]

Both Ascham's critique and the Recorder's originate inside the educational establishment; this is doubly true of the Recorder, since he is the satiric product of just such angry princoxes. They depict him as the lackey of Sir Raderick, an old-fashioned knight who typifies the decayed sort they aim to displace. The Recorder flatters Sir Raderick with a prediction of comeuppance for the "busy" youths.

> Rec.: Well, remember another day what I say: schollers are pryed into of late, and are found to bee busye fellowes, disturbers of the peace, Ile say no more, gesse at my meaning, I smel a ratt.
>
> Sir Rad.: I hope at length England will be wise enough, I hope so, I faith, then an old knight may haue his wench in a corner without any Satyres or Epigrams. (Lines 1228–35)

Even allowing for the satiric bent here, one might apply this criticism to men like Ascham, who is openly bonded to the old-fashioned order and hostile to youthful cleverness, at least of the wrong sort. Perhaps our picture of kindly, if querulous, old Ascham needs adjustment. To the Cambridge graduates, at least, the old order of Ascham (and Burghley) was by 1600 approaching senility.

In the course of outlining his new educational model for the production of a proper public servant, Ascham characterizes the too-clever courtier by using a trope for the devaluation of real abilities that was echoed throughout the era. There are two versions of this character; much the more familiar is his Italianate Englishman, a trope much developed in literary works (e.g., Gabriel Harvey's "Speculum Tuscanismi"[79]) but first given theoretical rigor by Ascham. He makes a sharp distinction between the earlier moral Italy of the high Renaissance and the more recent corrupt Italy, to which current "grand tourists" are inevitably subjected.[80] He likens such a tour to the travels of Ulysses through the regions of the Cyclopes, Calypso, the Sirens, and Circe. If a man should succumb like a swine to the blandishments of Circe's "Court," "quicklie shall he becum a dull Asse, to vnderstand either learnyng or honestie: and yet shall he be as sutle as a Foxe, in breedyng of mischief, in bringyng in misorder, with a busie head, a discoursing tong, and a factious harte, in euery priuate affaire, in all matters of state, with this pretie propertie, alwayes glad to commend the worse partie, and euer ready to defend the false opinion" (p. 227). These properties—busyness of the head, a discoursing tongue, intrusiveness in both private and public affairs, the subtlety of the fox, and a decadent morality—define the stereotype of the Italianate Englishman now infesting the court. Ascham is uncompromising in his judgment of the moral status of such a man: "If you thinke, we judge amisse, and write to sore against you, heare, what the *Italian* sayth of the English man, what the master reporteth of the scholer: who vttereth playnlie, what is taught by him, and what learned by you, saying, *Englese Italianato, e vn diabolo incarnato*, that is to say, you remaine men in shape and facion, but becum deuils in life and condition" (pp. 228–29). George B. Parks, in his fine study of the first Italianate Englishman, reports that this proverb, although Ascham was the first writer to use it in a literary context, can be found in popular use somewhat earlier, in a diplomatic report from 1546, for instance.[81] But Ascham's use of it in *The Scholemaster* coincides with the rise of Italianate evil to conventional status. The queen's excommunication in 1570 and the later discovery of the role played by the Florentine Ridolfi in the Norfolk conspiracy were contemporaneous with the publication of Ascham's work. Parks quotes two examples from 1572 to suggest that the trope of Italy as a land of devious evil was created here, in the middle of the Elizabethan period. The duke of Norfolk in his own defense denied that "he did ... lyke of such Italyon Devyces." And Archbishop Parker's history of the archbishops of Canterbury (1572) called Cardinal Pole Italianate in the conspiratorial sense, although such a term had never been used to describe him in his own lifetime, when he underwent much Reformation vilification.[82] (It is not unlikely, however, that the insult originated in Reformation politics. Luther notes in his *Tabletalk* [from 1538]: "Beware of an Italo-German! For as soon as a German learns epicureanism in Italy and adopts the hellish art, he becomes more deceitful than Italians."[83])

Although Ascham wrote his work before discovery of the explicitly conspiratorial evidence concerning Ridolfi, and before the excommunication bull *Regnans in Excelsis*, he fleshed out the construct of Italianate social psychology very completely. Italianate corruption both oppresses and arouses the mind, it seems, through quasi-educational forces.

He, that by liuing, & traueling in *Italie*, bringeth home into England out of *Italie*, the Religion, the learning, the policie, the experience, the maners of *Italie*. That is to say, for Religion, Papistrie or worse: for learnyng, lesse commonly than they caried out with them: for pollicie, a factious hart, a discoursing head, a mynde to medle in all mens matters: for experience, plentie of new mischieues neuer knowne in England before: for maners, varietie of vanities, and chaunge of filthy lyuing. These be the inchantementes of *Circes*, brought out of *Italie*, to marre mens maners in England:

much, by example of ill life, but more by preceptes of fonde bookes, of late
translated out of *Italian* into English, sold in euery shop in London, commended by honest titles the soner to corrupt honest maners: dedicated
ouer boldlie to vertuous and honorable personages, the easielier to begile
simple and innocent wittes. It is pitie, that those, which haue authoritie
and charge, to allow and dissallow bookes to be printed, be no more
circumspect herein, than they are. (Pp. 229–30)

It is not only travel to Italy that is at fault, but also the Italian writings available locally in England, especially in London.[84] These texts
suggest the other version of Ascham's "character," because they pur-
vey Italian wares domestically, and Ascham makes clear that English
Italianate courtiers are born and bred at home, directly sponsored by
the educational and political establishments. He presents the domestic version through his famous distinction between "quick wits" and
"hard wits."

Those, which be commonlie the wisest, the best learned, and best men
also, when they be olde, were neuer commonlie the quickest of witte, when
they were yonge. . . . Quicke wittes commonlie, be apte to take, vnapte to
keepe: soone hote and desirous of this and that: as colde and sone wery of
the same againe: more quicke to enter spedelie, than hable to pearse
farre. . . . Soch wittes delite them selues in easie and pleasant studies, and
neuer passe farre forward in hie and hard sciences. And therefore the
quickest wittes commonlie may proue the best Poetes, but not the wisest
Orators: readie of tonge to speake boldlie, not deepe of iudgement, either
for good counsell or wise writing. Also, for maners and life, quicke wittes
commonlie, be, in desire, newfangle, in purpose, vnconstant, light to
promise any thing, readie to forget euery thing: both benefite and iniurie:
and therby neither fast to frend, nor fearefull to foe: inquisitiue of euery
trifle, not secret in greatest affaires: bolde, with any person: busie, in euery
matter: sothing, soch as be present: nipping any that is absent: of nature
also, alwaies, flattering their betters, enuying their equals, despising their
inferiors: and, by quicknes of witte, verie quicke and readie, to like none so
well as them selues. . . . In yougthe also they be, readie scoffers, priuie
mockers, and euer ouer light and mery. In aige, sone testie, very waspishe,
and alwaies ouer miserable. (Pp. 188–89)[85]

Compared with these, hard wits learn slowly but well; they have stay-
ing power and will amount to something later in life. Ascham goes
into detail in describing hard wits, but what counts here is the con-
gruence between the quick wit and the Italianate Englishman. The
same emphasis falls on meddling, busyness, curiosity, skepticism,
newfangledness. In fact, Ascham has invented a domestic etiology for

intellectually courtly evil by tracing it to the court's debased humanism. This new history of evil refers not to Italy but to English schooling. (Perhaps Ascham's own profession is given a starring role in this
perversion of the public world, from which stage he may call for reform more effectively.) For the present situation derives in significant
part from "the ill chosing of scholers, to go to the vniuersities.
Whereof cummeth partelie, that lewde and spitefull prouerbe . . . that,
the greatest Clerkes be not the wisest men" (p. 192). Those already in
power find the quick wits more worthy of fostering than the hard wits
(finally, perhaps, because they are themselves quick wits, members of
the generation to whom Elyot first gave the call). And in turn, such
young quick wits will grow up to replace their Italianate elders.

At issue here is not only university education, but schooling in its
more pragmatic sense of life at court, or what Mark Curtis calls "the
resort of Aristippus." He quotes Gabriel Harvey for this distinction:
"Schollars in ower age ar rather nowe Aristippi then Diogenes: and
rather active then contemplative philosophers: covetinge above alle
thinges under heaven to appeare sumwhat more than schollars if
themselves wiste howe."[86]

We need only recall Elyot's fear of the "school" (p. 12) of Aristippus
a generation earlier (see p. 118 above) to perceive Harvey's Elizabethan reorientation. What was lechery in Elyot's time is for Harvey a
figure of the active life. (Compare the views of the two Coridons.) The
hostility of Elyot's friend Ascham to the educational character of
court life then takes on an even more old-fashioned tone.

> This euill, is not common to poore men, as God will haue it, but proper to
> riche and great mens children, as they deserue it. In deede from seuen, to
> seuentene, yong ientlemen commonlie be carefullie enough brought vp:
> But from seuentene to seuen and twentie (the most dangerous tyme of all a
> mans life, and most slipperie to stay well in) they haue commonlie the
> reigne of all licens in their owne hand, and speciallie soch as do liue in the
> Court. And that which is most to be merueled at, commonlie, the wisest
> and also best men, be found the fondest fathers in this behalfe. (Pp.
> 204–5)

The danger of this latter phase of life derives from the example of
one's corrupted elders. Ascham notes this repeatedly. "Take hede
therfore, ye great ones in ye Court, yea though ye be ye greatest of all,
take hede, what ye do, take hede how ye liue. For as you great ones vse
to do, so all meane men loue to do. You be in deed, makers or marrers,
of all mens maners within the Realme" (p. 220). He acknowledges the

presence of good examples but thinks the court is dominated by evil models.[87]

> For wisedom, and vertue, there be manie faire examples in this Court, for yong Ientlemen to folow. But they be, like faire markes in the feild, out of a mans reach, to far of, to shote at well. The best and worthiest men, in deede, be somtimes seen, but seldom taulked withall: A yong Ientleman, may somtime knele to their person, smallie vse their companie, for their better instruction.
>
> But yong Ientlemen ... be driuen to kepe companie with the worste: and what force ill companie hath, to corrupt good wittes, the wisest men know best.
>
> And not ill companie onelie, but the ill opinion also of the most part, doth moch harme, and namelie of those, which shold be wise in the trewe decyphring, of the good disposition of nature, of cumlinesse in Courtlie maners, and all right doinges of men.
>
> But error and phantasie, do commonlie occupie, the place of troth and iudgement. (P. 206)

The mode of this perversion will be familiar:

> For, if a yong ientleman, be demeure and still of nature, they say, he is simple and lacketh witte: if he be bashefull, and will soone blushe, they call him a babishe and ill brought vp thyng ... If he be innocent and ignorant of ill, they say, he is rude, and hath no grace, so vngraciouslie do som gracelesse men, misuse the faire and godlie word GRACE.
>
> But if ye would know, what grace they meene, go, and looke, and learne emonges them, and ye shall see that it is: First, to blush at nothing. And blushyng in youth, sayth *Aristotle* is nothyng els, but feare to do ill: which feare beyng once lustely fraid away from youth, then foloweth, to dare do any mischief, to contemne stoutly any goodnesse, to be busie in euery matter, to be skilfull in euery thyng, to acknowledge no ignorance at all. To do thus in Court, is counted of some, the chief and greatest grace of all. ....
>
> Moreouer, where the swing [i.e., power] goeth, there to follow, fawne, flatter, laugh and lie lustelie at other mens liking. To face, stand formest, shoue back: and to the meaner man, or vnknowne in the Court, to seeme somwhat solume, coye, big, and dangerous of looke, taulk, and answere: To thinke well of him selfe, to be lustie in contemning of others, to haue some trim grace in a priuie mock .... to be able to raise taulke, and make discourse of euerie rishe [rush, i.e., trifle]: to haue a verie good will, to heare him selfe speake. (Pp. 206–7)

In this arena, says Ascham, it is easy for the Italianate governor to reproduce himself. Those who should set the best example are too far away and too busy to have much influence; in fact, their own (presumably neglected) sons are most given to this base courtesy. The available models are senior quick wits like Parolles, who hawk perverted sprezzatura to the impressionable young Bertrams readiest to learn from those at hand. These guides readily transmute virtues of innocence into vices of silliness and make the newcomer mend (that is, mar) his ways quickly, lest he be thought to be what he is—innocent. In the absence of better teachers, Ascham fears, these men will shape the future of the nation.

This conflation of Italianate and quick-wit vices admittedly neglects Ascham's explicit argument that few quick wits "cum to shewe any great countenance, or beare any great authoritie abrode in the world, but either liue obscurelie, men know not how, or dye obscurelie, men marke not whan" (p. 189). In fact Ascham is inconsistent here, since he laments the infection of the court by just such behavior. If great countenance and authority equal, say, Privy Council status, then he may only be denying topical reference to the powerful. (The text was, in fact, posthumously published.) It may equally be the case that his slur on the future of quick wits is jussive in force. Whatever he means here, he certainly grieves elsewhere about Italianate quick wits' achieved "swing."

He extends their influence well beyond the courtly realm: "But I meruell the lesse, that thies misorders be emonges som in the Court, for commonlie in the contrie also euerie where, innocencie is gone: Bashfulnesse is banished: moch presumption in yougthe: small authoritie in aige: Reuerence is neglected: dewties be confounded: and to be shorte, disobedience doth ouerflowe the bankes of good order, almoste in euerie place, almoste in euerie degree of man" (p. 209). Such apocalyptic sorrow returns from the specificities of courtly demeanor to the universal echoes of original sin, vibrating daily in a world out of tune. The agency of sin is still Italianate, but now popish rather than Machiavellian (terms Ascham would have thought redundant): "For, all thies misorders, be Goddes iuste plages, by his sufferance, brought iustelie vpon vs, for our sinnes, which be infinite in nomber, and horrible in deede, but namelie, for the greate abhominable sin of vnkindnesse . . . in committing aduoultrie . . . with the doctrine of Babylon" (p. 209).

Ascham easily finds his way back and forth between the religious and secular infections of Italy, but for us to translate his abhorrence for contemporary courtliness into formulaic Protestant complaint would efface the deformed face he saw at court. There might be many reasons to decry courtly corruption; the things Ascham says were said many times and indeed have a formulaic weight. But we must also notice, indeed credit as equally formulaic, Ascham's interpretive perception. If the courtiers whom he hates see (and label) bashfulness as babisheness, he sees and labels their views as filth. One man's wit is another man's poison. The shapes of Castiglione's iconography press clearly through the satanic shroud Ascham would wrap them in. We can, for instance, readily connect the Italianate Englishman's aim to be "meruelous singular in all ... matters" or "ignorant of nothyng" (p. 236) with the perfect courtier's aim to stand out whenever he can, and (as Guazzo has it) to have a mouth for every matter. Ascham approves Castiglione by name (p. 218) but rejects the world that Castiglione's courtesy generates.[88] In so doing he reveals the same internal division we saw in Googe. Those who wield intellectual tools better than he does are subjected to detraction, perhaps not so enviously here, but with a partisan rhetorical flare that bonds him thoroughly to his rivals, a connection we have already noted in Burke's linking of competition and imitation.

Ascham's book thus takes its place beside Castiglione's enchiridion, the precipitate of another tutorial undertaking designed to reveal the false courtier in his true colors. What must again be said about such manuals is that, despite their combative vocabularies and projects of disenfranchisement, in practice they resulted in conversion rather than dismissal. Sir Humphrey Gilbert, another would-be tutor to the aristocracy, faces this synthetic future openly in his own plan for academic reformation:

> By erecting this Achademie, there shalbe heareafter, in effecte, no gentleman within this Realme but good for some what, Wheareas now the most parte of them are good for nothinge. And yet therby the Cowrte shall not onely be greatly encreased with gallant gentlemen, but also with men of vertue, wherby your Maiesties and Successors cowrtes shalbe for ever, in steade of a Nurserie of Idlenes, become a most noble Achademy of Chiuallric pollicy and philosophie, to your great fame. And better it is to haue Renowme among the good sorte, then to be lorde over the whole world.[89]

Gilbert dreams of an academy of chivalric policy that reverses Ascham's complaint (excised from his first draft, again perhaps for its brashness): "Tyme was, whan I dyd reioyce to see the court, in manye respects lyke to the vniversitie: and I am now evyn as sorye, to hear say, yt the Vniversities be ouer lyk the court."[90] This clean future, staffed with scoured good-for-nothings, matches Puttenham's vision of Elizabeth making the vile noble and valiant. Perhaps it also serves well enough to describe the scene Ascham so despised and feared: a scene in which his resentment of the Italianate quick wit gave rise to a combative vocabulary soon used by the very courtiers he despised, as one of many tools for attacking their own rivals. None of the tools of courtesy proved resistant to co-optation, whatever emotional heat had forged it. For the qualities Ascham saw and hated effectively brought one to court and kept one there; had this not been so, his hatred would have had no object. Such partisan detraction, however justified, testifies by its very existence to the "swing" of the Italianate English courtier, power owed in significant part to just such courteous tropes.

It must be noted, of course, that most if not all of the devices considered in this chapter might be ironically inverted; their range of deployment is nearly twice as wide as my analysis here has suggested. This fact may be formalized with the help of a more general observation Goffman makes regarding negative and positive social rites (of aversion and support): "Although one social relationship requires keeping away from a particular personal preserve, another relation will license and even oblige its penetration. All of these penetrative acts through which some persons are shown support are acts, which, if performed to other persons, would violate them."[91] If we map these actions onto a grid of hierarchical class categories (distinctions generally absent from Goffman's analyses of contemporary bourgeois culture), then we can see how many of the tactics reviewed here follow this logic, and match tropes of promotion by both inversion and similarity. The use of slanderous language for banter is perhaps the most obvious example, but della Casa provides a more explicit such match: "No one should place himself in such a position as to turn his back on anyone else, nor raise either of his legs so as to expose those parts of the body which are usually concealed. These things are done only in the presence of people who need not be treated with deference. In fact, if a gentleman were to behave in this way before a member of his household or even a friend of lesser degree than himself, it would be a sign of friendship and familiarity rather than arrogance."[92]

This example returns us at the close to the way in which the elements of the paradiastolic matrix interpenetrate fully, not only along the axis of support and rejection, but also along the axis of desert.

Chapters 4 and 5 might have been partitioned not by positive and negative, but by true (praise and blame) and false (flattery and slander). Such different allocations would have arranged the tropes differently, indeed, would have emphasized different tropes. In fact the particular choices made here usually rest upon the presence of familiar theoretical *topoi* in the courtesy corpus. But enough has been said of the performative logic of such tropes to suggest where to look further for such activities. Many similar operations never achieved the conventional status of a name. Since the symbolic functions we have examined could use any substantive action as a vehicle, and could flow along any vector, our field of view might finally extend to encompass all of human action. But this analysis must cease somewhere short of global inventory.

Afterword

Kenneth Burke founds his *Rhetoric of Motives*, he says, as much on the concept of "identification"—the ascription of categorical identity—as on that of persuasion. "Particularly when we come upon such aspects of persuasion as are found in 'mystification,' courtship, and the 'magic' of class relationship, the reader will see why the classical notion of clear persuasive intent is not an accurate fit, for describing the ways in which the members of a group promote social cohesion by acting rhetorically upon themselves and one another. As W. C. Blum has stated the case deftly, 'In identification lies the source of dedications and enslavements, in fact of cooperation.'"[1] The primary purpose of my exploration of the resources of courtesy has been the reanimation of a corpus of Renaissance texts vital for the production of such kinds of identity. And if on occasion the survey has reached far to reclaim the banal, I believe the explanation lies in the permeation of the unconscious actions of everyday life by symbolic operations of the social forms of dominance and cooperation. Pierre Bourdieu argues that such minutiae are momentous: "If all societies and, significantly, all the 'totalitarian institutions,' in Goffman's phrase, that seek to produce a new man through a process of 'deculturation' and 'reculturation' set such store on the seemingly most insignificant details of *dress*, *bearing*, physical and verbal *manners*, the reason is that, treating the body as a memory, they entrust to it in abbreviated and practical, i.e., mnemonic form the fundamental principles of the arbitrary content of the culture."[2] Recovery of this kind of experience from the literature of courtesy can add significantly to our understanding of the transition from one system of "arbitrary content" to another—from the medieval to the modern world—in at least two ways. First, such recovery reveals some of the workings of what was, in England, the transitional structure of absolutism. Burke notes that epideictic rhetoric "would become uppermost in periods of rhetorical decay, as when the democratic functions of public debate were curtailed in Rome after the fall of the Republic."[3] The Elizabethan era, the final surge of a Renaissance several centuries long, was such a period. Life, in the cultural center of London at least, was lived under the surveillance of a queen and class whose entire style of rule depended on guarding prerogative from interpretive challenge. The efflorescence of personal rhetoric considered in these pages was a response to this repressive absolutist climate. "At such time," Burke says, "the sturdiest rhetoric with ulterior motive would be found, not in public utterance, but in the unrecorded cabals of courtiers." Fortunately, such Elizabethan codes may be traced in the palimpsests that have come down to us in the forms of courtesy literature.

The second contribution to our understanding of the Renaissance transition has to do, as I have said, with a new notion of personal identity, one based on achieved rather than ascribed characteristics. We learn more all the time about separating, for instance, sexual roles from the regions of ascriptive destiny. (Gender is perhaps the last bastion of the Given.) At the same time we are working toward a better understanding of the complex extrinsic determinations of what is now called the subject, by both material and linguistic forces. It seems to me very important for the success of this enterprise that we recognize and comprehend one of the first conscious departures from the ascriptive: the gradual and halting realization of the human determination of social ranks. The move from a sense of *kinds* of humans to a sense of humans who *act* variously was a decisive change, and its causes were very complex indeed. The insights that courtesy literature has to offer this project reveal only part of the story, but a significant part. For this corpus is the precipitate of what was then a new kind of practice, which we have since come to regard as natural: the practice of being an individual. It is important to recall that this practice has a history, and beginnings. These origins can in part be discerned through the lens of courtesy literature, which can reveal "the real conditions of its genesis . . . the conditions in which its functions, and the means it uses to attain them" were originally defined.[4] This history is worth reading.

We have only begun to write it, however. We need to know more about how these courteous lives were lived, in public arenas ranging from Parliament to presence chamber, from evening games like Urbino's to class confrontation in the streets and at the theater. Much unconsidered evidence is preserved for us in the correspondence of the time, to which lode we should turn with more demanding (and respectful) questions than have so far been asked. Opportunity is even more plentiful in the silent interstices of the *Short Title Catalogue*. The answers we find will aid us in interpreting many literary works that depict or depend upon these lives, but the informed reading of such fictional texts will just as surely help us to construe the culture that they reflect and transform. Courtesy texts make it clear that intrinsic and extrinsic modes of interpretation cannot be kept separate. Rhyme is as historical as reason, and social practices of all kinds, be they debate, applause, conversation, or even the merest internal nod of endorsement, possess intrinsic structures that we can reconstruct, however invisible or universal they may have been to Renaissance consciousness. If the notion of text has freed us from the distinction between literary and nonliterary, it has also restored access to the structures of practice of many lost everyday lives. In this book I have sought to retrieve some Elizabethan struggles, and perhaps, along the way, to interrogate some of our own.

Notes

Chapter 1: Courtesy Literature and Social Change

1. Thomas Wilson, *The Arte of Rhetorique* (1560), ed. G. H. Mair (Oxford: Clarendon, 1909), the preface (sigs. A6v–7v). All references to this text are from the brief preface.

2. Michel Foucault, "Prison Talk," in *Power/Knowledge: Selected Interviews and Other Writings, 1972–77*, ed. Colin Gordon, trans. Colin Gordon et al. (New York: Pantheon Books, 1980), p. 39.

3. Foucault, "Two Lectures," in *Power/Knowledge*, p. 93.

4. Ibid., p. 83 (italics in original).

5. C. S. Lewis, *The Allegory of Love* (1936; reprint ed., Oxford: Oxford Univ. Press, 1958), p. 351.

6. Kenneth Burke, "Literature as Equipment for Living," in *The Philosophy of Literary Form: Studies in Symbolic Action*, 3d rev. ed. (Berkeley and Los Angeles: Univ. of California Press, 1973), p. 304.

7. Ibid., p. 303.

8. Pierre Bourdieu, *Outline of a Theory of Practice* (1972), trans. Richard Nice (Cambridge: At the University Press, 1977), p. 114. I have continually been stimulated by Bourdieu's subtle unfolding of the various practical logics of structures designed to generate the obvious, what he calls the *doxic*. See especially his Chap. 3: "Generative Schemes and Practical Logic: Invention within Limits."

9. Ibid., pp. 14–15 (italics in original).

10. Ibid., p. 2 (italics in original).

11. Ibid., p. 1.

12. Lawrence Stone, "Social Mobility in England, 1500–1700," *Past & Present* 33 (1966): 48, 16. I am indebted throughout my discussion to this seminal essay.

13. Ibid., pp. 18–20. See also David Cressy, "Describing the Social Order of Elizabethan and Stuart England," *Literature and History* 3 (1976): 29–44.

14. Cressy, "Describing the Social Order," p. 29.

15. See Wallace MacCaffrey's introduction to William Camden, *The History of the Most Renowned and Victorious Princess Elizabeth, Late Queen of England* [the *Annals*], selected chapters (Chicago: Univ. of Chicago Press, 1970), pp. xiii–xiv.

16. Ruth Kelso, *The Doctrine of the English Gentleman in the Sixteenth Century,* in *University of Illinois Studies in Language and Literature* 14 (1929): 18.

17. On these matters, see Elizabeth L. Eisenstein, *The Printing Press as an Agent of Change: Communications and Cultural Transformations in Early-Modern Europe* (Cambridge: At the University Press, 1979), vol. 1, chaps. 3–4 (especially "Toward Modern Forms of Consciousness" and "Resetting the Stage for the Reformation").

18. Wallace MacCaffrey, "Place and Patronage in Elizabethan Politics," in *Elizabethan Government and Society,* ed. S. T. Bindoff, Joel Hurstfield, and C. H. Williams (London: Athlone, 1961), pp. 95–96. (This remarkable essay continually influenced my thinking in writing this book.) For more detail on Henry VII's actions, see Margaret Condon, "Ruling Elites in the Reign of Henry VII," in *Patronage, Pedigree, and Power in Later Medieval England,* ed. Charles Ross (Totowa, N.J.: Rowman & Littlefield, 1979), pp. 109–42. See also Penry Williams, *The Tudor Regime* (Oxford: Clarendon, 1979).

19. A. G. Dickens, *The English Reformation* (New York: Schocken Books, 1964), p. 163. See further:

> Camden's visitation of Warwickshire in 1619 produced over 230 gentle pedigrees; the visitations of Surrey from 1530 to 1623 show about 240 and those of Lincolnshire between 1560 and 1660 nearly 1,000. In the two latter cases not all these families existed simultaneously, yet on the other hand the lists are incomplete, and they naturally omit all yeoman-families, even though some of these were more ancient and wealthy than many gentle families. The editor of the Lincolnshire pedigrees comments on the enormous rise in their numbers between 1562 and 1634. The pedigrees in the Essex heralds' visitations increase from 144 in 1558 to 336 in 1634. The same impression is given by the vast number of applications for the grant or confirmation of arms during the Elizabethan period and the seventeenth century. . . . [T]he growth in numbers . . . extended the relations of the gentry not upwards, but downwards and outwards into the professional, the farming, the trading classes. (pp. 163–64).

See also Lawrence Stone, *The Crisis of the Aristocracy, 1558–1641* (Oxford: Clarendon, 1965), p. 67.

20. Stone, "Social Mobility," p. 33.

21. Sir John Neale, "The Elizabethan Political Scene," in *Essays in Elizabe-*

than History (New York: St. Martin's Press, 1958), p. 61. See also MacCaffrey, "Place and Patronage," pp. 110–24.

22. MacCaffrey, "Place and Patronage," p. 97.

23. Stone, "Social Mobility," p. 35.

24. Ibid., pp. 23–24.

25. Stone, *Crisis of the Aristocracy*, chap. 3.

26. Gervase Holles, *Memorials of the Holles Family, 1493–1656*, ed. A. C. Wood, Camden Society, 3d. series, vol. 55 (London: Camden Society Publications, 1937), 94–95.

27. E. A. Wrigley and R. S. Schofield, *The Population History of England, 1541–1871: A Reconstruction* (Cambridge, Mass.: Harvard Univ. Press, 1981), table 7.8, pp. 208–9.

28. A recent estimate by Valerie Pearl (author of *London and the Outbreak of the Puritan Revolution* [New York: Oxford Univ. Press, 1961]), cited as a private communication by Margot Heinemann in *Puritanism and Theatre: Thomas Middleton and Opposition Drama under the Early Stuarts* (Cambridge: At the University Press, 1980), p. 4. Compare T. H. Hollingsworth, *Historical Demography* (Ithaca, N.Y.: Cornell Univ. Press, 1969), who estimates that there were some 150,000 adults (over the age of 16) in 1603 (p. 83).

29. Stone, "Social Mobility," pp. 23–24.

30. MacCaffrey, "Place and Patronage," pp. 98–99 (for ca. 1580–1590).

31. Ibid., p. 108.

32. Compare Stone, "Social Mobility," p. 22.

33. Ibid., pp. 28–29.

34. Ibid., p. 52.

35. MacCaffrey, "Place and Patronage," p. 102.

36. Ibid., p. 101. It is appropriate to emphasize here, given the terms of these demographic descriptions, that my concern in this book is with courtesy for *men* at court. I have chosen to bracket for the moment issues regarding courtesy and women, whose situations were distinctly different, both in life and in the literature, owing to complex interactions of social and gender codes. I hope to treat these matters elsewhere.

37. See Neale, "Elizabethan Political Scene," p. 61.

38. J. H. Hexter's "The Education of the Aristocracy in the Renaissance" (first published in *Journal of Modern History* in 1950, reprinted in his *Reappraisals in History* [New York: Harper & Row, 1961], pp. 45–70) was the first extended consideration of this problem. I have also consulted the following major studies: Mark H. Curtis, *Oxford and Cambridge in Transition, 1558–1642* (Oxford: Clarendon, 1959); Lawrence Stone, "The Educational Revolution in England, 1560–1640," *Past & Present* 28 (1964): 41–80; Kenneth Charlton, *Education in Renaissance England* (London: Routledge & Kegan Paul, 1965); Joan Simon, *Education and Society in Tudor England* (Cambridge: At the University Press, 1967); Hugh Kearney, *Scholars and*

Gentlemen: Universities and Society in Pre-Industrial Britain, 1500–1700 (Ithaca, N.Y.: Cornell Univ. Press, 1970); and James McConica, "Scholars and Commoners in Renaissance Oxford," in *The University in Society*, ed. Lawrence Stone, 2 vols. (Princeton: Princeton Univ. Press, 1974), I: 151–81. Stone presents the most detailed statistical analysis of the increase in gentry attendance.

39. Kearney, *Scholars and Gentlemen*, p. 19.

40. Ibid., pp. 20–22.

41. See Charlton, *Education in Renaissance England*, chaps. 2–3.

42. Ibid., p. 82.

43. Ibid., p. 85. Compare Stone: "The landed classes were converted, rightly or wrongly, by the arguments of the sixteenth-century humanists and educators, Colet, Elyot, Mulcaster and others, and were impressed by the new social ideals set out by Castiglione. They therefore sent their sons to school and university to pick up bookish, classically-orientated training which they had come to believe that every gentleman ought to have, whether to serve his Prince, to hold his audiences in the House of Commons or Lords, or to converse agreeably with men of his own standing" ("Educational Revolution," p. 70).

44. See his *Poetry and Courtliness in Renaissance England* (Princeton: Princeton Univ. Press, 1978). Although I frequently disagree with Javitch on political matters, let me record here at the outset my extensive indebtedness to the stimulus of his work. He has updated his views on such matters in "*Il Cortegiano* and the Constraints of Despotism," in *Castiglione: The Ideal and the Real in Renaissance Culture*, ed. Robert W. Hanning and David Rosand (New Haven: Yale Univ. Press, 1983), pp. 17–28. I still feel that he misreads courtly interaction, both in his stress on the monarch's role and his views on courtesy generally, as my discussion will reveal. (Javitch devotes some attention to class interaction at pp. 24–25.)

45. Charlton, *Education in Renaissance England*, pp. 140–68; Kearney, *Scholars and Gentlemen*, pp. 24–33.

46. Charlton, *Education in Renaissance England*, pp. 137–38: "It would seem that the governors were indeed sending their sons to the institutions of higher education in order to receive a training which would equip them for their future life of service at both local and national levels."

47. Kearney, *Scholars and Gentlemen*, pp. 26–27.

48. MacCaffrey, "Place and Patronage," p. 105. With this we may compare the mixture of functions lawyers performed: "Besides their purely litigious functions, common lawyers acted as accountants, brokers, financiers, entrepreneurs and land agents; the barrister's sphere of operations was far less restricted than it is today, partly because the responsibilities of attorneys and solicitors were equally ill-defined and partly because of the lack of other professional men of affairs" (from Wilfrid Prest, *The Inns of Court under Elizabeth I and the Early Stuarts, 1590–1640* [London: Longman, 1972], p. 22).

In university and Inns-of-Court training as in courtly and bureaucratic service, public and private alike, flexibility might often outweigh the virtues of special knowledge.

49. Simon, *Education and Society,* p. 358.

50. Ibid., p. 340.

51. Stone, "Educational Revolution," p. 56.

52. *Richard Mulcaster's Positions* (1581), abr. and ed. Richard L. DeMolen (New York: Teachers College Press, Columbia Univ., 1970), p. 146.

53. Ibid., p. 85. See also Francis Bacon, "Of Seditions and Troubles," *Essays* (1625; reprint ed., New York: Everyman's Library, 1906): "when more are bred scholars than preferments can take off . . . [it] doth speedily bring a state to necessity" (p. 45).

54. Charlton, *Education in Renaissance England,* p. 139.

55. Stone, "Social Mobility," pp. 19–20:

> Even in a prosperous and socially and intellectually advanced area like Oxfordshire or Worcestershire, between three-quarters and two-thirds of early seventeenth-century parish clergy were still of non-gentry origin. . . . The higher clergy were ruthlessly plundered under the Tudors, and their social origins were generally inferior to those of the lawyers. . . . The precise reason for this lowly status is hard to determine. Was it the vigorous and widespread anti-clericalism of the age which both lowered respect for the profession and frightened off prospective entrants of gentry stock? Or the lack of assured tenure during a period of theological upheaval? Or the substantially reduced financial rewards to be expected even from a successful career?

56. See Stone, "Educational Revolution," pp. 57–62.

57. McConica, "Scholars and Commoners," p. 179.

58. Ibid., p. 176. This pedagogical bias toward eristic strategies may have helped to eclipse the pressures of scarcity: marketplace strife might be read as proof of arrival in the public sphere rather than as evidence of failure. For examinations of this bias, see Jerrold E. Seigel, *Rhetoric and Philosophy in Renaissance Humanism: The Union of Eloquence and Wisdom, Petrarch to Valla* (Princeton: Princeton Univ. Press, 1968); Nancy Struever, *The Language of History in the Renaissance: Rhetorical and Historical Consciousness in Florentine Humanism* (Princeton: Princeton Univ. Press, 1970); Richard Lanham, "The Rhetorical Ideal of Life," in *The Motives of Eloquence* (New Haven: Yale Univ. Press, 1976), pp. 1–35; Arthur F. Kinney, "Rhetoric as Poetic: Humanist Fiction in the Renaissance," *ELH* 43 (1976): 413–43; Kinney, "Humanist Poetics and Elizabethan Fiction," in *Renaissance Papers, 1978,* pp. 31–45; Joel Altman, *The Tudor Play of Mind: Rhetorical Inquiry and the Development of Elizabethan Drama* (Berkeley and Los Angeles: Univ. of California Press, 1978).

59. Charlton, *Education in Renaissance England,* pp. 146–47.
60. Stone, "Educational Revolution," p. 70.
61. Prest, *Inns of Court,* p. 23.
62. Ibid., pp. 23–24.
63. Ibid., p. 21.
64. Ibid., p. 31. Compare also Stone's figures for the Middle Temple between 1570 and 1639, which suggest that a maximum of 19 percent of the entrants were of possible bourgeois or professional origin ("Educational Revolution," p. 58).
65. Stone, "Social Mobility," p. 46.
66. Stone, "Educational Revolution," p. 70.
67. Baldassare Castiglione, *The Book of the Courtier* (1528), trans. Sir Thomas Hoby (1561; reprint ed., New York: Dutton, Everyman, 1966), p. 29. All citations will be made from this edition in order to emphasize the Elizabethan reception of the work. The Elizabethan translation has been compared with the standard modern Italian text, *Il libro del cortegiano con una scelta delle opere minori,* 2d ed., ed. Bruno Maier (Turin: Unione Tipografico-Editrice Torinese, 1964). Page numbers from this edition are incorporated in the text following citation of the English edition, for convenience of reference. In these notes attention is occasionally focused on key words and phrases from Castiglione's Italian original. (The quotation here is from Maier, p. 100.)

Few readers have directly addressed the assheads passage. J. R. Woodhouse, in *Baldesar Castiglione: A Reassessment of "The Courtier"* (Edinburgh: Edinburgh Univ. Press, 1978), says that "the antagonistic attitude shown here to the 'presumptuous and inept' courtier is a further example of Castiglione's new professionalism" (p. 70). Here and at pp. 189–96 Woodhouse develops this idea of the "professional" courtier, in light of an early, discarded preface of Castiglione that says that "only recently has a profession been made of this court service, if we can call it that, only recently has it been refined to an art and a discipline" (p. 189) (translated from *Il libro del cortegiano del Conte Baldessar Castiglione, colla vita di lui scritta dal Sig. Abate Pierantonio Serassi* [Padua, 1766]). Although Woodhouse, unlike most English and American readers of Castiglione, sees that the text is grounded in the task of "survival and security in a hostile world" (p. 2), he does not locate the issue of assheads in relation to this hostility; class phenomena play a small role in his reading. I contend that, at least in its English reception, the text was consumed in an explicitly class-conscious fashion, in order to govern interactions in this competitive arena. The idea of "professionalism" reductively rationalizes the political struggle (which Woodhouse in general tends to see in contemplative and abstract terms).

Robert W. Hanning cites the asshead passage in "Castiglione's Verbal Portrait: Structures and Strategies," in *Castiglione: The Ideal and the Real,* p. 135. But his reference to the "touchstone" function of the idea of the ideal courtier, which can "put down" the assheads, is made merely in passing. His principal concern is with two idealist "portraits" existing in tension in the book: "the ideal, timeless portrait of themselves that the courtiers of Urbino collectively fabricate, and the enveloping, commemorative portrait of them that Castiglione offers us in the face of time's deadly reality" (p. 135). My concern is not with either of these contemplative notions, but with the active deployment of the ideal in the world of *negotium* and domination.

Thomas M. Greene addresses the issue indirectly in "*Il Cortegiano* and the Choice of a Game," *Renaissance Quarterly* 32 (1979): 173–86, reprinted in *Castiglione: The Ideal and the Real*, pp. 1–15 (citations are from the original study). Greene maintains that "the game really becomes a contest between the community's will to understand itself, to examine and know itself, and conversely its will to protect itself from excessive knowledge, in order to function politically and socially" (p. 180). Insofar as he agrees that the repressive devices often functioned better when the superior believed in the ontology of the hierarchy (see Chap. 3, note 31 below) and were endangered when this ontology had openly to be moored with fictions, Greene's view fits with mine. But if Castiglione's game is designed to evade this knowledge, then we must credit Castiglione himself with some awareness of what he was doing.

Jonas Barish considers what may be the final theoretical stroke in this mode of class struggle, Baudelaire's famous digression on the dandy in *The Painter of Modern Life* (1862). Barish adduces Castiglione without noting that the element of class struggle is as present in his original blow as in Baudelaire's final one.

> As Baudelaire expounds it, dandyism embodies a sociological protest, a last heroic flare-up, on the part of a self-appointed elite, against the levelling, brutalizing encroachments of democracy. Traditional aristocracy having collapsed following the Revolution, the dandy would forge a new one based on personal distinction. Instead of striving to please his prince or a noble patron, however, he aims to startle the bourgeois, but by similar means: by a cult of the self expressed in an endless preoccupation with his own elegance. We might be reminded of Castiglione, whose courtier is similarly devoted to the formation of a brilliant self, similarly driven by the need to arrest the gaze and compel the admiration of his beholders. Like the courtier, the dandy is an essentially theatrical construct, created for the values of parade, about whose inner life we possess only fragmentary hints. He aspires to indifference, it would appear, not so much for its own sake as because it enables him to satisfy two contradictory conditions simultaneously: it imposes a patrician distance between himself and the crowd, while at the same time riveting their attention onto his own ornamental person. It provokes their admiration while declaring his independence of them, his

awareness of belonging to a class which they cannot aspire to approach. (From *The Antitheatrical Prejudice* [Berkeley and Los Angeles: Univ. of California Press, 1981], pp. 353–54).

Barish makes numerous penetrating observations on the courtier's psychology here and elsewhere in this fine book.

68. *Tutte le opere di Matteo Bandello,* ed. Francesco Flora (Milan: A. Mondadori, 1934–35), 2: 229 (Epistle to Novel 57, Second Part); translation by Jackson Cope.

69. See B. M. Ward, *The Seventeenth Earl of Oxford, 1550–1604* (London, John Murray, 1928), pp. 81–82. (Ward's translation is from Oxford's Latin; see *B. Castilionis de curiale siue aulico libri quatuor. Ex Italico sermone in Latinum conuersi, B. Clerke interprete.* London, 1571 [STC 4782].)

70. This idea should be correlated with what may seem its reverse, Barish's view of the kind of self-fashioning derived from Castiglione as a component of an "identity dispersal," which was a culturewide phenomenon during the Renaissance. The puritan antitheatrical response was a reaction against this dispersal, meant "to resynthesize something felt to be coming apart" (*The Antitheatrical Prejudice,* p. 473). In my view, Castiglione's plan was designed as part of this holding action, although its effect was as often dispersive as restorative of the identity of hierarchical rank.

71. Count Annibale Romei, *The Courtiers Academie* (1585), trans. I. Kepers (1598; reprint ed., New York: Da Capo Press, 1969), sig. A3r. Subsequent references will appear in the text.

72. John Ferne, *The Blazon of Gentrie* (1586; reprint ed., New York: Da Capo Press, 1973), sig. A6r. Subsequent references will appear in the text.

73. Michel Foucault, "Nietzsche, Genealogy, History," in *Language, Counter-Memory, Practice,* ed. Donald F. Bouchard, trans. Bouchard and Sherry Simon (Ithaca, N.Y.: Cornell Univ. Press, 1977), p. 151. Compare also, "if interpretation is the violent or surreptitious appropriation of a system of rules, which in itself has no essential meaning, in order to impose a direction, to bend it to a new will, to force its participation in a different game, and to subject it to secondary rules, then the development of humanity is a series of interpretations" (pp. 151–52).

74. For a related but much more ambitious argument that partly anticipates this point, see Norbert Elias, *The History of Manners* (1939), (*The Civilizing Process,* vol. 1), trans. Edmund Jephcott (New York: Urizen, 1978), especially, for instance, pp. 100–101. Elias continues the argument in *Power and Civility* (1939), (*The Civilizing Process,* vol. 2), trans. Edmund Jephcott (New York: Pantheon Books, 1982), which appeared in English too late for me to make use of it. Elias is concerned with tracing the institutions of public and private social control from the twelfth to the twentieth centuries, by analyzing the internalization of a sense of "proper" behavior. His work is at once more general than mine (covering a much wider time span and dealing with the notion of "civiliza-

tion") and more narrow (focusing on the manners of the body—such as blowing the nose). He does make the point that courtesy writings both restricted and enabled the spread of those manners that signified aristocratic identity. On the whole, however, he is less concerned than I with the activities of social conflict and its mediations in mobility.

75. Javitch, for instance, claims that "only the poet is endowed with the verbal manners necessary to promote virtuous action" in the English ruling "enclave" (*Poetry and Courtliness*, pp. 100–101). The poets made this kind of claim often, of course; Javitch alludes to the concept quoted as Philip Sidney's "awareness." But it is an error to *believe* these claims instead of *analyzing* them. In any case, the language of sheer morality ("virtuous action") offers a far too narrow context in which to explain these poetic claims.

76. See on this issue Philip J. Finkelpearl, *John Marston of the Middle Temple: An Elizabethan Dramatist in His Social Setting* (Cambridge, Mass.: Harvard Univ. Press, 1969); R. C. Bald, *John Donne: A Life* (Oxford: Oxford Univ. Press, 1970); *The Diary of John Manningham of the Middle Temple*, ed. Robert Parker Sorlien (Hanover, N.H.: Univ. Press of New England, 1976); Ann Jennalie Cook, *The Privileged Playgoers of Shakespeare's London, 1576–1642* (Princeton: Princeton Univ. Press, 1981).

77. See *The Life of the Renowned Sr. Philip Sidney*, in *The Works in Verse and Prose Complete of the Right Honourable Fulke Greville, Lord Brooke*, ed. A. B. Grosart, 4 vols. (1870; reprint ed., New York: AMS Press, 1966), 4: 5–224; James M. Osborn, *Young Philip Sidney, 1572–1577* (New Haven: Yale Univ. Press, 1972).

78. See Julia Cartwright, *Baldassare Castiglione, the Perfect Courtier: His Life and Letters*, 2 vols. (London: John Murray, 1908).

79. See Clifford Geertz, "Ideology as a Cultural System," in *The Interpretation of Cultures* (New York: Basic Books, 1973), pp. 193–233.

80. Barish, *Antitheatrical Prejudice*, p. 213.

81. Woodhouse, *Baldesar Castiglione*, p. 195.

82. Francis Bacon, *De Augmentis*, in *The Works of Francis Bacon*, ed. James Spedding, Robert Leslie Ellis, and Douglas Denon Heath, 15 vols. (New York: Hurd and Houghton, 1869), vol. 9: 8.1.235.

83. Francesco Guicciardini, *Maxims and Reflections [Ricordi]*, trans. Mario Domandi (Philadelphia: Univ. of Pennsylvania Press, 1965), Series C, item 179, p. 86. Subsequent references will appear in the text, identified by series and item number (e.g., C179).

84. Edmund Spenser, *Poetical Works*, ed. J. C. Smith and E. de Selincourt, Oxford Standard Authors Series (Oxford: Oxford Univ. Press, 1912), p. 603. The sonnet is dated July 18, 1586, from Dublin, but Virginia F. Stern believes that it was probably written some years earlier, to accompany a volume of satirical writings eventually withheld from publication to avoid offense. See her *Gabriel Harvey: His Life, Marginalia, and Library* (Oxford: Clarendon, 1979), p. 77n.

85. On Elyot see K. J. Wilson's edition of *The Letters of Sir Thomas Elyot, Studies in Philology* 73, no. 5 (1976), i–xxx, 1–37; on Harvey see Stern, *Gabriel Harvey*, pp. 3–134.

86. From Gabriel Harvey, *Three proper wittie familar Letters*, in *Works*, ed. A. B. Grosart, 3 vols. (1884; reprint ed., AMS Press, 1966), 1: 70–73.

87. MacCaffrey, "Place and Patronage," p. 97.

88. Williams, *Tudor Regime*, p. 305.

89. Ibid., p. 303.

90. Simon, *Education and Society*, p. 359.

91. Quoted by George B. Parks in "The First Draft of Ascham's *Scholemaster*," *Huntington Library Quarterly*, 1 (1938): 324.

92. I would like to acknowledge here my extensive local and general indebtedness to Harry Berger's largely unpublished writings on reascription and cultural change, especially his book-length "Blueprint for Curricula: A General Theory of Culture Change." A brief introduction has appeared as "Outline of a General Theory of Cultural Change" in *CLIO* 2 (1972): 49–63.

93. *The Letter-Book of Gabriel Harvey, A.D. 1573–1580*, ed. E. J. L. Scott (London: Camden Society Publications, 1884), p. 78. Harvey was certainly among these would-be activists himself, in the search for tactical instruction. See, for instance, Caroline Ruutz-Rees's report of his extensive annotation of his Hoby *Courtier*, in "Some Notes of Gabriel Harvey's in Hoby's Translation of Castiglione's *Courtier*," *PMLA* 25 (1910): 608–39; *Gabriel Harvey's Marginalia*, comp. and ed. G. C. Moore-Smith (Stratford-upon-Avon: Shakespeare Head Press, 1913), *passim*; John L. Lievsay, *Stefano Guazzo and the English Renaissance, 1575–1675* (Chapel Hill: Univ. of North Carolina Press, 1961), pp. 88–96; Stern, *Gabriel Harvey*, p. 17. Harvey's typical hypertrophy is apparent in the epigraph to this book, transcribed by Lievsay from Harvey's copy of Lodovico Domenichi's *Facetie, et motti di diverse persone* (1571) (see Lievsay, *Stefano Guazzo*, p. 93).

94. Harvey, *Letter-Book*, pp. 78–79.

95. Harvey, *Three . . . Letters*, in *Works*, 1:69.

96. Curtis, *Oxford and Cambridge in Transition*, pp. 135–37.

97. Thomas M. Greene, "The Flexibility of the Self in Renaissance Literature," in Peter Demetz, Thomas Greene, and Lowry Nelson, Jr., eds., *The Disciplines of Criticism: Essays in Literary Theory, Interpretation, and History* (New Haven: Yale Univ. Press, 1968), p. 250.

98. Daniel Javitch, "Rival Arts of Conduct in Elizabethan England: Guazzo's *Civile Conversation* and Castiglione's *Courtier*," *Yearbook of Italian Studies* 1 (1971): 180–81.

99. The number and distribution of English Renaissance editions of basic courtesy texts are shown in the following table. (Complete bibliographic information is given elsewhere.) The array of reprints strongly suggests that this counts as an Elizabethan corpus, published and read throughout the period.

Author/Work	Editions	Dates
Elyot, *Governor*	8	1531, 1537, 1544, 1546, 1553, 1557, 1584, 1585
Wilson, *Arte of Rhetorique*	8	1553, 1560, 1562, 1563, 1567, 1580, 1584, 1585
Institucion	2	1555, 1568
Castiglione, *Courtier* (trans. Hoby)	4	1561, 1577, 1588 (Italian, French, English parallel text), 1603
Ascham, *Scholemaster*	5	1570, 1571, 1573, 1579, 1589
Castiglione, *Courtier* (trans. Clerke)	6	1571, 1577, 1585, 1593, 1603, 1612
Philibert, *Philosopher of the Court*	1	1575
Della Casa, *Galateo*	2	1576, 1630
Guazzo, *Civile Conversation*	2	1581 (bks. 1–3), 1586
Jovius, *Worthy Tract*	1	1585
Ferne, *Blazon of Gentrie*	2	1586, 1586
Puttenham, *Arte of English Poesie*	1	1589
Bacon, *Essays*	15	1597, 1598, 1606, 1612, 1612, 1613, 1613, 1613, 1614, 1624, 1625, 1625, 1629, 1632, 1639
Romei, *Courtiers Academie*	1	1598

(For a discussion of the complexities of the number and dates of the early editions of Ascham, see Lawrence V. Ryan, *Roger Ascham* [Stanford: Stanford Univ. Press, 1963], pp. 250–51. I have followed Ryan's list here instead of the *Short Title Catalogue*, the source for the rest of the figures.)

100. Bourdieu, *Outline of a Theory of Practice*, p. 105 (italics in original).

101. See Thomas Dekker, *The Guls Horn-Booke: or, Fashions to please all sorts of Guls* (1609), in *Non-Dramatic Works*, ed. A. B. Grosart (1885; reprint ed., New York: Russell & Russell, 1963), 2: 202; Kenneth Burke, *A*

Rhetoric of Motives (1950; reprint ed., Berkeley and Los Angeles, 1969), p. 98. Javitch glances at this pattern in "Rival Arts," p. 191.

102. See Burke, "Literature as Equipment." Guazzo was of course a collector of proverbs; see Lievsay's chapter entitled "Finding a Staff to Beat a Dog" (a Guazzo proverb adapted), in *Stefano Guazzo*, pp. 114–44.

103. Jean Bodin, *The Six Bookes of a Commonweale* (1576 in French, 1586 in Bodin's Latin), trans. Richard Knolles (from both versions, 1606; reprint ed., Cambridge, Mass.: Harvard Univ. Press, 1962), 3.8.396.

104. The most famous discontinuity in Castiglione, the question of the proper relation between Books 1–3 and Book 4 (that is, the relation between private and public politics), has received considerable attention. See, among others, Lawrence V. Ryan, "Book IV of Castiglione's *Courtier*: Climax or Afterthought?" *Studies in the Renaissance* 19 (1972): 156–79; Dain A. Trafton, "Structure and Meaning in *The Courtier*," *English Literary Renaissance* 2 (1972): 283–97; Wayne Rebhorn, *Courtly Performances: Masking and Festivity in Castiglione's "Book of the Courtier"* (Detroit: Wayne State Univ. Press, 1978), pp. 197–204. My point here is a more abstract version of the problem of this and the many other debates internal to *The Courtier*: the perception, denial, or explanation of this famous discontinuity involves the same operations as would be applied to construing *any* local or momentarily coherent facet of the nature of the proper courtly life. These critics in fact act like the dialogues's interlocutors and Renaissance readers and quoters of Castiglione: data are conjoined or distinguished according to the argumentative needs (social, critical, or intellectual) of the moment or person. The chasm (or bridge) between Books 1–3 and 4 of *The Courtier* is simply an obtrusively special case, not in my view much more recalcitrant or organic, but obtaining at a higher level of abstraction than many other gaps in arguments elsewhere in the book. Characters and readers alike are occupied with construing these data, which are presented, as it were, either problematically preconstrued or insufficiently construed. Where Renaissance readers saw a social opportunity, we see a critical problem.

105. [Paolo Giovio], *The Worthy Tract of Paulus Iovius* (1585), trans. Samuel Daniel, together with Giovio's *Dialogo dell 'Imprese et Amorose*, intro. by Norman K. Farmer, Jr. (reprint ed., Delmar, N.Y.: Scholars' Facsimiles & Reprints, 1976).

106. *The Civile Conversation of M. Steeven Guazzo* (1574), trans. George Pettie (Books 1–3, 1581) and Bartholomew Young (Book 4, 1586), the Tudor Translations, 2 vols. (London: Constable, 1925). Subsequent references will appear in the text, noted by citing the physical volumes (1–2) of this edition rather than the work's internal books (1–4). The Elizabethan translation has been compared with *La civile conversatione del Sig. Stefano Guazzo* (Vinegia, 1575), to which reference is occasionally made for clarification. But the translation history of the book is very complex, including an intervening

French translation and several revised editions by Guazzo; no attempt has been made to match all citations to passages in the Italian. For a discussion of the translations, see Lievsay, *Stefano Guazzo*, chap. 2.

107. J. B. Leishman, ed., *The Three Parnassus Plays (1598–1601)* (London: Ivor Nicholson & Watson, 1949). Subsequent references will appear in the text.

108. See C6: "It is a great error to speak of the things of this world absolutely and indiscriminately and to deal with them, as it were, by the book. In nearly all things one must make distinctions and exceptions because of differences in their circumstances. These circumstances are not covered by one and the same rule. Nor can these distinctions and exceptions be found written in books. They must be taught by discretion."

109. Sir Walter Raleigh, *Maxims of State*, in *The Works of Sir Walter Ralegh , Kt.*, ed. Thomas Birch, 8 vols. (Oxford: Oxford Univ. Press, 1829), 8: 1–34.

110. John E. Mason emphasized that Bacon should be considered under this rubric, in his pioneering *Gentlefolk in the Making: Studies in the History of English Courtesy Literature and Related Topics from 1531 to 1774* (Philadelphia: Univ. of Pennsylvania Press, 1935), pp. 44–45.

111. Simon, *Education and Society*, p. 352.

112. Sir Thomas Elyot, *The Book named the Governor* (1531), ed. S. E. Lehmberg (New York: Dutton, Everyman, 1962). Subsequent references will appear in the text.

113. *The Institucion of a Gentleman* (1555; reprint ed., Norwood, N.J.: Walter J. Johnson, 1974). Subsequent references will appear in the text.

114. Giovanni della Casa, *Galateo* (1558), trans. R. S. Pine-Coffin (Harmondsworth: Penguin Books, 1958). The standard Italian text is *Opere di Baldassare Castiglione, Giovanni della Casa, Benvenuto Cellini*, ed. Carlo Cordie (Milan and Naples: Ricciardi, 1960); references to the English and Italian texts are specified in that order.

115. Sir Humphrey Gilbert, *Queene Elizabethes Achademy* (after 1562), Early English Text Society Extra Series 8 (London: Trubner, 1869). Subsequent references will appear in the text. This treatise was presented to Queen Elizabeth as a proposed reform of the education of the queen's wards (in whose future the state had numerous kinds of interest). An earlier plan to the same end, devised by Sir Nicholas Bacon when he was attorney of the Court of Wards, was entitled *Articles devised for the bringinge up in vertue and leringe of the Queenes Majesties wardes beinge heires Males* (after 1561). This plan has little relevance to courtesy, but it helps put Gilbert's proposal in context. See J. Payne Collier, "One Sir Nicholas Bacon, Lord Keeper; with extracts from some of his unprinted papers and speeches," *Archaeologia* 36 (1855): 344; H. E. Bell, *An Introduction to the History and Records of the Court of Wards and Liveries* (Cambridge: At the University Press, 1953), pp.

120–21; Curtis, *Oxford and Cambridge in Transition*, pp. 67–68; Joel Hurstfield, *The Queen's Wards: Wardship and Marriage under Elizabeth I* (Cambridge: Harvard Univ. Press, 1958), pp. 25–27 and *passim.*

116. Roger Ascham, *The Scholemaster* (1570), in *English Works*, ed. William Aldis Wright (1904; reprint ed., Cambridge: At the University Press, 1970). Subsequent references will appear in the text.

117. George Puttenham, *The Arte of English Poesie* (1589), ed. Gladys Doidge Willcock and Alice Walker (Cambridge: At the University Press, 1936). Subsequent references will appear in the text.

118. See Bacon, *Works*, vol. 13, p. 313; compare vol. 8, p. 438.

119. Thomas Blundeville, *The True Order and Methode of Wryting and Reading Hystories* (1574; reprint ed., Norwood, N.J.: Walter J. Johnson, 1979), sigs. H3v–4r. I have sought to follow Blundeville's advice in reading the literature and in writing this book, which may then, I hope, take on certain resemblances to the Elizabethan courtier's grasped sense of the corpus.

120. Jovius, *Worthy Tract*, sig. *5r.

121. W. H. Woodward, *Studies in Education during the Age of the Renaissance, 1400–1600* (Cambridge: At the University Press, 1906), p. 295. The remark is apparently quoted by Woodward, without identification. I have been unable to trace its origin. It (or Woodward) is repeated by C. G. Osgood in *The Voice of England* (New York: Harper & Bros., 1935), p. 147 (I owe this citation to William Ringler); and by Simon in *Education and Society*, p. 366. Neither documents it.

122. Wallace MacCaffrey notes that "a great many royal servants, although nominally assigned to specific posts in the household or one of the public offices, in fact performed quite other tasks, as the Queen or privy council directed. The floating and indefinite nature of their assignments involved them in diplomatic, fiscal, judicial, or ceremonial tasks as need dictated" ("Place and Patronage," pp. 104–5).

123. Richard Lanham, *Revising Prose* (New York: Scribner's, 1979), p. 65.

124. See Neale, "Elizabethan Political Scene," pp. 59–84; Joel Hurstfield, *Freedom, Corruption, and Government in Elizabethan England* (Cambridge, Mass.: Harvard Univ. Press, 1973), p. 3; Williams, *Tudor Regime*, chaps. 11–12.

125. Burke, *Rhetoric of Motives*, p. 220.

Chapter 2: Rhetorical Semiotics at Court

1. See Ernst Cassirer, *The Individual and the Cosmos in Renaissance Philosophy* (1927), trans. Mario Domandi (1963; reprint ed., Philadelphia: Univ. of Pennsylvania Press, 1972), p. 84. In harmony with Cassirer's use here of the scholastic notion of being (*esse*), I regularly employ the philosophical term *ontology* to refer to the older notion of social identity as provided abso-

lutely at birth, prior to and independent of human action: given, that is, as an aspect of existence.

2. See Fredric Jameson, "Marxism and Historicism," *New Literary History* 11 (1979): 57.

3. Thomas Middleton, *A Mad World, My Masters* (1604–06), ed. Standish Henning (Lincoln: Univ. of Nebraska Press, 1965), 2.1.55–57.

4. I. M., *A Health to the Gentlemanly Profession of Serving-Men* (1598; reprint ed., London: Oxford Univ. Press, 1931), sigs. F3v–F4r; cf. sig. E3v.

5. Jean-Paul Sartre, *Anti-Semite and Jew*, trans. George J. Becker (1946; reprint ed., New York: Schocken Books, 1965), pp. 34, 37. Subsequent references will appear in the text.

6. To Sartre's use of this substantive ("thing") we may compare observations of Penry Williams and Stephen Greenblatt. Williams notes that "the multiplication of life tenures, the scramble for reversions, and the attempt to make posts hereditary are all indications that offices were coming to be regarded as forms of property rather than as jobs to be done" (*The Tudor Regime* [Oxford: Clarendon, 1979], p. 87). Greenblatt writes in similar terms of power at court, "directly linked, as always, to wealth, status, and the monopoly of violence, but also thought of as something quite independent, a possession to be wrested from another, an object of intellectual interest, a consummate manifestation of human energy" (*Renaissance Self-Fashioning, from More to Shakespeare* [Chicago: Univ. of Chicago Press, 1980], p. 140). The substantiation records the phenomenological coincidence of office, power, and inalienable status.

7. For related arguments, see Pierre Bourdieu on the "economy of logic" of ideology in traditional society, and on "making use of indeterminacy," in *Outline of a Theory of Practice* (1972), trans. Richard Nice (Cambridge: At the University Press, 1977), pp. 109–14, 140–43.

8. Baldassare Castiglione, *The Book of the Courtier* (1528), trans. Sir Thomas Hoby (1561; reprint ed., New York: Dutton, Everyman, 1966); cited with *Il libro del cortegiano con una scelta delle opere minori*, 2d ed., ed. Bruno Maier (Turin: Unione Tipografico-Editrice Torinese, 1964). Subsequent references from these editions will appear in the text.

9. There are interesting resonances in "wonder at him" (*di lui si maravigliasse*): the notion of the marvelous was a key critical term in sixteenth-century theoretical discussions for the desired effect worked by literature.

10. George Puttenham, *The Arte of English Poesie* (1589), ed. Gladys Doidge Willcock and Alice Walker (Cambridge: At the University Press, 1936). Subsequent references will appear in the text.

11. Kenneth Burke, *A Rhetoric of Motives* (1950; reprint ed., Berkeley and Los Angeles: Univ. of California Press, 1969), pp. 285–86.

12. *The Civile Conversation of M. Steeven Guazzo* (1574), trans. George Pettie (Books 1–3, 1581) and Bartholomew Young (Book 4, 1586), the Tudor Translations, 2 vols. (London: Constable, 1925). Subsequent references will

appear in the text, noted by citing the physical volumes (1–2) of this edition rather than the work's internal books (1–4).

13. From a letter from Raleigh to his son, copied into a manuscript of the *Instructions to his Son*, MS Additional 22587 (in the British Library), unearthed by Agnes M.C. Latham, in "Sir Walter Raleigh's *Instructions to his Son*," in *Elizabethan and Jacobean Studies Presented to Frank Percy Wilson in Honour of His Seventieth Birthday* (Oxford: Clarendon, 1959), pp. 207–8.

14. For a related reading of Guidobaldo's role, see Robert W. Hanning, "Castiglione's Verbal Portrait: Structures and Strategies," in *Castiglione: The Ideal and the Real in Renaissance Culture*, ed. Hanning and David Rosand (New Haven: Yale Univ. Press, 1983). Guidobaldo's courtiers are "his prize works of art, the human analogues to the beautiful books" in his library (p. 136). "Guidobaldo has become a connoisseur of courtliness, which connoisseurship, combined with his political power, has made him the artist-creator of his superlative courtiers as well" (p. 137). The courtiers seek (and, for Hanning, find) worthiness by subjecting themselves to the duke's judgments, both aesthetic and political. In my view these judgments tend to coalesce.

15. A similar notion is put forward by Fredric Jameson in his analysis of Sartre's *Critique of Dialectical Reason*, in *Marxism and Form* (Princeton: Princeton Univ. Press, 1971), pp. 247–57. If Sartre's terms for describing a mass society (seriality and the genuine "revolving thirds" group) can be applied to late sixteenth-century England, then it seems that the Elizabethan ruling elite did not fully achieve genuine group status, but instead partook of the alienations of seriality.

16. Greenblatt, *Renaissance Self-Fashioning*, p. 31.

17. I am indebted here to Kenneth Burke's discussion of Jeremy Bentham's analysis of eulogistic, neutral, and dyslogistic epithets (*Rhetoric of Motives*, pp. 90–101), but my concern is with the *interconvertibility* of eulogistic and dyslogistic in a political arena, not with the pursuit of the neutral by demystification. Indeed, *paradiastole* underwrites the *flight* from the neutral. Compare also Burke's discussion of classical rhetoric, pp. 55–90.

Examples of the trope appear in *The Institucion of a Gentleman* (1555; reprint ed., Norwood, N.J.: Walter J. Johnson, 1974), sig. B4r; Roger Ascham's *The Scholemaster* (in *English Works*, ed. William Aldis Wright [1904; reprint ed., Cambridge: At the University Press, 1970]), p. 206; Thomas Wyatt's "Mine Own John Poyntz" (in *Complete Poems*, ed. R. A. Rebholz [New Haven: Yale Univ. Press, 1978]), pp. 187–88 (lines 61–75); William Shakespeare, *King Lear* (2.2.97–106; cited from *The Complete Signet Classic Shakespeare*, ed. Sylvan Barnet [New York: Harcourt, Brace & World, 1963]; all references to Shakespeare will be taken from this edition and are cited in the text). The earliest specimen of paradiastole I have found occurs in Thucydides' *The Peloponnesian War* (III, x, 189–90) (trans. Richard Crawley [New York: Modern Library, 1951]). This occurrence sets up useful links with the Sophists and with Machiavelli, both conceptually relevant here. The term seems to have originated with Quintilian (*Institutes* 9. 3. 65), according to Liddell and Scott, who also adduce Rutilius and Isidorus Harpalensis.

It is worth considering the logic of this odd device, since it amounts to describing something as its opposite. Puttenham's liberal unthrift is a convenient example. Both an unthrift and a liberal gentleman share the attribute of ready spending. Relabeling the former as the latter suppresses the element that differentiates them: what the money is spent on. The unthrift wastes his money on trifles; the liberal gentleman is generous in making worthwhile expenditures. Paradiastole hides this difference, allowing one to evade undesired elements of a label by substituting for it another, similar label that lacks those elements.

Daniel Javitch considers this trope in Puttenham, in essentially aesthetic terms: "wit may always allow whoever possesses it to transform ostensible impropriety into its opposite"; "the courtly practice of hiding a disagreeable sense under an agreeable expression warrants the need for the poet to command this figure. Puttenham is not concerned, as is [the rhetorician, the elder Henry] Peacham, with [paradiastole's] moral or epistemological dubiousness, but with its aesthetic effect." My reading actively applies the term to the politics of conversation. (For the quotations, see Javitch's "Poetry and Court Conduct: Puttenham's *Arte of English Poesie* in the Light of Castiglione's *Cortegiano*," *MLN* 87 [1972]: 868, 877.)

18. Greenblatt, *Renaissance Self-Fashioning*, p. 100.

19. Ibid., pp. 108–9 and chap. 2.

20. See Javitch, "Poetry and Court Conduct," p. 876, on the elder Peacham.

21. For a related treatment of the demystification of a ruling elite by means of linguistic emphasis on a variety of the "literal," see my "Ideology and Class Conduct in *The Merchant of Venice*," *Renaissance Drama*, n.s. 10 (1979), pp. 93–115, esp. pp. 103–4.

22. My reading of these matters is obviously at variance with those readings which speak of Duke Guidobaldo's departure as radically liberating to the interlocutors of the dialogue. Hanning, for instance, sees the retirement as "clearing a play space for the courtiers' game of reproducing themselves as verbal, rather than living, works of art" ("Castiglione's Verbal Portrait," in *Castiglione: The Ideal and the Real*, p. 137). Thomas M. Greene properly denies this distinction between verbal and living activity, positing the game as a conquest of *negotium* by *otium*, but he too posits an insulated "enclosure" (one enhanced by Guidobaldo's absence) and stresses the group's resilient capacity to evade or to repress unwelcome perceptions. (See his "*Il Cortegiano* and the Choice of a Game," *Renaissance Quarterly*, 32 (1979): 173–86; reprinted in *Castiglione: The Ideal and the Real*, pp. 1–15.) I propose to emphasize both the mutually rhetorical dominations implicit in the gradations of power and legitimacy that would pervade any such gathering at a

Renaissance court and the internal hierarchies that thrive with the intro-jected witness inside each courtier. Indeed, I think the game replicates—in the author's consciousness, among its participants, and within each of them—the fissures of its historical context at large. Still, though I disagree with the breadth of embrace that Greene imputes to the game and to the group's "resiliency" (its capacity to deflect, actually, into personal interiors, unwanted awarenesses), his essay is an extremely subtle examination of some of the relevant phenomena of the situation.

23. Daniel Javitch, "*The Philosopher of the Court*: A French Satire Misun-derstood," *Comparative Literature* 23 (1971): 97–124; see also Greenblatt, *Renaissance Self-Fashioning*, pp. 163–64.

24. Count Annibale Romei, *The Courtiers Academie* (1585), trans. I. Ke-pers (1598; reprint ed., New York: Da Capo Press, 1969). Subsequent refer-ences will appear in the text.

25. Giovanni della Casa, *Galateo* (1558), trans. R. S. Pine-Coffin (Har-mondsworth: Penguin Books, 1958), p. 93; *Opere di Baldassare Castiglione, Giovanni della Casa, Benvenuto Cellini*, ed. Carlo Cordie (Milan and Na-ples: Ricciardi, 1960), p. 431.

26. Ibid., pp. 93–94/431.

27. John Ferne, *The Blazon of Gentrie* (1586; reprint ed., New York: Da Capo Press, 1973). Subsequent references will appear in the text.

28. For a bridge between this notion and the similar principles of modern advertising, see Jonson's *Alchemist*, where Subtle plans a protoneon sign for Drugger's tobacco shop: "I will haue his name / Form'd in some mystick char-acter; whose *radij*, / Striking the senses of the passers by, / Shall, by a vertuall influence, breed affections" (2.6.14–17; from *Ben Jonson*, ed. C. H. Herford, Percy Simpson, and Evelyn Simpson, 11 vols. [Oxford: Clarendon, 1925–52], 5:337). See also Chap. V, note 56, below. Advertising scientizes the magic of courtliness.

29. The social formation shapes consciousness in ranges much deeper and more general than is usually supposed. For further exploration of such deter-minations see, for instance, William Kerrigan, "The Articulation of the Ego in the Renaissance," in Joseph H. Smith, M.D., ed., *The Literary Freud: Mech-anisms of Defense and the Poetic Will*, Psychiatry and the Humanities (New Haven: Yale Univ. Press, 1980), 4: 261–308; and Arthur F. Marotti, "Coun-tertransference, the Communication Process, and the Dimensions of Psy-choanalytic Criticism," *Critical Inquiry* 4 (1978): 471–89, especially the fol-lowing passage: "A sociocultural system not only inculcates certain ideals, values, sublimations—that is, superego formations—but also, as object-re-lations psychoanalysis has taught us, the very shapes of (instinctive) desire and need, from the basic modes of taking in reality in infancy—related pri-marily to feeding and other forms of maternal care—to the most sophisti-cated forms of adult relationships" (p. 486). We might fruitfully follow these leads by investigating deeper structures of relation with the self and others in

those social frames dominated by rigorous hierarchical stratification, where rank marks different *kinds* of humans, a distinction similar in ontological potency to more familiar (if equally problematic) conceptions of race and gender. Burke's work on "identification" is relevant here, in relation to his sense of humans as "classifying animals." Especially relevant is his examination of the individual-for-group misunderstanding involved in the notion of the "inferiority complex": we experience "a difference between *this* being and *that* being as a difference between *this kind* of being and *that kind* of being" (*Rhetoric of Motives*, p. 282). Different categories of "kind" will receive various emphases in different social formations. Burke is especially acute in noting the revealing effects of the *loss* of such categorial relation, speaking of those who have broken away from their class or race, such as "Negro intellectuals, liberal Jews, or Gentiles who have notably altered their social position for better or worse" (p. 282). We might well learn more about the Renaissance elite's sense of social class by considering the experience of transsexuals today, as ontologically mobile beings. See, for instance, Harold Garfinkel, "Passing and the Managed Achievement of Sex Status in an Intersexed Person, Part I," in *Studies in Ethnomethodology* (Englewood Cliffs, N.J.: Prentice-Hall, 1967), pp. 116–85, 285–88.

30. This point has been noted by Dain A. Trafton, "Structure and Meaning in *The Courtier*," *English Literary Renaissance* 2 (1972): 290; and by J. R. Hale, "Castiglione's Military Career," in *Castiglione: The Ideal and the Real*, p. 160.

31. Williams, *Tudor Regime*, p. 81.

32. And if the prince or other adequate audience figures are absent, one can turn the performance or experience of war to useful rhetorical account afterward. Sir John Harington writes from Ireland (on duty with Essex) of how he will employ the experience when back at court: "I have informed myself reasonably well of the whole state of the country, by observation and conference; so that I count the knowledge I have gotten here worth more than half the three hundred pounds this jorney hath cost me: and as to warr, joyning the practise to the theory, and reading the book you so prays'd, and other books of Sir Griffin Markham's, with his conference and instructions, I hope at my coming home to talk of counterscarpes, and cazamats, with any of our captains" (from *The Letters and Epigrams of Sir John Harington*, ed. Norman Egbert McClure [Philadelphia: Univ. of Pennsylvania Press, 1930], p. 74).

33. Francesco Guicciardini, *Maxims and Reflections* [*Ricordi*], trans. Mario Domandi (Philadelphia: Univ. of Pennsylvania Press, 1965). Subsequent references will appear in the text, identified by series and item number.

34. Francis Bacon, "Of Negociating," *Essays*, (1625; reprint ed., New York: Everyman's Library, 1906), p. 144.

35. Bacon, "Of Vain-Glory," *Essays*, p. 158; "Of Honour and Reputation," p. 160.

36. Sir Robert Naunton, *Fragmenta Regalia*, ed. Edward Arber, English Reprints (1653; reprint ed., London, 1870), p. 16.

37. Wallace MacCaffrey, "Place and Patronage in Elizabethan Politics," in *Elizabethan Government and Society*, ed. S. T. Bindoff, Joel Hurstfield, and C. H. Williams (London: Athlone, 1961), p. 108. See also Rosemary O'Day, "Ecclesiastical Patronage: Who Controlled the Church?" in *Church and Society in England: Henry VIII to James I*, ed. Felicity Heal and Rosemary O'Day (London: Macmillan, 1977); and Guy Fitch Lytle and Stephen Orgel, eds., *Patronage in the Renaissance* (Princeton: Princeton Univ. Press, 1981).

38. Sir Walter Raleigh, *Maxims of State*, in *The Works of Sir Walter Raleigh, Kt.*, ed. Thomas Birch, 8 vols. (Oxford: Oxford Univ. Press, 1829), 8:13–14.

39. Bacon, "Of Followers and Friends," *Essays*, p. 147.

40. For a related discussion of the political mounting of the linguistic situation, compare Pierre Bourdieu, "The Economics of Linguistic Exchanges," trans. Richard Nice, *Social Science Information* 16 (1977): 645–68.

41. See Walter J. Ong, "Oral Residue in Tudor Prose Style," in *Rhetoric, Romance, and Technology: Studies in the Interaction of Expression and Culture* (Ithaca, N.Y.: Cornell Univ. Press, 1971), pp. 23–47.

42. Bacon, "Of Simulation and Dissimulation," *Essays*, p. 18.

43. Bacon, "Of Seditions and Troubles," *Essays*, pp. 46–47.

44. For a brief but suggestive analysis of "comeliness," see Thomas M. Greene, "Roger Ascham: The Perfect End of Shooting," *ELH* 26 (1960): 620–21.

45. For a somewhat different view of the function of delay, see Javitch, *Poetry and Courtliness in Renaissance England* (Princeton: Princeton Univ. Press, 1978), p. 58.

46. Williams, *The Tudor Regime*, p. 440. M. E. James has made an interesting close study of this gradual diffusion of centralist ideas of order into the more isolated parts of the realm; see "The Concept of Order and the Northern Rising of 1569," *Past & Present* 60 (1973): 49–83.

47. I have elsewhere analyzed the effects of such obligations on the practice of letter-writing for preferment; see "The Rhetoric of Elizabethan Suitors' Letters," *PMLA* 96 (1981): 864–82.

48. George Gascoigne, *Complete Works*, ed. John W. Cunliffe, 2 vols. (1907; reprint ed., New York: Greenwood Press, 1969), 1:5, 8. Subsequent references will appear in the text.

49. For a statement of this restricted view, see Paula Glatzer, *The Complaint of the Poet: The Parnassus Plays—A Critical Study of the Trilogy Performed at St. John's College, Cambridge, 1598–99—1601–02, Authors Anonymous* (Salzburg: Institut für Englische Sprache und Literatur, 1974).

50. J. B. Leishman, ed., *The Three Parnassus Plays (1598–1601)* (London: Ivor Nicholson & Watson, 1949). Subsequent references will appear in the text.

51. Lawrence Stone, *The Crisis of the Aristocracy, 1558–1641* (Oxford: Clarendon, 1965), p. 707.

52. Samuel Daniel, *Delia* 48 (1592 text), in *Poems and A Defence of Ryme*, ed. A. C. Sprague (1930; reprint ed., Chicago: Univ. of Chicago Press, 1965), p. 34.

53. See "In Doctissimi Viri Rogeri Aschami Laudem Sylva" (An Elegy on the Most Learned Man Roger Ascham), in George Burke Johnson, ed., *Poems by William Camden, Studies in Philology,* 72, no. 5 (1975), 54–59. The text quoted is from p. 54, lines 24–25; the translation (by Johnson) is from p. 55, lines 26–28. This text was published in 1575, in Edward Grant's edition of Ascham's letters and poems, *Disertissimi Viri Rogeri Aschami Angli, Regiae Olim Majestati a Latinis Epistolis* (STC 826); it was Camden's first published work.

54. Richard Mulcaster, *The First Part of the Elementarie* (1582; reprint ed., Menston, England: Scolar Press, 1970), sigs. *2r–*3r.

55. As Ingenioso's words to the doorman (lines 249–56) suggest, the intellectual hireling's skills may threaten as well as praise. There is one situation in which they do both at once—when they intimidate the employer with their excellence or correctness, as Ingenioso intimidates Gullio. When Ingenioso delivers "Gullio's" poems to his lady, she rejects them, denying that he wrote them and saying that his Latin is false. Gullio replies to this news with a defensive response that frees him from the rules by claiming transcendence: "my Lattin was pure Lattin, and such as they speake in Rhems and Padua. Why, it is not the custome in Padua to obserue such base ruls as Lilie, Priscian, and such base companions haue sett downe; wee of the better sorte haue a priueledge to create Lattin, like knightes, and to saye, Rise upp, Sr phrase" (lines 1431–37).

Other satiric uses can be found in Donne: "He is worst, who (beggarly) doth chaw / Others' wits' fruits, and in his ravenous maw / Rankly digested, doth those things out spew, / As his own things" (Satire II, lines 25–28, in *John Donne: The Complete English Poems,* ed. A. J. Smith [Harmondsworth: Penguin Books, 1973], p. 158); in Jonson: "If shee loue wit, giue verses, though you borrow 'hem of a friend, or buy 'hem, to haue good" (*Epicoene* 4.1.97–99: in *Ben Jonson,* ed. Herford, Simpson, and Simpson, 5:221); and in George Wither's *Abuses Stript and Whipt* (1613): "Sith Dunces can have Sonnets fram'd, and send them / As their inventions, when some others pend them" (quoted in *The Works of Michael Drayton,* ed. J. William Hebel et al., 5 vols. [1931; reprint ed., Basil Blackwell, 1961], 5:140).

56. Drayton, *Idea* 21 (1619 text), in *Works* 2:321.

57. A copy of a letter from Overbury to Carr (probably written in 1613, while Overbury was in the tower) is preserved in the Cotton MS Titus B VII, fn. 483, and printed in Sir Ralph Winwood, *Memorials of Affairs of State in the Reigns of Q. Elizabeth and K. James I,* 3 vols. (London, 1725), 3:478–79. Overbury berates Carr for allowing him to languish in the tower, angrily

referring to him as one who "knoweth that *what he speakes and writes howerly is mine*," and indicts him for abandoning him "*when you fell in Love with that Woman, as soon as you had wonne her by my Letters*, and after all the Difficulties [had] past" (p. 479). Beatrice White determines (apparently on the basis of this letter) that "it was Overbury who translated into the burning words and phrases dear to lovers the passion of his inarticulate patron" (in her study, broadly based on manuscript as well as printed sources, *Cast of Ravens: The Strange Case of Sir Thomas Overbury* [New York: Braziller, 1965], p. 28). See also D. H. Willson, *King James VI and I* (New York: Oxford Univ. Press, 1967), p. 342.

58. George Turberville provides another nonsatiric example of the service of vicarious seduction:

> Then for my friends (as divers loved me well)
> Endite I must some light devise of love,
> And in the same my friends affection tell,
> Whom nothing mought from beauties bar remove:
> My pen must plead the sillie Suters case,
> I had my hire, so he mought purchase grace.
>
> Some otherwhile, when beautie bred disdaine,
> And feature forst a pride in hawtie brest,
> So as my friend was causelesse put to paine,
> And for good will might purchace slender rest;
> Then must my quill to quarels flatly fall,
> Yet keepe the meane twixt sweete and sower brall.
>
> Somtimes I must commend their beauties much
> That never came where any beautie lay,
> Againe somwhiles my mates would have me tutch
> The quicke, bicause they had received the nay:
> And thus my pen, as change of matter grew,
> Was forst to grief, or els for grace to sue.

> (Quoted by C. T. Prouty from *Tragical Tales and Other Poems*, in
> *George Gascoigne: Elizabethan Courtier, Soldier, and Poet*
> [New York: Columbia Univ. Press, 1942], p. 118)

59. See B. M. Ward's edition of *A Hundreth Sundrie Flowres* (1573) (London: Etchells and Macdonald, 1926); the same author's "Further Research on *A Hundreth Sundrie Flowres*," *Review of English Studies* 4 (1938): 35–48; C. T. Prouty's introduction to his edition of the *Flowres* (Columbia: Univ. of Missouri Press, 1942); and Eric St. John Brooks, *Sir Christopher Hatton* (London: Jonathan Cape, 1946), pp. 104–10.

60. Erving Goffman, "The Nature of Deference and Demeanor," in *Interaction Ritual: Essays on Face-to-Face Behavior* (Garden City, N.Y.: Doubleday, Anchor Books, 1967), p. 58.

61. Sir Humphrey Gilbert, *Queene Elizabethes Achademy* (after 1562), Early English Text Society Extra Series 8 (London: Trubner, 1869). Subsequent references will appear in the text.

62. Erving Goffman, *Strategic Interaction* (Philadelphia: Univ. of Pennsylvania Press, 1969), pp. 67–69.

63. See Michel Foucault, *Discipline and Punish*, trans. Alan Sheridan (New York: Random House, Vintage Books, 1979).

64. Wayne Rebhorn, *Courtly Performances: Masking and Festivity in Castiglione's "Book of the Courtier"* (Detroit: Wayne State Univ. Press, 1978), p. 30.

65. Sir Harris Nicolas, *Memoirs of the Life and Times of Sir Christopher Hatton, K.G.* (London: Richard Bentley, 1847), p. 165. The letter is anonymous and undated, but it must predate 1584, since it deals with Elizabeth's possible marriage to the duke of Alençon, who died June 10, 1584.

Chapter 3: Tropes of Social Hierarchy: Gentle and Base

1. *The Civile Conversation of M. Steeven Guazzo* (1574), trans. George Pettie (Books 1–3, 1581) and Bartholomew Young (Book 4, 1586), the Tudor Translations, 2 vols. (London: Constable, 1925). Subsequent references will appear in the text, noted by citing the physical volumes (1–2) of this edition rather than the work's internal books (1–4).

2. Kenneth Burke, *A Rhetoric of Motives* (1950; reprint ed., Berkeley and Los Angeles: Univ. of California Press, 1969), p. 210.

3. Ibid., p. 115.

4. Baldassare Castiglione, *The Book of the Courtier* (1528), trans. Sir Thomas Hoby (1561; reprint ed., New York: Dutton, Everyman, 1966); cited with *Il libro del cortegiano con una scelta delle opere minori*, 2d ed., ed. Bruno Maier (Turin: Unione Tipografico-Editrice Torinese, 1964). Subsequent references to these editions will appear in the text.

5. George Puttenham, *The Arte of English Poesie* (1589), ed. Gladys Doidge Willcock and Alice Walker (Cambridge: At the University Press, 1936). Subsequent references will appear in the text.

6. Francis Beaumont and John Fletcher, *Philaster* (1609), ed. Andrew Gurr, The Revels Plays (London: Methuen, 1969), 4.5.90–92.

7. *The Institucion of a Gentleman* (1555; reprint ed., Norwood, N.J.: Walter J. Johnson, 1974). Subsequent references will appear in the text.

8. Sir Thomas Elyot, *The Book named the Governor* (1531), ed. S. E. Lehmberg (New York: Dutton, Everyman, 1962). Subsequent references will appear in the text.

9. Niccolo Machiavelli, *The Prince* (1513), in *The Portable Machiavelli*, trans. and ed. Peter Bondanella and Mark Musa (Harmondsworth: Penguin Books, 1979), pp. 130–33.

10. Arthur B. Ferguson, *The Indian Summer of English Chivalry* (Dur-

ham, N.C.: Duke Univ. Press, 1960), pp. 190–92. The reverse can be argued for courtesy manuals as well. The earl of Oxford's preface to Clerke's Latin translation of Castiglione credits the author with having been able to "lay down principles for the guidance of the very Monarch himself" (B. M. Ward, *The Seventeenth Earl of Oxford, 1550–1604* [London: John Murray, 1928], p. 81). And Stanford Lehmberg believes that the injunctions of *The Book named the Governor* are aimed principally at Elyot's prince; see *Sir Thomas Elyot: Tudor Humanist* (Austin: Univ. of Texas Press, 1960), p. 37.

11. Burke, *Rhetoric of Motives*, p. 115.

12. Passages like these, and there are many, need to be set beside those where Javitch notes that Guazzo "condemns aristocratic exclusiveness as 'incivilitie and churlishnesse'" ("Rival Arts of Conduct in Elizabethan England: Guazzo's *Civile Conversation* and Castiglione's *Courtier*," *Yearbook of Italian Studies* 1 [1971]: 193) before we can properly assess class attitudes in Guazzo. The "marvelous payment" of the gentleman's mere presence is far from anything like mutuality serving "to strengthen the fabric of society" (p. 193), though the ideology aims to inculcate that apparent effect.

13. Edmund Spenser, *Poetical Works*, ed. J. C. Smith and E. de Selincourt, Oxford Standard Authors Series (Oxford: Oxford Univ. Press, 1912), p. 337.

14. Count Annibale Romei, *The Courtiers Academie* (1585), trans. I. Kepers (1598; reprint ed., New York: Da Capo Press, 1969). Subsequent references will appear in the text.

15. Lawrence Stone, *The Crisis of the Aristocracy, 1558–1641* (Oxford: Clarendon, 1965), p. 36.

16. John Nichols, *The Progresses and Public Processions of Queen Elizabeth* (1823; reprint ed., New York: Burt Franklin, n.d.), 3:1–22. Elizabeth sometimes gave more individualized gifts; see the pages of miscellaneous gift records following p. 22.

17. Ibid., 3:2.

18. Ibid., 3:1.

19. Ibid., 3:15. The archaic abbreviations in this quotation can be decoded by using the following table:

dim. quarter	⅛ oz.	dim. dim. quarter	⅝ oz.
quarter	¼ oz.	iii quarters	¾ oz.
quarter dim.	⅜ oz.	iii quarters dim.	⅞ oz.
dim.	½ oz.		

(See A. J. Collins, *Jewels and Plate of Queen Elizabeth I: The Inventory of 1574* [London: British Museum, 1955], p. 257). I have been aided in deciphering these records by David Beasley and Christine Lance of the library of the Worshipful Company of Goldsmiths, and by Leslie Greene, assistant curator for decorative arts at the Los Angeles County Museum of Art.

20. Hugh Keele and Sir Richard Martyn were prominent goldsmiths, Martyn being the more eminent because he had close connections with the

Royal Mint (see C. E. Challis, *The Tudor Coinage* [Manchester: Manchester Univ. Press, 1978]). David Beasley tells me that despite the identification of these pieces by maker, it is likely that "one could only assess the importance of the gifts from the weights indicated." Another marker noted in the Nichols inventory is one "L," whose identity I have not been able to determine, though it probably lies hidden in Sir Charles James Jackson's *English Goldsmiths and Their Marks* (London: Macmillan, 1921).

21. John Husee's report of his presentation in 1538 of a New Year's gift to Henry VIII on behalf of his master, Lord Lisle, is a fascinating (and presumably rudimentary, by Elizabethan standards) version of this ceremony. See *The Lisle Letters*, ed. Muriel St. Clare Byrne, 6 vols. (Chicago: Univ. of Chicago Press, 1981), 5:10 (letter 1086). Henry had a secretary on hand to record all presentations.

22. Sir John Neale, "The Elizabethan Political Scene," in *Essays in Elizabethan History* (New York: St. Martin's Press, 1958), p. 71; quoted from Arthur Collins, *Sydney Papers* 1:382.

23. Ibid., p. 72; quoted from Lansdowne MS 47, fols. 8ff.

24. This functionary, John Astely, who signed this and many other records of New Year's gifts, was a full-scale courtier. He offers a perfect example of the Elizabethan public servant's synthesis of bureaucratic and courtly functions. He was Master of the Jewel House (1558–95), sat in three Parliaments (1570, 1586, and 1588–89), wrote a treatise on horsemanship (1584), was married to the Chief Gentlewoman of the Privy Chamber, and was a guest at the dinner from which, Ascham tells us, the idea for *The Scholemaster* emerged (see Roger Ascham, *The Scholemaster* [1570], in *English Works*, ed. William Aldis Wright [1904; reprint ed., Cambridge: At the University Press, 1970], p. 175). According to Gabriel Harvey, Pietro Bizarro, "a learned Italian," proposed Astely as "a perfect Patterne of Castilios Courtier" (*Pierce's Supererogation*, in *Works*, ed. A. B. Grosart, 3 vols. [1884; reprint ed., New York: AMS Press, 1966], 2: 99). (Caroline Ruutz-Rees refers this quotation erroneously to a Giles edition, presumably confusing Grosart with Ascham's editor; see her "Some Notes of Gabriel Harvey's in Hoby's Translation of Castiglione's *Courtier*," *PMLA* 25 [1910]: 615.) See also Collins, *Jewels and Plate*, pp. 199–230. However, Bizarro seems to have been, like Harvey himself, an exaggerated courtier not to be taken quite seriously. For mockery of his ornate postures by Hubert Languet and Philip Sidney, see James M. Osborn, "Sidney and Pietro Bizari," *Renaissance Quarterly* 24 (1971): 344–54.

25. Francis Bacon, "Of Seditions and Troubles," *Essays* (1625; reprint ed., New York: Everyman's Library, 1906), p. 46.

26. Quoted by Stone without identification from Inner Temple MSS 538.44, fol. 13, in *Crisis of the Aristocracy*, p. 49.

27. John Ferne, *The Blazon of Gentrie* (1586; reprint ed., New York: Da Capo Press, 1973). Subsequent references will appear in the text.

28. Some critics have a tendency to employ this dismissive vocabulary un-

reflectively. Rebhorn, for instance, says that the doors of symposia like Castiglione's "are closed to keep out riff-raff" (Wayne Rebhorn, *Courtly Performances: Masking and Festivity in Castiglione's "Book of the Courtier"* [Detroit: Wayne State Univ. Press, 1978], p. 164). Such terms should offer a subject for, not a mode of, criticism.

29. Again, compare Daniel Javitch: "Because Guazzo's hierarchy is primarily moral, its exclusions show none of Castiglione's vertical criteria" ("Rival Arts," p. 194). Javitch habitually uncouples Guazzo from Castiglione's courtly and hierarchical values, borrowing from John L. Lievsay's more extreme position, with some appropriate caveats (see Lievsay's *Stefano Guazzo and the English Renaissance, 1575–1675* [Chapel Hill: Univ. of North Carolina Press, 1961], especially chap. 1). But Javitch fails to address Guazzo's explicitly courtly Book 4, an omission that is the more serious insofar as Book 4 is exemplary of the precepts stated in the earlier books. It is headed: "The Fourth Booke . . . In the which is set downe the fourme of Civile Conversation, by an example of a Banquet . . . betweene six Lords, and foure Ladies" (2: 115). As will become clear, Book 4 is profoundly concerned with "vertical criteria" of a social sort.

It may be that Javitch means to offer a moral content for what he calls "the shift from an ideal of the 'cortegiano' to one of the 'gentiluomo'" ("Rival Arts," p. 179). But in English applications of the ideal (Javitch's stated subject), it is erroneous to see the gentleman of the sixteenth century as uncourtly. It was once thought correct to mark off the gentleman from the noble and to ally him with "middle classes." Sir Edward Sullivan applied this notion to Guazzo, in fact, in his introduction to the Tudor Translations reprint: "Guazzo never intended his book to be regarded as anything but a treatise that confined itself strictly to the great middle classes as distinguished from the patricians of a higher social order" (1: xxviii). But it has been clear for some time that this view is untenable. See, for instance, J. H. Hexter's pronouncement: "However respectable its sponsors [he alludes here to Tawney], a view that separates the gentry from the titled nobility and binds them to merchants and tradesmen finds little justification in Tudor habits of thought" ("Education of the Aristocracy," in *Reappraisals in History* [New York: Harper & Row, 1961], p. 50; see also "The Myth of the Middle Class in Tudor England," pp. 71–116 in the same volume). As the studies by Stone and Cressy cited in Chap. 1 also make clear, nobles and gentles must be grouped together, in specific contradistinction to all their base inferiors. It is the members of this exclusive group who read Guazzo in England, at university and at court, and who shared values with him and with each other. Not until the seventeenth century do we find a significantly anticourtly sector of the ruling elite in England. Before that time, I believe, Castiglione and Guazzo were read by the same sort of readers and were used for the same set of hierarchical purposes.

30. Friedrich Nietzsche characteristically cites two explicitly religious versions of this transport (though he misquotes the first) in *The Genealogy of*

Morals, trans. Francis Golffing (Garden City, N.Y.: Doubleday, Anchor Books, 1956), 1: 15: pp. 182–85. The examples are from Aquinas and Tertullian. Aquinas says, in the *Summa Theologica*, "Et ideo, ut beatitudo sanctorum eis magis complaceat, et de ea uberiores gratias Deo agant, datur eis ut poenas impiorum perfecte videant." ("In order that the happiness of the saints may be more delightful to them and that they may render more copious thanks to God for it, they are allowed to see perfectly the sufferings of the damned.") See the Supplement to the Third Part, Ques. 94, Art. 1, from *Opera Omnia*, 25 vols. (New York: Musurgia, 1948), 4: 658. The translation is from R. M. Hutchins and Mortimer Adler, eds., *Great Books of the Western World* (New York: Encyclopedia Brittanica, 1952), vol. 20, *Thomas Aquinas II*, trans. the Fathers of the English Dominican Province, rev. by Daniel J. Sullivan, p. 1041. Aquinas also says "Sancti de poenis impiorum gaudebunt, considerando in eis divinae justitiae ordinem, et suam liberationem, de qua guadebunt." ("The saints will rejoice in the punishment of the wicked, by considering therein the order of Divine justice and their own deliverance, which will fill them with joy.") (Ques. 94, Art. 3, pp. 659, 1042, respectively.) The tortures are not pleasing in themselves, but rather because they signify the ordering power of God, which elevated the witnesses to their viewpoint.

The other parallel occurs in the famous rhetorical conclusion to Tertullian's *De Spectaculis*: the pleasures of watching the gory tortures of the damned are compared to the lesser earthly pleasures of viewing the gladiatorial spectacles (see the Loeb edition, trans. T. R. Glover [London: Heinemann, 1931], pp. 299–301).

Shakespeare offers yet another example, more ambiguous if equally shrill: the anxious laughter of Gratiano in acts 4–5 of *The Merchant of Venice*.

31. See, for instance, Georg Lukacs, "Class Consciousness," in *History and Class Consciousness*, trans. Rodney Livingstone (Cambridge, Mass.: MIT Press, 1971), p. 60; Louis Althusser, "Marxism and Humanism," in *For Marx*, trans. Ben Brewster (London: NLB, 1977), p. 235.

32. *Richard Mulcaster's Positions* (1581), abr. and ed. Richard L. DeMolen (New York: Teachers College Press, Columbia Univ., 1970), p. 167.

33. This passage is rearranged by Peacham in praise of poetry: "And if Mechanicall Arts hold their estimation by their effects in base subiects, how much more deserueth this to be esteemed, that holdeth so soueraigne a power ouer the minde, can turne brutishnesse into Ciuilitie, make the lewd honest (which is *Scaligers* opinion of *Virgils* Poeme) turne hatred to loue, cowardise into valour, and in briefe, like a Queene command ouer all affections?" (Henry Peacham, *The Compleat Gentleman* [1622; reprint ed., New York: Da Capo Press, 1968], p. 80). Here the metamorphic power is attributed not to the princely poet but to poetic persuasion itself.

Another assertion of Elizabeth's creative facility appears in the earl of Oxford's preface to Clerke's Castiglione, where he lauds the wisdom of dedicating the book to the queen: "For there is no pen so skilful or powerful, no kind of speech so clear, that is not left behind by her own surpassing virtue" (Ward, *Seventeenth Earl of Oxford*, p. 83).

34. Francesco Guicciardini, *Maxims and Reflections* [*Ricordi*], trans. Mario Domandi (Philadelphia: Univ. of Pennsylvania Press, 1965). Subsequent references will appear in the text, identified by series and item number.

35. Bacon, "Of Great Place," *Essays*, p. 33.

36. George McGill Vogt surveys such stipulation of nobility by virtue in "Gleanings for the History of a Sentiment: Generositas Virtus, non Sanguis," *Journal of English and Germanic Philology* 24 (1925): 102–24.

37. For a similar argument, concerning the apodictic determination of "correct" linguistic usage by a restricted social group ("Phrases, words, and nuances are good *because* they, the members of the social elite, use them"), see Norbert Elias, *The History of Manners* (1939) (*The Civilizing Process*, vol. 1), trans. Edmund Jephcott (New York: Urizen, 1978), pp. 111–12.

38. See J. W. Saunders, "The Stigma of Print: A Note on the Social Bases of Tudor Poetry," *Essays in Criticism* 1 (1951): 139–64; and Steven W. May, "Tudor Aristocrats and the Mythical 'Stigma of Print,'" *Renaissance Papers 1980*, pp. 11–18. May demonstrates that the code was regularly transgressed, but he does not offer an account of the nonetheless frequent assertions of its postulates, which register a characteristically self-depictive upper-class posture.

39. Ruutz-Rees, "Some Notes of Gabriel Harvey's," pp. 631–32.

40. Compare Romei's ranking "aboue all others, the Arte of Warre, and studie of the Lawes: For the one preserueth, and the other gouerneth a Common-wealth" (p. 203).

41. This is a theme of Shakespeare's *Henry VI, Part One*. J. R. Hale emphasizes Castiglione's neglect of the technicalities of warfare: "In his book Castiglione selects only those military topics that would concern the civilian. Living in a generation that saw and discussed rapid changes in weapons, tactics, brigading, siegecraft, and the design of fortifications, he ignores them. He says nothing, either, about the officer class to which, contractually, he belonged, nothing about the campaigns—and there were so many of them!—in which they fought. There is no treatment of the art of war in the *Courtier*." (See "Castiglione's Military Career," in *Castiglione: The Ideal and the Real in Renaissance Culture*, ed. Robert W. Hanning and David Rosand [New Haven: Yale Univ. Press, 1983], p. 159.)

42. See, among others, Frances Yates, *Astraea: The Imperial Theme in the Sixteenth Century* (London: Routledge & Kegan Paul, 1975); Roy Strong, *Splendor at Court: Renaissance Spectacle and the Theater of Power* (Boston: Houghton Mifflin, 1973); Norman Council, "O Dea Certe: The Allegory of the Fortress of Perfect Beauty," *Huntington Library Quarterly* 39 (1976): 329–42, and his "Ben Jonson, Inigo Jones, and the Transformation of Tudor Chivalry," *ELH* 47 (1980): 259–75; Louis Adrian Montrose, "Celebration

and Insinuation: Sir Philip Sidney and the Motives of Elizabethan Courtship," *Renaissance Drama*, n.s. 8 (1977), pp. 3–35; and Richard C. McCoy's forthcoming book on Elizabethan chivalry.

43. Sir Philip Sidney, *Prose Works*, ed. Albert Feuillerat, 4 vols. (1912; reprint ed., Cambridge: At the University Press, 1962), 3: 125. See also the advice to a nephew given by Francis Walsingham, quoted in Conyers Read, *Mr. Secretary Walsingham and the Policy of Queen Elizabeth* (Oxford: Clarendon, 1925), 1: 18–20.

44. Castiglione's view is that from the art of drawing "there ensue many commodities, and especially in warre, to draw out Countries, Platformes, Rivers, Bridges, Castels, Holdes, Fortresses, and such other matters, the which though a man were able to keepe in minde (and that is a hard matter to doe) yet can he not shew them to others" (pp. 78/173). For the denial, see pp. 77/172. See also *Book named the Governor*, pp. 23–28.

45. Machiavelli, *The Prince*, chap. 14, p. 125.

46. See, for instance, Joan Simon, *Education and Society in Tudor England* (Cambridge: At the University Press, 1967), pp. 333–37.

47. Sir Humphrey Gilbert, *Queene Elizabethes Achademy* (after 1562), Early English Text Society Extra Series 8 (London: Trubner, 1869). Subsequent references will appear in the text.

48. This will be a possible reading if the *Oxford English Dictionary's* sixth meaning of "ordinary" is applied here: "Not distinguished by rank or position; belonging to the commonalty; of low degree. . . ." This meaning is not surely noted before 1659. "Price" in Gilbert's time could have meant "personal or social worth; excellency, honourableness" (sb. II 6b) or ". . . honour, glory, renown" (sb. III 9). For a related usage, compare a remark of Walsingham's about a deserving candidate for appointment: "If he lived in any other country than this, where martial men presently bear no price, he should not have been so long kept underfoot" (quoted from Arthur Collins, *Sydney Papers*, 1: 70–71, by Wallace MacCaffrey, "Place and Patronage in Elizabethan Politics," in *Elizabethan Government and Society*, ed. S. T. Bindoff, Joel Hurstfield, and C. H. Williams [London: Athlone, 1961], p. 101).

49. Compare Raleigh's similar rule for "preserving of an oligarchy by sophisms." He suggests that the aristocracy generously allow the poorer sorts to absent themselves from lawmaking assemblies and office, "under colour of sparing them" the pains and charge thereof. Their betters do not mind the pains, of course (though they are to be fined if they avoid them). See Sir Walter Raleigh, *Maxims of State*, in *The Works of Sir Walter Raleigh, Kt.*, ed. Thomas Birch, 8 vols. (Oxford: Oxford Univ. Press, 1829), 8: 27.

50. Quoted by Paul Lucas from *The Records of the Honourable Society of Lincoln's Inn: The Black Book* (London, 1897–98), ii. 81 (in "Blackstone and the Reform of the Legal Profession," *English Historical Review* 77 [1962]: 471). The Tudor-Stuart issues are treated at pp. 462–74.

51. Burke, *Rhetoric of Motives*, p. 131.

52. Quoted by F. J. Fisher in "The Development of London as a Centre of Conspicuous Consumption in the Sixteenth and Seventeenth Centuries," *Transactions of the Royal Historical Society,* 4th series, 30 (1948), pp. 38 – 39 (from Botero, p. 65). Compare also Marvell's "An Horatian Ode upon Cromwell's Return from Ireland." Cromwell's departure from the "peaceful" rivalries within his own party to actual war is twice described: "The forward youth that would appear / Must now forsake his muses dear," and "(For 'tis all one to courage high / The emulous or enemy)" (from Andrew Marvell, *The Complete Poems,* ed. E. S. Donno [Harmondsworth: Penguin Books, 1972], lines 1–2, 17–18 [p. 55]).

53. George Peele, *Polyhymnia* (1590), from *The Life and Minor Works of George Peele,* ed. David H. Horne (New Haven: Yale Univ. Press, 1952), pp. 231–43.

54. Strange and Gerrarde are a possible exception:

> He mountes him bravely for his friendlie foe,
> And at the head he aimes, and in his aime
> Happily thrives, and breakes his Azure staves.
> Whom gentle Gerrarde, all in white and greene,
> Collours (belike) best serving his conceit,
> Lustilie meetes, mounted in seate of steele,
> With flourishing plume and faire Caparison,
> And then at everie shocke the shivers flie,
> That recommend their honors to the skie.

(Lines 53–61)

At line 55 Strange breaks lances on Gerrarde's head, a feat worth double credit in the scoring. (See Sidney Anglo, "Archives of the English Tournament: Score Cheques and Lists," *Journal of the Society of Archivists* 2 [1960– 64]: 157. The breaking of a lance on the opponent's body was the basic increment; hitting the helm, a smaller target, was worth two points: "Hunsdon 'brake xiiij staves whereof one was on the vissarde wiche is allowid for ij staves Broken'" [p. 157].) Thus Strange "thrives" (line 55). But Gerrarde, not unhorsed, meets him lustily; the flying shivers recommend *their* honors to the sky. Each in fact just "does well." Other passages also suggest that the language of winning simply means "fighting well." Of Carey and Graham, Peele says: "And breake they doo, they misse not as I weene, / And all was done in honour of their Queene" (lines 171–72). And the meeting of Knowles and Bowes makes a sound "as [if] horse and man had both bene borne to ground" (line 220). But we are not told *which* horse and man bit the dust. (I owe the Anglo reference to Richard C. McCoy. See also Anglo's "Financial and He- raldic Records of the English Tournament," *Journal of the Society of Archi- vists* 2 [1960–64]: 183–95.)

55. See Claude Levi-Strauss, *The Savage Mind* (Chicago: Univ. of Chicago Press, 1966), p. 32. "Games thus appear to have a *disjunctive* effect: they end

in the establishment of a difference between individual players or teams where originally there was no indication of inequality. And at the end of the game they are distinguished into winners and losers. Ritual, on the other hand, is the exact inverse; it *conjoins*, for it brings about a union . . . or in any case an organic relation between two initially separate groups."

56. Anglo, "Archives," p. 157.

57. Ibid., p. 158, n. 17.

58. Spenser details the attitudes that might develop if an inferior did successfully compete with a superior in serious matters, without successfully dismissive redefinition. In *A View of the Present State of Ireland* (1598), ed. W. L. Renwick (Oxford: Clarendon, 1970), Eudoxus, speaking of Hugh McHugh, says: "Surely I can commend him that being of himself of so base condition, hath through his own hardiness lifted himself up to that height that he now dares front princes, and make terms with great potentates; the which as it is honourable to him, so it is to them most disgraceful to be bearded of such a base varlet, that being but late grown out of the dunghill beginneth not to overcrow so high mountains" (pp. 117–18). The mobile upstart is viewed in two ways in this passage (flatteringly and unflatteringly), but those he "fronts" are simply disgraced.

59. Kenneth Burke, *A Grammar of Motives* (1945; reprint ed., Berkeley and Los Angeles: Univ. of California Press, 1969), p. 430; see also pp. 430–40.

60. Jean Bodin, *The Six Bookes of a Commonweale* (1576 in French, 1586 in Bodin's Latin), trans. Richard Knolles (from both versions, 1606; reprint ed., Cambridge, Mass.: Harvard Univ. Press, 1962), I.6.47; see also III.8.389.

61. Stephen Greenblatt, "Improvisation and Power," from *Literature and Society*, ed. Edward Said, English Institute Essays (Baltimore: Johns Hopkins Univ. Press, 1980), p. 83.

62. Raymond Williams, *Marxism and Literature* (Oxford: Oxford Univ. Press, 1977), pp. 115–16.

63. See Edwin Greenlaw, "Elizabethan Fact and Modern Fancy," in *Studies in Spenser's Historical Allegory* (Baltimore: Johns Hopkins Univ. Press, 1932), pp. 59–103; Sidney Anglo, "The *British History* in Early Tudor Propaganda," *Bulletin of the John Rylands Library* 44 (1961): 17–48; Angus Fletcher, *The Prophetic Moment* (Chicago: Univ. of Chicago Press, 1971), pp. 106–21.

64. Fredric Jameson, *Marxism and Form* (Princeton: Princeton Univ. Press, 1971), p. 258.

65. Sir Philip Sidney, *An Apology for Poetry*, ed. Geoffrey Shepherd (Manchester: Manchester Univ. Press, 1973), p. 125.

Chapter 4. Tropes of Personal Promotion: Praise and Flattery

1. William Harrison, *The Description of England* (1577, 1587), ed. Georges Edelen, Folger Documents of Tudor and Stuart Civilization (Ithaca, N.Y.: Cornell Univ. Press, 1968), p. 114.

2. Richard Lanham, *The Motives of Eloquence* (New Haven: Yale Univ. Press, 1976), p. 157.

3. Baldassare Castiglione, *The Book of the Courtier* (1528), trans. Sir Thomas Hoby (1561; reprint ed., New York: Dutton, Everyman, 1966); cited with *Il libro del cortegiano con une scelta delle opere minori,* 2d ed., ed. Bruno Maier (Turin: Unione Tipografico-Editrice Torinese, 1964). Subsequent references to these editions will appear in the text.

4. In "Politics and the Praise of Women," in *Castiglione: The Ideal and the Real in Renaissance Culture,* ed. Robert W. Hanning and David Rosand (New Haven: Yale Univ. Press, 1983), Dain A. Trafton cites this passage as evidence that "the games [*The Courtier*] records, refined and fascinating though they are, do not represent the real business of courtiers" (p. 32). He argues for the serious political weight of Castiglione's Book 3, the transition to which the passage in question is said to mark. Without addressing Trafton's entire argument (which I find problematic), I will say that his reading of this passage differs from mine because he focuses on the *gap* the analogy registers, whereas I stress the *link* it records. The high quality of Urbino's gaming is presented as evidence of the high quality of its serious practices.

5. Sir Thomas Elyot, *The Book named the Governor* (1531), ed. S. E. Lehmberg (New York: Dutton, Everyman, 1962). Subsequent references will appear in the text.

6. Caroline Ruutz-Rees, "Some Notes of Gabriel Harvey's in Hoby's Translation of Castiglione's *Courtier*," *PMLA* 25 (1910): 635.

7. Sir Harris Nicolas, *Memoirs of the Life and Times of Sir Christopher Hatton, K. G.* (London: Richard Bentley, 1847), p. 329.

8. *The Civile Conversation of M. Steeven Guazzo* (1574), trans. George Pettie (Books 1–3, 1581) and Bartholomew Young (Book 4, 1586), the Tudor Translations, 2 vols. (London: Constable, 1925). Subsequent references will appear in the text, noted by citing the physical volumes (1–2) of this edition rather than the work's internal books (1–4).

9. Neville Williams, *Elizabeth, Queen of England* (1967; reprint ed., London: Sphere, 1971), p. 186.

10. Compare Eduardo Saccone: "What the courtier is playing at is no game, or if it is, it is like that of the trapeze artist, who plays without the net" ("*Grazia, Sprezzatura,* and *Affettazione* in Castiglione's *Book of the Courtier*," trans. Susan G. Beecher, *Glyph* 5 [1979]: 50; reprinted in *Castiglione: The Ideal and the Real,* pp. 45–67). Subsequent citations (from the original article) will appear in the text.

11. Saccone's analysis diverges from mine in its history-of-ideas view of these variables. He does see the region of relevant action as specific to "a single class, whose ambition is to lead" (p. 44), but he does not confront the issues of power and privilege that identify this class and its actions. "Leadership" as a concept suppresses important elements of *rule,* for one thing, and it is reductive to call this class a "club" (p. 43). (I have not seen an Italian original of this piece; the translation may blur distinctions made there.) Still, Sac-

cone's explication of the gradual universalization of the realm of *grazia* and *sprezzatura* is extremely useful.

12. Roslyn Brogue Henning, "The Paideia of a Renaissance Gentleman: Castiglione's *Book of the Courtier*," in *Renaissance Men and Ideas*, ed. Robert Schwobel (New York: St. Martin's Press, 1971), p. 109.

13. I. M., *A Health to the Gentlemanly Profession of Serving-Men* (1598; reprint ed., London: Oxford Univ. Press, 1931), sig. F2v.

14. Jean-Paul Sartre, *Anti-Semite and Jew*, trans. George J. Becker (1946; reprint ed., New York: Schocken Books, 1965), pp. 22–23.

15. For the germ of this idea I am indebted to Robert Shephard; compare also Daniel Javitch, "Rival Arts of Conduct in Elizabethan England: Guazzo's *Civile Conversation* and Castiglione's *Courtier*," *Yearbook of Italian Studies* 1(1971): 188–89.

16. Erving Goffman, "On Face-Work," in *Interaction Ritual: Essays on Face-to-Face Behavior* (Garden City, N.Y.: Doubleday, Anchor Books, 1967), p. 7.

17. Erving Goffman, "Where the Action Is," in *Interaction Ritual*, p. 218. I am indebted throughout my discussion to this essay.

18. Giovanni della Casa, *Galateo* (1558), trans. R. S. Pine-Coffin (Harmondsworth: Penguin Books, 1958), pp. 21–22; *Opere di Baldassare Castiglione, Giovanni della Casa, Benvenuto Cellini*, ed. Carlo Cordie (Milan and Naples: Ricciardi, 1960), p. 368.

19. Francis Bacon, "Of Ceremonies and Respects," *Essays* (1625; reprint ed., New York: Everyman's Library, 1906), p. 154. Isabella is the queen of Spain; this is not a cognate reference to Elizabeth I, as might appear. Compare Bacon's apothegm no. 99: "Queen Isabell of Spain used to say; *Whosoever hath a good presence and a good fashion, carries letters of recommendation*" (*The Works of Francis Bacon*, ed. James Spedding, Robert Leslie Ellis, and Douglas Denon Heath, 15 vols. [New York: Hurd and Houghton, 1869], 13:350).

20. Bacon, "Of Empire," *Essays*, p. 57.

21. Niccolo Machiavelli, *The Prince* (1513), in *The Portable Machiavelli*, trans. and ed. Peter Bondanella and Mark Musa (Harmondsworth: Penguin Books, 1979), chap. 18, p. 135.

22. Jonas Barish, *The Antitheatrical Prejudice* (Berkeley and Los Angeles: Univ. of California Press, 1981), p. 183. See also Barish's examination of what seems to him to be Castiglione's mandate for fakery in painting, at pp. 172–73.

23. Bacon, "Of Discourse," *Essays*, p. 103.

24. Bacon, "Of Vain-Glory," *Essays*, p. 158.

25. George Puttenham, *The Arte of English Poesie* (1589), ed. Gladys Doidge Willcock and Alice Walker (Cambridge: At the University Press, 1936). Subsequent references will appear in the text.

26. Sir Philip Sidney, *An Apology for Poetry*, ed. Geoffrey Shepherd (Manchester: Manchester Univ. Press, 1973), p. 123.

27. E. R. Curtius, *European Literature and the Latin Middle Ages*, trans.

Willard R. Trask (1953; reprint ed., New York: Harper & Row, 1963), p. 408.

28. Bacon, "Of Vain-Glory," *Essays*, p. 159.

29. *A Health to the Gentlemanly Profession of Serving-Men*, sig. C2v.

30. A pattern made more common by structural inadequacies of the early modern bureaucracy. See Penry Williams, *The Tudor Regime* (Oxford: Clarendon, 1979), p. 107, for a description of the relatively primitive state of affairs existing in England at this time.

31. For further discussion of this structure, see J. W. Saunders, "The Stigma of Print: A Note on the Social Bases of Tudor Poetry," *Essays in Criticism* 1 (1951): 139–64, especially pp. 145–47.

32. Bacon, "Of Friendship," *Essays*, p. 86.

33. Frances Yates gives a rich account of Sidney's use of this trope in the *Arcadia*; see *Astraea: The Imperial Theme in the Sixteenth Century* (London: Routledge, 1975), pp. 88–94.

34. Less so is his own material reward for state service. In 1539 he and his wife were permitted to buy a large parcel of confiscated monastic land, for which privilege he had petitioned Cromwell in 1536. In order to relieve "indigence" incurred in state service, he says, "I therefor moste humbly desyre you my speciall goode lorde so to bryng me into the kinges moste noble remembran[ce] that of his moste bounteouse liberality it may like his highnesse to reward me with some convenyent porcion of his Suppressid landes" (*The Letters of Sir Thomas Elyot*, ed. K. J. Wilson, *Studies in Philology*, 73, no. 5 [1976]: 31); see also letter 11, n. 6; p. xix; and Stanford Lehmberg, *Sir Thomas Elyot: Tudor Humanist* (Austin: Univ. of Texas Press, 1960), pp. 157–58.

Elyot's harping rhetoric of penury is an interesting counterpoint to his ascetic writings on the relations between state service and material elevation. These pressures grew much more dramatic under Elizabeth, given the queen's habit of rewarding courtiers with credit or suspension of debt owed to the crown. Both ostentation and indebtedness rose spectacularly, increasing dependence on the queen.

35. Saint Augustine, *On Christian Doctrine*, trans. D. W. Robertson (Indianapolis: Bobbs-Merrill, 1958), I.iii (p. 9).

36. At the very least, it is *statistically* unlikely that every spicy courtier will please the prince's palate and so be used. As Walter J. Schnerr puts it, "It is easy to imagine a group of extremely versatile men, but it is less easy to visualize very many of them actually in a position to exercise the kind of influence here [in Castiglione's Book 4] expected of them" ("Two Courtiers: Castiglione and Rodrigues Lobo," *Comparative Literature* 13 [1961]: 152). For the rest, pleasure is its own reward, and the instrumental justification is sheer ideology.

Another way of construing this quantitative segregation has been proposed by Joseph A. Mazzeo:

The old sharp antithesis between active and contemplative ideals of life survives in Castiglione as the contrast between the one man who rules and possesses the art of commanding, and all the rest of the people who are ruled, possess the art of obeying and, if they are courtiers, of advising the ruler. The love theory which Bembo presents in Book IV of the *Courtier* offers a contemplative ideal for all men, or at least all gentlemen, but it scarcely affects the political and social realities, the status of the ruler's subjects. It is by no means insignificant that Castiglione left the knowledge of government to one man and offered harmless erotic ecstasies to the rest. ("Castiglione's *Courtier*: The Self as a Work of Art," in *Renaissance and Revolution: Backgrounds to Seventeenth-Century Literature* [New York: Random House, Pantheon Books, 1965], p. 137)

This view is based on the assumptions that advising the prince is a minimally political activity; that Castiglione viewed the prince as being politically skilled; and that the Neoplatonic elevation (or preoccupation) of a privileged class is politically insignificant. I disagree on all counts and prefer to locate the segregation below the courtly folk, instead of between them and their prince.

For a related treatment of mystifications of political ascendancy by erotic myth, see Eugene Vance, "Signs of the City: Medieval Poetry as Detour," *New Literary History* 4 (1973): 557–74.

37. Aristotle sets the positive here: "Noble also are those actions whose advantage may be enjoyed after death, as opposed to those whose advantage is enjoyed during one's lifetime: for the latter are more likely to be for one's own sake only" (*Rhetoric*, trans. W. Rhys Roberts [New York: Modern Library, 1954], p. 58: I.9,1367a).

38. Della Casa, *Galateo*, pp. 94–95/432.

39. For some history of this aversion to cosmetics, especially in regard to Tertullian and the Christian tradition, see Barish, *Antitheatrical Prejudice*, pp. 49–50, 158.

40. This is not, of course, to deny the long tradition of antifeminist criticism of female falsehood, present during the Renaissance in medieval monastic aspersions of Eve and continued by Puritans such as Philip Stubbes. The functions of such criticism shift with changes in the status of women, sexuality, and self-fashioning in general. What is of interest here is the Elizabethan *courtly* male's antipathy to female *cosmesis*. In each case the social function of the criticism must be determined. (See, for instance, Bosola's critique of the Old Lady in Webster's *The Duchess of Malfi*.)

Neville Williams reports a major leap in the importation, use, and criticism of women's cosmetics later in the sixteenth century: "The contrast between the first and second halves of the century is indeed most remarkable" (*Powder and Paint: A History of the Englishwoman's Toilet* [London: Longman, 1957], p. 2). Until this time there had been relatively few references in the literature of misogyny to facial cosmetics. Lengthy works like the fourteenth-century *Book of Vices and Virtues* rebuked fascination with mirrors and the combing of hair but never mentioned painting (p. 1). But new distinctions became available to the court lady as a result of luxurious ingredients gained from increased international trade. Williams cites Stubbes's angry phrase from *The Anatomie of Abuses* (1583): the "cunningly couched" ingredients are "both farre fetched and deer bought" (*Powder and Paint*, p. 3). The trade in mirrors now increased greatly; even men carried them at court, in their hats (p. 12). With this increase in use came a great increase in comment. For examination of this comment in the drama, see two studies by Annette Drew-Bear: "Face-Painting in Ben Jonson's Plays," *Studies in Philology* 77 (1980): 388–401; and "Face-Painting in Renaissance Tragedy," *Renaissance Drama*, n.s. 12 (1981): 71–93.

We need to know more about the dispersion of these cosmetic signifiers throughout the social scale. Their luxury commodity status makes it likely that at least at first, such behavior was identified with the ruling elite. (Did the queen lead the way?) If so, then the allegorical link I am proposing between cosmetics and cosmesis in the larger sense seems unadventurous; courtly male opposition would have involved a willed self-delusion.

Much goes unsaid here about cosmetics in relation to the state of women during the Renaissance, of course. But whatever conclusions we draw, we must avoid the opaque moralism of the shrill Elizabethan male if we are to avoid simply repeating his views.

J. R. Woodhouse notes a version of courtly rejection that repeats the pattern noted here but operates by absence: "The noun *cortegiana*, with its undertones of 'prostitute,' was studiously avoided by Castiglione, who stated that, instead, he would call his court-lady a *donna di palazzo*, but the prejudice there shown against the feminine equivalent of *cortegiano* was just that —male prejudice which preferred to ignore the moral servility of the male courtier's own situation" (*Baldesar Castiglione: A Reassessment of "The Courtier"* [Edinburgh: Edinburgh Univ. Press. 1978], pp. 54–55). As with painting, the rejection denies the resemblance.

For an investigation of a range of behavior intimately related to cosmetics, the rhetorical government of bodily functions (urination, spitting, nose-blowing, sexual behaviors), see Norbert Elias, *The History of Manners* (1939) (*The Civilizing Process*, vol. 1), trans. Edmund Jephcott (New York: Urizen, 1978).

41. The debate between Clerimont and Truewit in Jonson's *Epicoene* is of great interest on this score; see 1.1 and 4.1 (*Ben Jonson*, ed. C. H. Herford, Percy Simpson, and Evelyn Simpson, 11 vols. [Oxford: Clarendon, 1925–52], vol. 5).

42. Della Casa, *Galateo*, pp. 36/381.

43. We must often understand the presentation of an idealized self-image as an avoidance of accurate perception. Wayne Rebhorn neglects this point in

preferring a positive definition of self-creation: "Castiglione assumes his courtier will possess the abilities his image suggests"; he will use image-generation techniques to "effectively proclaim abilities and talents he may not be able to demonstrate convincingly at first sight or sufficiently often.... [A]lthough the courtier's image making may begin as compensation for the inadequacy of human perception, it clearly becomes a distinct advantage as it allows him to make himself into a much more enticing and compelling figure than he might otherwise be" (*Courtly Performances: Masking and Festivity in Castiglione's "Book of the Courtier"* [Detroit: Wayne State Univ. Press, 1978], p. 38). Castiglione's courtier may, as an ideal form, have all the abilities he seems to have, but the ordinary man trying to live by his precepts will often use them to struggle with the *adequacy* of human perception, not its blindness.

44. K. J. Wilson deals subtly and at some length with this general problem in Elyot, in his introduction to Elyot's letters and prologues.

45. Ibid., p. xx.

46. Roger Ascham, *The Scholemaster* (1570), in *English Works*, ed. William Aldis Wright (1904; reprint ed., Cambridge: At the University Press, 1970). Subsequent references will appear in the text.

47. Fulke Greville, Lord Brooke, *The Life of the Renowned Sr. Philip Sidney*, in *The Works in Verse and Prose Complete of the Right Honourable Fulke Greville, Lord Brooke*, ed. A. B. Grosart, 4 vols. (1870; reprint ed., New York: AMS, 1966), 4:152–53.

48. Cicero, *De Oratore*, II, 18; quoted from *Cicero on Oratory and Orators* [a translation of *De Oratore* and *Brutus*], trans. J. S. Watson (Carbondale: Southern Illinois Univ. Press, 1970), p. 103.

49. Greville, *Life of ... Sidney*, pp. 153–54.

50. Daniel Javitch, *Poetry and Courtliness in Renaissance England* (Princeton: Princeton Univ. Press, 1978), p. 60.

51. Greville, *Life of ... Sidney*, pp. 155–56.

52. Compare Rebhorn's discussion of this technique in *Courtly Performances*, p. 152.

53. It is interesting to note John Webster's adaptation of this saw: "To reprehend princes is dangerous: and to over-commend some of them is palpable lying" (*The White Devil* [1612], 5.3.67–68; ed. John Russell Brown [London: Methuen, 1960]). The ameliorations of "over-commend" and "some of them" suggest that in 1612 the saying still held true, for Webster anyway.

54. Daniel Javitch, "Poetry and Court Conduct: Puttenham's *Arte of English Poesie* in the Light of Castiglione's *Cortegiano*," *MLN* 87 (1972): 865–82. Arguments about Javitch and Puttenham similar to those I present here have been made independently by Louis Adrian Montrose in "Of Gentlemen and Shepherds: The Politics of Elizabethan Pastoral Form," *ELH* 50 (1983): 415–59, which appeared in print too late for me to use.

55. Javitch, *Poetry and Courtliness*, p. 120.

56. Javitch, "Poetry and Court Conduct," p. 881.

57. Ibid.

58. Ibid., p. 866.

59. For a similar consideration of deniability in Wyatt, see Stephen Greenblatt, *Renaissance Self-Fashioning, from More to Shakespeare* (Chicago: Univ. of Chicago Press, 1980), p. 121.

60. For a fascinating contemporary discussion comparing the pros and cons of life at court with those of ruling-class life at an outland administrative center, see Lawrence Stone, "Office under Queen Elizabeth: The Case of Lord Hunsdon and the Lord Chamberlainship in 1585," *Historical Journal* 10 (1967): 279–85.

61. K. J. Wilson, *Letters of Sir Thomas Elyot*, pp. xv, xvii, 47.

62. Ibid., p. 48; see also p. xvii.

63. Sir Walter Raleigh, *Maxims of State*, in *The Works of Sir Walter Raleigh, Kt.*, ed. Thomas Birch, 8 vols. (Oxford: Oxford Univ. Press, 1829), 8: 8–9.

64. *The Letters and Epigrams of Sir John Harington*, ed. Norman Egbert McClure (Philadelphia: Univ. of Pennsylvania Press, 1930), p. 80.

65. Ibid., p. 109.

66. Steven W. May, ed., *The Poems of Edward De Vere, Seventeenth Earl of Oxford, and of Robert Devereux, Second Earl of Essex, Studies in Philology*, 77, no. 5 (1980): 47. The poem is thought to have been sent to the queen from Ireland in 1599. See also Edward Doughtie, "The Earl of Essex and Occasions for Contemplative Verse," *English Literary Renaissance* 9 (1979): 355–63.

67. Nicolas, *Sir Christopher Hatton*, p. 282.

68. For a suggestive consideration of this formal device of self-embedding, or the kleinform, see Walter J. Ong, "Voice and Opening Closed Systems," in *Interfaces of the Word: Studies in the Evolution of Consciousness and Culture* (Ithaca, N.Y.: Cornell Univ. Press, 1977), pp. 319–20.

69. See Marcel Mauss, *The Gift*, trans. Ian Cunnison (1954; reprint ed., New York: Norton, 1967).

70. Burke, *Rhetoric of Motives*, p. 220.

71. *The Institucion of a Gentleman* (1555; reprinted., Norwood, N.J.: Walter J. Johnson, 1974). Subsequent references will appear in the text.

72. Henry Peacham, *The Compleat Gentleman* (1622; reprint ed., New York: Da Capo Press, 1968), p. 188.

73. *Sir Walter Raleigh's Instructions to his Son and to Posterity*, in *Works*, 8: 557. For an interesting consideration of the issues involved in this hard public attitude toward friendship and other such matters, see Agnes M. C. Latham, "Sir Walter Raleigh's *Instructions to his Son*," in *Elizabethan and Jacobean Studies Presented to Frank Percy Wilson in Honour of His Seventieth Birthday* (Oxford: Clarendon, 1959), pp. 199–218. It is, she thinks, a matter of "how to avoid making friends and being influenced by people" (p. 215).

74. Bacon, "Of Discourse," *Essays*, p. 103.

75. Under many other circumstances, of course, the gentleman and the

servant are one and the same. Elias quotes Jean du Peyrat, the translator of della Casa's *Galateo* into French, who in his introduction specifies the civil as well as the martial and erotic virtues required of the courtly knight: "There is, in addition, service at table before kings and princes, the manner of adjusting one's language toward people according to their rank and quality, their glances, gestures, and even the smallest signs or winks they might give" (*The History of Manners* [1939], [*The Civilizing Process*, vol. 1], trans. Edmund Jephcott [New York: Urizen, 1978], p. 216).

Chapter 5: Tropes of Personal Rivalry: Blame and Slander

1. Sir Thomas Elyot, *The Book named the Governor* (1531), ed. S. E. Lehmberg (New York: Dutton, Everyman, 1962). Subsequent references will appear in the text.

2. Baldassare Castiglione, *The Book of the Courtier* (1528), trans. Sir Thomas Hoby (1561; reprint ed., New York: Dutton, Everyman, 1966); cited with *Il libro del cortegiano con una scelta delle opere minori*, 2d ed., ed. Bruno Maier (Turin: Unione Tipografico-Editrice Torinese, 1964). Subsequent references to these editions will appear in the text.

3. Francis Bacon, "Of Honour and Reputation," *Essays* (1625; reprint ed., New York: Everyman's Library, 1906), p. 160.

4. *The Civile Conversation of M. Steeven Guazzo* (1574), trans. George Pettie (Books 1–3, 1581) and Bartholomew Young (Book 4, 1586), the Tudor Translations, 2 vols. (London: Constable, 1925). Subsequent references will appear in the text, noted by citing the physical volumes (1–2) of this edition rather than the work's internal books (1–4).

5. George Puttenham, *The Arte of English Poesie* (1589), ed. Gladys Doidge Willcock and Alice Walker (Cambridge: At the University Press, 1936). Subsequent references will appear in the text.

6. There may be an omission of some sort in Puttenham's text at this point; how it would affect what is present we cannot tell. See my "A Lacuna in Puttenham's *Arte of English Poesie*," in *English Language Notes*, in press (Fall 1984).

7. Jonson knows this type. *Epicoene*'s Jack Daw "will not be out, at the best friends hee has, to the talent of his wit" (*Ben Jonson*, ed. C. H. Herford, Percy Simpson, and Evelyn Simpson, 11 vols. [Oxford: Clarendon, 1925–52], 5: 191, 2.4.112–13). Earlier, Jonson had jokingly so described himself, as Horace in *Poetaster*, who "wil sooner lose his best friend, then his least iest" (*Ben Jonson* 4: 269, 4.3.110–11). For Drummond in 1619 the description was no joke: he described Jonson as "a great lover and praiser of himself, a contemner and Scorner of others, given rather to losse a friend, than a Jest" (*Ben Jonson* 1:151, "Ben Jonson's Conversations with William Drummond of Hawthornden," lines 680–81).

8. I will not wade far into the murky waters of legal history, but the follow-

ing points may be summarized to establish the context. The offense of defamation was tried during the Middle Ages by ecclesiastical courts, "*pro custodia morum* of the community and *pro salute animae* of the delinquent" (Van Vechten Veeder, "The History and Theory of the Law of Defamation," *Columbia Law Review* 3 [1903]: 551). With the Reformation such problems passed largely to the secular courts; "during the reigns of Elizabeth, James I, and Charles I, the reports teem with such cases, and the bulk of litigation in defamation at once assumed very large proportions" (Veeder, "Law of Defamation," p. 557.) The state's attempt to suppress the increasingly common habit of dueling was also a major factor in this increase, according to R. C. Donnelly ("The History of Defamation," *Wisconsin Law Review*, 1949, p. 113). But the law as illogically evolved (a matter of exasperation for legal historians) addressed only certain accusations: of having committed an indictable crime; of having syphilis, leprosy, or the plague (but not similar communicable diseases such as smallpox); of demonstrating incompetence or inadequacy in one's office or trade; or of performing an act that had already resulted in some special damage, usually financial (Veeder, "Law of Defamation," p. 558). There was also the criminal offense of *scandalum magnatum* : casting aspersion upon the reputation of a magnate, tending to arouse civil unrest. In 1606 one Roughton was found guilty of slandering the earl of Lincoln with this statement: "My lord is a base earl, and a paltry lord, and keepeth none but rogues and rascals like himself." These words were held either to raise contempt between the earl and the people or to arouse the king's indignation against him (Donnelly, "History of Defamation," p. 109; see also Veeder, "Law of Defamation," pp. 553–54). In 1609 Sir Edward Coke laid the foundations of the modern libel law (a distinction hitherto unobserved in England) with an adaptation of the Roman legal concept of *libellus famosus*, a principle designed to be invoked against anonymous (and scurrilous or seditious) pasquinades and epigrams. The actionability depended for the first time upon the mere form of the defamation, as written. Here, as with scandalum magnatum, the offense was seen to rest in the danger of a breach of the peace, supposedly amplified by the agency of print (Veeder, "Law of Defamation," pp. 563–73).

In such a context it is clear that the relation between slander and truth must be obscure. Fowler V. Harper and Fleming James, Jr. observe that "the origin and development of the rule that 'truth' is a defense to a civil action for defamation are shrouded in considerable mystery" (in *The Law of Torts* [Boston: Little, Brown, 1956], p. 415). In criminal actions (based on scandalum magnatum and libellus famosus), in fact, a common dictum was "the greater the truth, the greater the libel," when sedition might be amplified by truthfulness. Not until the nineteenth century, it seems, did our more modern sense of truth as a complete defense for civil slander become firmly established (Harper and James, *Law of Torts*, p. 415).

9. If I understand him rightly, Stephen Greenblatt offers a related sense of

the derivative nature of excess in his treatment of Guyon's destruction of the Bower of Bliss. In each case, excess derives not from transcendental categories but from political interaction—the attempt to limit or control. See *Renaissance Self-Fashioning, from More to Shakespeare* (Chicago: Univ. of Chicago Press, 1980), p. 177.

10. Virgil, *Aeneid*, trans. H. Rushton Fairclough, Loeb Classical Library (Cambridge, Mass.: Harvard Univ. Press, 1947), 1:423–37.

11. Virgil, *Georgics*, trans. H. Rushton Fairclough, Loeb Classical Library (Cambridge, Mass.: Harvard Univ. Press, 1947), 4:88–101. The parallels with Hal and Falstaff are striking.

12. Pliny, *Natural History*, trans. Harris Rackham, Loeb Classical Library (Cambridge, Mass.: Harvard Univ. Press, 1940), bk. 11, x.25, xxi.67. See also D. T. Starnes, "Shakespeare and Elyot's *Governour*," *University of Texas Studies in English* 7 (1927): 112–32.

13. The Georgic opposition between the noble captains gleaming bright and the ignoble broad paunch irresistibly recalls Falstaff, another case of muted fratricide, or rather parricide: "Let the nobler reign in the palace alone." For an argument concerning the use of bee lore to present Hal's displacement of his *biological* father, see R. P. Corballis, "'Buzz, Buzz': Bee-Lore in *2 Henry IV*," *Notes and Queries* 226 (1981): 127–28.

14. Thomas Wilson, *The Arte of Rhetorique* (1560), ed. G. H. Mair (Oxford: Clarendon, 1909), the preface, sig. A7v.

15. The extent of her investment can be estimated by reviewing the catalog of the queen's enormous wardrobe, made in 1600 and preserved by John Nichols in his *Progresses and Public Processions of Queen Elizabeth* (1823; reprint ed., New York: Burt Franklin, n.d.), 3:500–12. G. P. V. Akrigg reports the assertion of the weird if not mentally unstable Charles, Lord Stanhope, that the staggering sum of £60,000 was realized from the sale of her wardrobe after her death (see Akrigg, "The Curious Marginalia of Charles, Second Lord Stanhope," in *Joseph Quincy Adams Memorial Studies* [Washington, D.C.: Folger Shakespeare Library, 1948], p. 794). See also Greenblatt, *Renaissance Self-Fashioning*, pp. 28–29.

16. *The Institucion of a Gentleman* (1555; reprint ed., Norwood, N.J.: Walter J. Johnson, 1974). Subsequent references will appear in the text.

17. See Lawrence Stone, *The Crisis of the Aristocracy, 1558–1641* (Oxford: Clarendon, 1965), p. 562. The issuers of proclamations tried to keep up with the fluctuations in style by adding new details, according to Frederic A. Youngs, *The Proclamations of the Tudor Queens* (Cambridge: At the University Press, 1976), p. 162. And plans were made to supervise the producers directly. A proclamation of 1562 specified that "the Mayor of London, and all other officers in their jurisdictions and liberties, [are] to make or cause to be made search once within every eight days in every hosier's house to see what kind of hose they shall make" (from Paul L. Hughes and James F. Larkin, eds., *Tudor Royal Proclamations*, 3 vols. [New Haven: Yale Univ. Press, 1969], Proclama-

tion 493, 2:190). Anyone providing information as to the breaking of this proclamation's rules was "to enjoy, if the party be convicted, such part of the penalty as by the said law is appointed" (p. 189). A problem with fraudulent informing can be seen to have arisen within four years of its issuance. Proclamation 542 (1566) adjured informers "to observe the contents of these orders and not to abuse the meaning thereof with any fraud" (2:283).

18. From Mary Ellen Rickey and Thomas B. Stroup, eds., *Certaine Sermons or Homilies, Appointed to be Read in Churches in the Time of Queen Elizabeth I (1547–1571): A Facsimile Reproduction of the Edition of 1623* (Gainesville, Fla.: Scholars' Facsimiles & Reprints, 1968), p. 102.

19. Hughes and Larkin, *Tudor Royal Proclamations*, Proclamation 542 (1566), 2:281.

20. Proclamation 646 (1580) explicitly recognized this problem of invention: "If any person shall in contempt and defrauding of this proclamation devise any new kind or form of apparel, and for garnishing thereof, and thereby shall be at greater charge than appertaineth to his degree and quality, as is here above mentioned and intended: then the said person [is] to sustain the like punishment for his contempt as if the said garment or garnishing had been especially prohibited" (ibid., 2:460).

21. William Camden, *Remains Concerning Britain* (1605; reprint ed., East Ardsley, England: EP Publishing, 1974), pp. 219–20.

22. Edmund Spenser, *A View of the Present State of Ireland* (1598), ed. W. L. Renwick (Oxford: Clarendon, 1970), pp. 69–70. Renwick notes that the passage Spenser cites is not in Aristotle but compares Herodotus, 1:158.

23. Count Annibale Romei, *The Courtiers Academie* (1585), trans. I. Kepers (1598; reprint ed., New York: Da Capo Press, 1969). Subsequent references will appear in the text.

24. Hughes and Larkin, *Tudor Royal Proclamations*, Proclamation 493 (1562), 2:187–89.

25. Ibid., Proclamation 601 (1574), 2:382–83.

26. Ibid., Proclamation 646 (1580), 2:454.

27. It seems possible that as one moves down the orders of enforcement, the influence of puritan social thought grows. This would mean that the higher-level governors at court would more likely be offenders, and the lower-level governors in the country would more likely be offended. If this was the case, then the mutual animosity between the libertarian court and the radical puritans would in part be articulated symbolically by the sumptuary issue. The court-city hostilities would also figure in this equation. Internal divisions between various sectors of the governing elite were nowhere more complex than where they entailed religious differences.

28. Frances Elizabeth Baldwin, "Sumptuary Legislation and Personal Regulation in England, "*Johns Hopkins University Studies in Historical and Political Science*, 44, no. 1 (1926): 1–282.

29. Ibid., p. 159.

30. Ibid., pp. 167–68.

31. Wilfrid Hooper, "The Tudor Sumptuary Laws," *English Historical Review* 30 (1915): 441–42. Ostentation with regard to food might be related to the perquisites of servants. I. M., the author of *A Health to the Gentlemanly Profession of Serving-Men* (1598; reprint ed., London: Oxford Univ. Press, 1931) suggests that cutting corners on food not only undermines hospitality but also deprives the servant of his right: "Now, yf they haue but two or three dyshes, What should they neede so many Attendantes: So wanting seruice wherein to imploy them, there they cut off an other charge: this affoordes them a doble benefite, it cuts off the charge of Men, and many Dyshes . . . yet what shall answere the hungrie appetites of the attendantes that hath long fasted in hope of this reuertion?" (sig. H1r).
A similar inversion of the effects of sumptuous behavior may be noted at this point. I. M. also objects to the technological advance of the closed coach:

> Yf their Mistres ryde abrode, she must have vi or viii Servingmen to attende her, she must haue one to carrie her Cloake and Hood, least it raine, an other her Fanne, if she vse it not her selfe, an other her Boxe with Ruffes and other necessaries, an other behinde whom her Mayde or Gentlewoman must ryde, and some must be loose to open Gates, and supply other seruices that may be occasioned. Now to deminish and cut of this charge, aswell of Horse as Men, there is now a new inuention, and that is, she must haue a Coach, wherein she, with her Gentlewomen, Mayde, and Chyldren, and what necessaries as they or any of them are to vse, may be caryed and conueyed with smaller charge, lesse cost, and more credite, as it is accompted: for one or two Men at the most, besides the Coachman, are sufficient for a Gentlewoman or Lady of worthy parentage. (Sig. H1r–v)

Here, as everywhere in his text, the author perceives elite ostentation as creating a niche of employment and decries the newfangled modes, which discard the numerous human services required by the older modes. But in fact his aim is to widen the exclusive niche just enough to contain gentle servants, while still keeping the requirements rigorous enough to filter out ungentle upstarts. I. M.'s lament is in the end conservative, although he calls for wider dispersion of material benefits; his status as a functionary affiliate, the gentle servant, explains this apparent anomaly. I. M. wants the benefits spread only somewhat more widely; the door is briefly opened, then slammed in the face of the "vnciuill sottes [who] gape after . . . wealth, worth, credite, and preferment" (sigs. E4v–F1r). It is the ambitious artisan or peasant who is continually the villain in I. M.'s tract.

32. See G. R. Elton, *Reform and Reformation: England, 1509–1558* (Cambridge, Mass.: Harvard Univ. Press, 1977), p. 227.

33. Hooper, "Tudor Sumptuary Laws," p. 436.

34. Hughes and Larkin, *Tudor Royal Proclamations*, Proclamation 464 (1559), 2:136.

35. Ibid., Proclamation 601 (1574), 2:381.

36. Ibid., Proclamation 786 (1597), 3:175.

37. *The Statutes of the Realm, from Magna Carta to the End of the Reign of Queen Anne*, 11 vols. (London, 1810–28), 3:430 (abbreviations expanded).

38. Youngs notes (*Proclamations of the Tudor Queens*, p. 161) that Hughes and Larkin mistakenly label as Proclamation 495 an official summary of a statute, and so come up with the incorrect total of ten proclamations for the reign, the figure to which Stone alludes in *Crisis of the Aristocracy*, p. 29.

39. Baldwin, "Sumptuary Legislation," p. 150.

40. Ibid., p. 154.

41. Youngs, *Proclamations of the Tudor Queens*, p. 178.

42. Ibid., p. 162.

43. Ibid., p. 177.

44. Baldwin, "Sumptuary Legislation," p. 220.

45. Youngs, *Proclamations of the Tudor Queens*, p. 177.

46. Baldwin, "Sumptuary Legislation," p. 249. Statutes dealing obliquely with sumptuary prohibitions were passed in 1563, 1566, and 1571, but each of these had primary reference to the economic protection of English industry (the traditional goal of such legislation)—either by restricting to the upper classes the purchase of such luxury imports as velvet caps or by requiring the wearing of English woolen caps on Sundays by all except the elite (ibid., pp. 207–12). The 1571 statute was the last such law passed in the reign of Elizabeth (ibid., p. 213).

47. Joan Kent, "Attitudes of Members of the House of Commons to the Regulation of 'Personal Conduct' in Late Elizabethan and Early Stuart England," *Bulletin of the Institute of Historical Research*, 46, no. 113 (1973): 62.

48. Youngs, *Proclamations of the Tudor Queens*, p. 166.

49. Quoted in Conyers Read, *Lord Burghley and Queen Elizabeth* (1960; reprint ed., London: Jonathan Cape, 1965), pp. 528–29.

50. Hughes and Larkin, *Tudor Royal Proclamations*, Proclamation 493 (1562), 2:187. See also Kent, "Attitudes of Members of the House of Commons," pp. 48–49.

51. Youngs, *Proclamations of the Tudor Queens*, p. 167.

52. Quoted by Hooper ("Tudor Sumptuary Laws," p. 441) from City Corporation Records, Repertorium 15, fol. 414b.

53. Hughes and Larkin, *Tudor Royal Proclamations*, Proclamation 493 (1562), 2:188.

54. Quoted by Baldwin ("Sumptuary Legislation," pp. 237–38) from Court Leet Records (Southampton), 1:161, par. 98.

55. Hughes and Larkin, *Tudor Royal Proclamations,* Proclamation 601 (1574), 2:381.

56. It is fascinating to compare John Berger's analysis of the workings of advertising publicity with this Elizabethan function.

> Publicity is effective precisely because it feeds upon the real. Clothes, food, cars, cosmetics, baths, sunshine are real things to be enjoyed in themselves. Publicity begins by working on a natural appetite for pleasure. But it cannot offer the real object of pleasure and there is no convincing substitute for a pleasure in that pleasure's own terms. The more convincingly publicity conveys the pleasure of bathing in a warm, distant sea, the more the spectator-buyer will become aware that he is hundreds of miles away from that sea and the more remote the chance of bathing in it will seem to him. This is why publicity can never really afford to be about the product or opportunity it is proposing to the buyer who is not yet enjoying it. Publicity is never a celebration of a pleasure-in-itself. Publicity is always about the future buyer. It offers him an image of himself made glamorous by the product or opportunity it is trying to sell. The image then makes him envious of himself as he might be. Yet what makes this self-which-he-might-be enviable? The envy of others. Publicity is about social relations, not objects. Its promise is not of pleasure, but of happiness: happiness as judged from the outside by others. The happiness of being envied is glamour.
>
> Being envied is a solitary form of reassurance. It depends precisely upon not sharing your experience with those who envy you. You are observed with interest but you do not observe with interest—if you do, you will become less enviable. In this respect the envied are like bureaucrats; the more impersonal they are, the greater the illusion (for themselves and for others) of their power. The power of the glamorous resides in their supposed happiness: the power of the bureaucrat in his supposed authority. It is this which explains the absent, unfocused look of so many glamour images. They look out *over* the looks of envy which sustain them. (*Ways of Seeing* [London: British Broadcasting Corporation and Penguin Books, 1972], pp. 132–33)

The process that Berger describes results from the long revolution of social patterns away from ascription toward achievement; the way in which the sumptuary schedules may have aroused envy eventually led to actions designed to get the rewards detailed in the schedules. The relation between the sumptuary schedules and the advertising Berger writes about is that between what one (supposedly) *cannot* have and what one *does not* have but can buy; between denial that flatters the denier and intentional temptation.

Such descriptions can also repel, of course. Francis M. Kelly describes a remarkable caricature of Queen Elizabeth as a gaudy turkeycock in her "flaunting ruff," in "Queen Elizabeth and Her Dresses," *The Connoisseur* 113 (1944): 78–79.

57. Roger Ascham, *The Scholemaster* (1570), in *English Works*, ed. William Aldis Wright (1904; reprint ed., Cambridge: At the University Press, 1970). Subsequent references will appear in the text.

58. See Youngs, *Proclamations of the Tudor Queens*, pp. 168, 177.

59. Kent, "Attitudes of Members of the House of Commons," p. 52. This remark comes from a debate about the enforcement of rules for church attendance, but Kent presents the argument in parallel with arguments about apparel.

60. Ibid.

61. Hooper, "Tudor Sumptuary Laws," p. 437 (referring to a letter in the City Corporation Records, Journal 17, fol. 168, 8 November 1559: "Letter of the Privy Council of this date read and considered and commons exhorted to observe the same").

62. Kent, "Attitudes of Members of the House of Commons," p. 54.

63. Ibid., p. 56.

64. The full circumstances of this repeal are confusing. Again, the dangers of lawmaking by royal fiat were certainly feared, but a new view of sumptuary regulation seems also to have been influential. See Hooper, "Tudor Sumptuary Laws," pp. 448–49; Kent, "Attitudes of Members of the House of Commons," pp. 56–57.

65. Baldwin, "Sumptuary Legislation," p. 249. For later interventions in the sumptuary behavior of men at the Inns of Court, see Wilfrid Prest, *The Inns of Court under Elizabeth I and the Early Stuarts 1590–1640* (London: Longman, 1972), pp. 93–94, 101–14.

66. Bacon, "Of Followers and Friends," *Essays*, p. 146.

67. Torquato Tasso, *Aminta* (1573), trans. Henry Reynolds (1628), as *Torquato Tasso's Aminta Englisht. To this is added Ariadne's Complaint in imitation of Anguillara; written by the translator of Tasso's Aminta*; first chorus reprinted in Frank Kermode, ed., *English Pastoral Poetry, from the Beginnings to Marvell* (1952; reprint ed., New York: Norton, 1972), pp. 82–83.

68. Ibid., p. 81.

69. Barnabe Googe, "Egloga Tertia," in *Eglogs, Epytaphes, & Sonettes* (1563), ed. Edward Arber, English Reprints (London, 1871), pp. 39, 41. This poem contains religious criticism of the Marian regime, but the social issue of the association of wit with social mobility remains pertinent, whatever the doctrinal historicity of the poem. Googe's affiliations with the up-and-coming Cecil do not, of course, preclude occasional alienation, especially in poetry.

70. Timothy Cook has offered a topical explanation for this curiosity, in "Who Were Barnabe Googe's Two Coridons?" *Notes and Queries* 222 (1977): 497–99. He argues that Googe is "making acquaintances of his speak under assumed names, as Spenser did later, and that he is telling us

that the persecutor has the same surname as one of these acquaintances" (p. 498). The Coridons then turn out probably to be Barnabe Rich and Richard Rich, the latter lord chancellor of England from 1548 to 1551 and a major persecutor of Protestants (a subject to which the poem makes clear allusion). My interest in the poem presumes a thematic emphasis on the name-sharing (rather than historical allegory) and focuses on the complex of wit and carterly social mobility, seen from the position of the traditional conservative, in the vocabulary of the mobile. Cook treats such elements of this matrix as he considers in a chiefly denotative sense; I focus on their connotations. He considers the name-sharing to be biographically determined; I see it as a constituent of a text, the tensions of which are not exhausted by his topical equations. The issues of evil intelligence and education are not touched by the identification, nor are the ambivalent views of rural origins (shepherds and clowns). From these issues arise the tensions I note. Perhaps a partial accommodation can be achieved by noting the first-name link between Googe and Rich the poet, whereby the latter might substitute for the former, but this leaves untouched the gap between Cook's sense of the country Coridon's clear rejection of his governor-cousin, and my sense of his ambivalence.

For further discussion of the topical reference, see William E. Sheidley, *Barnabe Googe* (Boston: Twayne, 1981), pp. 76–78; and J. D. Alsop, "The Dramatis Personae in Barnabe Googe's Critique of the Marian Persecution," *Notes and Queries* 226 (1981): 512–16.

71. Bacon, "Of Ambition," *Essays*, p. 113.

72. Steven W. May, ed., *The Poems of Edward De Vere, Seventeenth Earl of Oxford, and of Robert Devereux, Second Earl of Essex, Studies in Philology*, 77, no. 5 (1980): 31.

73. Bacon, "Of Envy," *Essays*, p. 25.

74. Ibid., p. 26.

75. Ibid., p. 28.

76. Ibid., pp. 24–25. The quotation is adapted from Plautus, *Stichus* (trans. Paul Nixon, Loeb Classical Library [London: Heinemann, 1960], vol. 5), 1.3. 208.

77. Francesco Guicciardini, *Maxims and Reflections* [Ricordi], trans. Mario Domandi (Philadelphia: Univ. of Pennsylvania Press, 1965). Subsequent references will appear in the text, identified by series and item number.

78. J. B. Leishman, ed., *The Three Parnassus Plays (1598–1601)* (London: Ivor Nicholson & Watson, 1949). Subsequent references will appear in the text.

79. See Edmund Spenser, *Poetical Works*, ed. J. C. Smith and E. de Selincourt, Oxford Standard Authors Series (Oxford: Oxford Univ. Press, 1912), pp. 625–26.

80. Ascham also distinguished between travel in Italy and travel elsewhere on the Continent. The first version of *The Scholemaster* (written in 1563–64) contained a passage, later omitted, in praise of travel elsewhere than in Italy. See George B. Parks, "The First Draft of Ascham's *Scholemaster*," *Hunting-*

ton Library Quarterly 1 (1938): 324. Walter F. Staton has pointed out an early letter of Ascham (dated 1544) in which he explicitly dreams of professional work in foreign diplomacy. The letter is translated by Staton from the Latin in the Giles edition of Ascham's *Works*, 1: 45: "If you would ask the business of my life . . . I would reply the knowledge of the word of God, accompanied by the reading as of an aid or ancilla thereto of Plato, Aristotle, and Cicero . . . But in truth if the choice were given me and permission granted by my Lord of York . . . nothing would I wish more than that I might for a few years accompany some nobleman who should be sent by the King's Majesty to foreign nations . . . You perchance will judge this foolish and like some childish dream; but be that as it may, I would like your assistance if it becomes a definite possibility" (Staton's "Roger Ascham's Theory of History Writing," *Studies in Philology* 56 [1959]: 127). Perhaps Ascham's experiences while traveling on the Continent in the early 1550s altered this open attitude; certainly the reign of Mary must have amplified the hostility to papistry later recorded in the *Scholemaster*.

81. George B. Parks, "The First Italianate Englishmen," *Studies in the Renaissance* 8 (1961): 199.

82. Ibid., pp. 198–99, 211–12. A converse kind of evidence can be seen in the statement in William Thomas's *Historie of Italie* (1549) that the Italians can be commended, "that they woull not lightlye meddle with other mennes mattiers" (fol. 4v, quoted by Parks, p. 205.) The typifying element of the "meddling mind" had not yet been soldered to the Italianate mentality.

83. See Martin Luther, *Luther's Works*, ed. and trans. Theodore G. Tappert, gen. ed. Helmut T. Lehman, 54 vols. (Philadelphia: Fortress Press, 1967), 54: 310.

84. It is suggestive of courtly and political applications that the English study of the Italian language, and of the texts of *The Prince* and *The Book of the Courtier*, first received attention in the circle of Cromwell, Edmund Bonner, and Elyot. See Pearl Hogrefe, "Elyot and 'The Boke Called Cortegiano in Ytalion,'" *Modern Philology* 27 (1930): 303–9; and George B. Parks, "The Genesis of Tudor Interest in Italian," *PMLA* 77 (1962): 529–35.

85. Most of this material regarding quick wits and hard wits was a late addition, after the draft of 1563–64, according to Parks ("First Draft," p. 317). The entire section on Italy was much revised (p. 316). For a discussion of the influence of Quintilian on the section, see Lawrence V. Ryan, *Roger Ascham* (Stanford: Stanford Univ. Press, 1963), p. 265. I have not been concerned with issues of source and originality such as this, or Cicero's influence on Castiglione; my concern throughout has been with Elizabethan consumption and application.

86. *The Letter-Book of Gabriel Harvey, A.D. 1573–1580*, ed. E. J. L. Scott (London: Camden Society Publications, 1884), p. 78; see also Mark H. Curtis, *Oxford and Cambridge in Transition, 1558–1642* (Oxford: Clarendon, 1959), pp. 126–48.

87. It is worth noting that in his first draft, Ascham had explicitly excepted his queen from submission to this environment: "She from hir cradle, brought vp among all courtlye pleasures, hath led hir life, as litle subiect to the vayne delites of eye & eare, as ever wer Balnea Dianae in the vale of the hill Parnassus; so, that not onlie, she may be an example of learnynge to all ientlemen, but a Mistres of womanhod to all wemen, & a mirrour of cumlie & orderlie Lyving to all her court" (Parks, "First Draft," p. 323). Perhaps Ascham felt that even the argument of exception was unwise, in that it brought the queen too close to the negative environment. Daniel Javitch suggests that those who criticize the court often simultaneously laud the queen and her courtiers, revealing "a persistent Elizabethan belief in the myth of perfect courtliness" (*Poetry and Courtliness in Renaissance England* (Princeton: Princeton Univ. Press, 1978), p. 119). In my view, this simultaneity suggests rather the conviction that it was unhealthy not to exclude the queen and her (usually unnamed) inner circle from general criticism of the evil ones at court.

88. Javitch has noted this tension in *Poetry and Courtliness* (p. 122).

89. Sir Humphrey Gilbert, *Queene Elizabethes Achademy* (after 1562), Early English Text Society Extra Series 8 (London: Trubner, 1869), p. 12. The use of the trope of education invites the assumption of courtly metamorphosis rather than purging. Thomas Blundeville writes to the same effect in *Of Councils and Counselors* (1570), his translation of Federico Furio Ceriol's *El consejo i consejeros del principe* (1550):

> If the Prince delight in wise, learned, and vertuous counselers, mine Author sayth, that he dare aduenture his heade that a number of Barrons and Knightes in fewe yeres, woulde become most sufficient counselers. And for proofe thereof, wisheth that some Prince would put these his preceptes in vre, not doubting, but that in so doing, hee should quickly see such an alteration in his Courte, as those that doe now leawdely spende their tyme in ydleness, vayne pastymes, and in wantonnesse of life, would giue themselues to lawdable exercises, and therby make the Court to become a schoole of vertue, and knowledge. Which should be to the great honour of the Prince, to the profite of the common wealth, and to the glorye of God. (Sigs. Q3v–4r)

(See the Scholars' Facsimiles & Reprints text, ed. Karl-Ludwig Selig [Gainesville, Florida, 1963], pp. 138–39.)

90. Parks, "First Draft," p. 324.

91. Erving Goffman, *Relations in Public: Microstudies of the Public Order* (New York: Harper & Row, 1971), p. 64.

92. Giovanni della Casa, *Galateo* (1558), trans. R. S. Pine-Coffin (Harmondsworth: Penguin Books, 1958), p. 32; *Opere di Baldassare Castiglione, Giovanni della Casa, Benvenuto Cellini*, ed. Carlo Cordie (Milan and Naples: Ricciardi, 1960), p. 377.

Afterword

1. Kenneth Burke, *A Rhetoric of Motives* (1950; reprint ed., Berkeley and Los Angeles: Univ. of California Press, 1969), p. xiv.

2. Pierre Bourdieu, *Outline of a Theory of Practice* (1972), trans. Richard Nice (Cambridge: At the University Press, 1977), p. 94.

3. Burke, *Rhetoric of Motives*, p. 71.

4. Bourdieu, *Outline of a Theory of Practice*, p. 114.

Bibliography

Primary Sources

Aquinas, St. Thomas. *Summa Theologica*. From *Opera Omnia*. 25 vols. New York: Musurgia, 1948.

Aristotle. *Rhetoric*. Translated by W. Rhys Roberts. New York: Modern Library, 1954.

Ascham, Roger. *The Scholemaster*. 1570. In *English Works*. Edited by William Aldis Wright. 1904. Reprint. Cambridge: At the University Press, 1970.

St. Augustine. *On Christian Doctrine*. Translated by D. W. Robertson. Indianapolis: Bobbs-Merrill, 1958.

Bacon, Francis. *Essays*. 1625. Reprint. New York: Everyman's Library, 1906.

———. *The Works of Francis Bacon*. Edited by James Spedding, Robert Leslie Ellis, and Douglas Denon Heath. 15 vols. New York: Hurd and Houghton, 1869.

Bacon, Nicholas. *Articles devised for the bringinge up in vertue and lerninge of the Queenes Majesties wardes beinge heires Males*. After 1561. In John Payne Collier, "One Sir Nicholas Bacon, Lord Keeper; with extracts from some of his unprinted papers and speeches." *Archaeologia* 36 (1855): 339–48.

Bandello, Matteo. *Tutte le opere di Matteo Bandello*. Edited by Francesco Flora. Milan: A. Mondadori, 1934–35.

Beaumont, Francis, and John Fletcher. *Philaster*. 1609. Edited by Andrew Gurr. The Revels Plays. London: Methuen, 1969.

Blundeville, Thomas. *Of Councils and Counselors*. 1570. (A translation of Federico Furio Ceriol's *El consejo i consejeros del principe* [1550].) Edited by Karl-Ludwig Selig. Gainesville, Fla.: Scholars' Facsimiles & Reprints, 1963.

———. *The True Order and Methode of Wryting and Reading Hystories*. 1574. Reprint. Norwood, N.J.: Walter J. Johnson, 1979.

Bodin, Jean. *The Six Bookes of a Commonweale*. 1576 in French, 1586 in Bodin's Latin. Translated by Richard Knolles (from both versions). 1606. Reprint. Cambridge, Mass.: Harvard Univ. Press, 1962.

Camden, William. *The History of the Most Renowned and Victorious Princess Elizabeth, Late Queen of England.* Edited by Wallace MacCaffrey. Chicago: Univ. of Chicago Press, 1970. Selected chapters.

———. *Poems by William Camden.* Edited by George Burke Johnson. *Studies in Philology,* 72, no. 5 (1975).

———. *Remains Concerning Britain.* 1605. Reprint. East Ardsley, England: EP Publishing, 1974.

Castiglione, Baldassare. *Il libro del cortegiano con una scelta delle opere minori.* Edited by Bruno Maier. 2d. ed. Turin: Unione Tipografico-Editrice Torinese, 1964.

———. *The Book of the Courtier.* 1528. Translated by Sir Thomas Hoby. 1561. Reprint. New York: Dutton, Everyman, 1966.

Cicero. *Cicero on Oratory and Orators.* Translated by J. S. Watson. Carbondale: Southern Illinois Univ. Press, 1970.

Daniel, Samuel. *Delia.* 1592. In *Poems and a Defence of Ryme.* Edited by A. C. Sprague. 1930. Reprint. Chicago: Univ. of Chicago Press, 1965.

Dekker, Thomas. *The Guls Horn-Booke: or, Fashions to please all sorts of Guls.* 1609. In *Non-Dramatic Works.* Edited by A. B. Grosart. 1885. Reprint. New York: Russell & Russell, 1963.

della Casa, Giovanni. *Galateo.* 1558. In *Opere di Baldassare Castiglione, Giovanni della Casa, Benvenuto Cellini.* Edited by Carlo Cordie. Milan and Naples: Ricciardi, 1960.

———. *Galateo.* Translated by R. S. Pine-Coffin. Harmondsworth: Penguin Books, 1958.

Donne, John. *The Complete English Poems.* Edited by A. J. Smith. Harmondsworth: Penguin Books, 1973.

Drayton, Michael. *The Works of Michael Drayton.* Edited by J. William Hebel et al. 5 vols. 1931. Reprint. London: Basil Blackwell, 1961.

Elyot, Sir Thomas. *The Book named the Governor.* 1531. Edited by S. E. Lehmberg. New York: Dutton, Everyman, 1962.

———. *The Letters of Sir Thomas Elyot.* Edited by K. J. Wilson. *Studies in Philology,* 73, no. 5 (1976).

Ferne, John. *The Blazon of Gentrie.* 1586. Reprint. New York: Da Capo Press, 1973.

Gainsford, Thomas. *The Secretaries Studie.* 1616. Reprint. Norwood, N.J.: Walter J. Johnson, 1974.

Gascoigne, George. *A Hundreth Sundrie Flowres.* 1573. Edited by B. M. Ward. London: Etchells and Macdonald, 1926.

———. *A Hundreth Sundrie Flowres.* 1573. Edited by C. T. Prouty. University of Missouri Studies, vol. 17, no. 2. Columbia: Univ. of Missouri Press, 1942.

———. *Complete Works.* Edited by J. W. Cunliffe. 2 vols. 1907. Reprint. New York: Greenwood Press, 1969.

Gilbert, Sir Humphrey. *Queene Elizabethes Achademy.* After 1562. Early English Text Society Extra Series 8. Reprint. London: Trubner, 1869.

Giovio, Paolo. *The Worthy Tract of Paulus Iovius.* 1585. Reprint. Translated by Samuel Daniel, together with Giovio's *Dialogo dell 'Imprese et Amorose.* Intro. Norman K. Farmer, Jr. Delmar, N.Y.: Scholars' Facsimiles & Reprints, 1976.

Googe, Barnabe. *Eglogs, Epytaphes, & Sonettes.* 1563. Edited by Edward Arber. English Reprints. London, 1871.

Greville, Fulke, Lord Brooke. *The Life of the Renowned Sr. Philip Sidney.* In *The Works in Verse and Prose Complete of the Right Honourable Fulke Greville, Lord Brooke,* edited by A.B. Grosart. 4 vols. 1870. Reprint. New York: AMS Press, 1966.

Guazzo, Stefano. *La civile conversatione del Sig. Stefano Guazzo.* Vinegia, 1575.

———. *The Civile Conversation of M. Steeven Guazzo.* 1574. Translated by George Pettie (Books 1–3, 1581) and Bartholomew Young (Book 4, 1586). The Tudor Translations. 2 vols. London: Constable, 1925.

Guicciardini, Francesco. *Maxims and Reflections [Ricordi].* Translated by Mario Domandi. Philadelphia: Univ. of Pennsylvania Press, 1965.

Harington, Sir John. *The Letters and Epigrams of Sir John Harington.* Edited by Norman Egbert McClure. Philadelphia: Univ. of Pennsylvania Press, 1930.

Harrison, William. *The Description of England.* 1577, 1587. Edited by Georges Edelen. Folger Documents of Tudor and Stuart Civilization. Ithaca, N.Y.: Cornell Univ. Press, 1968.

Harvey, Gabriel. *The Letter-Book of Gabriel Harvey, A.D. 1573–1580.* Edited by E.J.L. Scott. London: Camden Society Publications, 1884.

———. *Gabriel Harvey's Marginalia.* Compiled and edited by G.C. Moore-Smith. Stratford-upon-Avon: Shakespeare Head Press, 1913.

———. *Works.* Edited by A.B. Grosart. 3 vols. 1884. Reprint. New York: AMS Press, 1966.

Holles, Gervase. *Memorials of the Holles Family, 1493–1656.* Edited by A.C. Wood. Camden Society, 3d. series, vol. 55. London: Camden Society Publications, 1937.

Hughes, Paul L., and James F. Larkin, eds. *Tudor Royal Proclamations.* 3 vols. New Haven: Yale Univ. Press, 1969.

The Institucion of a Gentleman. 1555. Reprint. Norwood, N.J.: Walter J. Johnson, 1974.

Jonson, Ben. *Ben Jonson.* Edited by C.H. Herford, Percy Simpson, and Evelyn Simpson. 11 vols. Oxford: Clarendon, 1925–52.

Leishman, J.B., ed. *The Three Parnassus Plays (1598–1601).* London: Ivor Nicholson & Watson, 1949.

The Lisle Letters. Edited by Muriel St. Clare Byrne. 6 vols. Chicago: Univ. of Chicago Press, 1981.

Luther, Martin. *Luther's Works*. Edited and translated by Theodore G. Tappert, gen. ed. Helmut T. Lehman. 54 vols. Philadelphia: Fortress Press, 1967.

M., I. *A Health to the Gentlemanly Profession of Serving-Men*. 1598. Reprint. London: Oxford Univ. Press, 1931.

Machiavelli, Niccolo. *The Prince*. 1513. In *The Portable Machiavelli*. Translated and edited by Peter Bondanella and Mark Musa. Harmondsworth: Penguin Books, 1979.

Manningham, John. *The Diary of John Manningham of the Middle Temple*. Edited by Robert Parker Sorlien. Hanover, N.H.: Univ. Press of New England, 1976.

Marvell, Andrew. *The Complete Poems*. Edited by E. S. Donno. Harmondsworth: Penguin Books, 1972.

May, Steven W., ed. *The Poems of Edward DeVere, Seventeenth Earl of Oxford, and of Robert Devereux, Second Earl of Essex*. In *Studies in Philology*, 77, no. 5 (1980).

Middleton, Thomas. *A Mad World, My Masters*. 1604–06. Edited by Standish Henning. Lincoln: Univ. of Nebraska Press, 1965.

Mulcaster, Richard. *The First Part of the Elementarie*. 1582. Reprint. Menston, England: Scolar Press, 1970.

———. *Richard Mulcaster's Positions*. 1581. Abridged and edited by Richard L. DeMolen. New York: Teachers College Press, Columbia Univ., 1971.

Naunton, Sir Robert. *Fragmenta Regalia*. 1653. Reprint. Edited by Edward Arber. English Reprints. London, 1870.

Nichols, John. *The Progresses and Public Processions of Queen Elizabeth*. 3 vols. 1823. Reprint. New York: Burt Franklin, n.d.

Nicolas, Sir Harris. *Memoirs of the Life and Times of Sir Christopher Hatton, K.G.* London: Richard Bentley, 1847.

Peacham, Henry. *The Compleat Gentleman*. 1622. Reprint. New York: Da Capo Press, 1968.

Peele, George. *Polyhymnia*. 1590. In *The Life and Minor Works of George Peele*, edited by David H. Horne. New Haven: Yale Univ. Press, 1952.

Plautus. *Stichus*. In *Plautus*. Translated by Paul Nixon. 5 vols. Loeb Classical Library. London: Heinemann, 1960.

Pliny. *Natural History*. Translated by Harris Rackham. 10 vols. Loeb Classical Library. Cambridge, Mass.: Harvard Univ. Press, 1940.

Puttenham, George. *The Arte of English Poesie*. 1589. Edited by Gladys Doidge Willcock and Alice Walker. Cambridge: At the University Press, 1936.

Quintilian. *Institutio Oratoria*. Translated by H. E. Butler. 4 vols. Loeb Classical Library. London: Heinemann, 1921–22.

Raleigh, Sir Walter. *The Works of Sir Walter Raleigh, Kt.* Edited by Thomas Birch. 8 vols. Oxford: Oxford Univ. Press, 1829.

Rickey, Mary Ellen, and Thomas B. Stroup, eds. *Certaine Sermons or Homilies, Appointed to be Read in Churches in the Time of Queen Elizabeth I (1547–1571): A Facsimile Reproduction of the Edition of 1623*. Gainesville, Fla.: Scholars' Facsimiles & Reprints, 1968.

Romei, Count Annibale. *The Courtiers Academie*. 1585. Translated by I. Kepers. 1598. Reprint. New York: Da Capo Press, 1969.

Shakespeare, William. *The Complete Signet Classic Shakespeare*. Edited by Sylvan Barnet. New York: Harcourt, Brace & World, 1963.

Sidney, Sir Philip. *An Apology for Poetry*. Edited by Geoffrey Shepherd. Manchester: Manchester Univ. Press, 1973.

――――. *Prose Works*. Edited by Albert Feuillerat. 4 vols. 1912. Reprint. Cambridge: At the University Press, 1962.

Spenser, Edmund. *Poetical Works*. Edited by J.C. Smith and E. de Selincourt. Oxford Standard Authors Series. Oxford: Oxford Univ. Press, 1912.

――――. *A View of the Present State of Ireland*. 1598. Edited by W.L. Renwick. Oxford: Clarendon, 1970.

Statutes of the Realm, from Magna Carta to the End of the Reign of Queen Anne. 11 vols. London, 1810–28.

Tasso, Torquato. *Aminta*. 1573. Translated by Henry Reynolds. 1628. First chorus in Frank Kermode, ed., *English Pastoral Poetry, from the Beginnings to Marvell*. 1952. Reprint. New York: Norton, 1972, pp. 81–83.

Tertullian. *De Spectaculis*. Translated by T.R. Glover. Loeb Classical Library. London: Heinemann, 1931.

Thucydides. *The Peloponnesian War*. Translated by Richard Crawley. New York: Modern Library, 1951.

Virgil. Translated by H. Rushton Fairclough. 2 vols. Loeb Classical Library. Cambridge, Mass.: Harvard Univ. Press, 1947.

Webster, John. *The White Devil*. 1612. Edited by John Russell Brown. The Revels Plays. London: Methuen, 1960.

Wilson, Thomas. *The Arte of Rhetorique*. 1560. Edited by G.H. Mair. Oxford: Clarendon, 1909.

Winwood, Sir Ralph. *Memorials of Affairs of State in the Reigns of Q. Elizabeth and K. James I*. 3 vols. London, 1725.

Wyatt, Sir Thomas. *Complete Poems*. Edited by R.A. Rebholz. New Haven: Yale Univ. Press, 1978.

Secondary Sources

Akrigg, G.P.V. "The Curious Marginalia of Charles, Second Lord Stanhope." In *Joseph Quincy Adams Memorial Studies*. Washington, D.C.: Folger Shakespeare Library, 1948, pp. 785–801.

Alsop, J.D. "The Dramatis Personae in Barnabe Googe's Critique of the Marian Persecution." *Notes and Queries* 226 (1981): 512–16.

Althusser, Louis. "Marxism and Humanism." In *For Marx*, translated by Ben Brewster. London: NLB, 1977, pp. 219–47.

Altman, Joel. *The Tudor Play of Mind: Rhetorical Inquiry and the Development of Elizabethan Drama*. Berkeley and Los Angeles: Univ. of California Press, 1978.

Anglo, Sidney. "The *British History* in Early Tudor Propaganda." *Bulletin of the John Rylands Library* 44 (1961): 17–48.

———. "Archives of the English Tournament: Score Cheques and Lists." *Journal of the Society of Archivists* 2 (1960–64): 153–62.

———. "Financial and Heraldic Records of the English Tournament." *Journal of the Society of Archivists* 2 (1960–64): 183–95.

Bald, R. C. *John Donne: A Life*. Oxford: Oxford Univ. Press, 1970.

Baldwin, Frances Elizabeth. "Sumptuary Legislation and Personal Regulation in England." *Johns Hopkins University Studies in Historical and Political Science* 44, no. 1 (1926): 1–282.

Barish, Jonas. *The Antitheatrical Prejudice*. Berkeley and Los Angeles: Univ. of California Press, 1981.

Bell, H. E. *An Introduction to the History and Records of the Court of Wards and Liveries*. Cambridge: At the University Press, 1953.

Berger, Harry. "Blueprint for Curricula: A General Theory of Culture Change."

———. "Outline of a General Theory of Cultural Change." *CLIO* 2 (1972): 49–63.

Berger, John. *Ways of Seeing*. London: British Broadcasting Corporation and Penguin Books, 1972.

Bourdieu, Pierre. "The Economics of Linguistic Exchanges." Translated by Richard Nice. *Social Science Information* 16 (1977): 645–68.

———. *Outline of a Theory of Practice*. 1972. Translated by Richard Nice. Cambridge: At the University Press, 1977.

Brooks, Eric St. John. *Sir Christopher Hatton*. London: Jonathan Cape, 1946.

Burke, Kenneth. *A Grammar of Motives*. 1945. Reprint. Berkeley and Los Angeles: Univ. of California Press, 1969.

———. *A Rhetoric of Motives*. 1950. Reprint. Berkeley and Los Angeles: Univ. of California Press, 1969.

———. "Literature as Equipment for Living." In *The Philosophy of Literary Form: Studies in Symbolic Action*. 3d rev. ed. Berkeley and Los Angeles: Univ. of California Press, 1973, pp. 293–304.

Cartwright, Julia. *Baldassare Castiglione, the Perfect Courtier: His Life and Letters*. 2 vols. London: John Murray, 1908.

Cassirer, Ernst. *The Individual and the Cosmos in Renaissance Philosophy*. 1927. Translated by Mario Domandi. 1963. Reprint. Philadelphia: Univ. of Pennsylvania Press, 1972.

Challis, C. E. *The Tudor Coinage*. Manchester: Manchester Univ. Press, 1978.

Charlton, Kenneth. *Education in Renaissance England*. London: Routledge & Kegan Paul, 1965.

Collins, A. J. *Jewels and Plate of Queen Elizabeth I: The Inventory of 1574*. London: British Museum, 1955.

Condon, Margaret. "Ruling Elites in the Reign of Henry VII." In *Patronage, Pedigree, and Power in Later Medieval England*, edited by Charles Ross. Totowa, N.J.: Rowman & Littlefield, 1979, pp. 109–42.

Cook, Ann Jennalie. *The Privileged Playgoers of Shakespeare's London*. Princeton: Princeton Univ. Press, 1981.

Cook, Timothy. "Who Were Barnabe Googe's Two Coridons?" *Notes and Queries* 222 (1977): 497–99.

Corballis, R. P. "'Buzz, Buzz': Bee-Lore in *2 Henry IV*." *Notes and Queries* 226 (1981): 127–28.

Council, Norman. "O Dea Certe: The Allegory of the Fortress of Perfect Beauty." *Huntington Library Quarterly* 39 (1976): 329–42.

———. "Ben Jonson, Inigo Jones, and the Transformation of Tudor Chivalry." *ELH* 47 (1980): 259–75.

Cressy, David. "Describing the Social Order of Elizabethan and Stuart England." *Literature and History* 3 (1976): 29–44.

Curtis, Mark H. *Oxford and Cambridge in Transition, 1558–1642*. Oxford: Clarendon, 1959.

Curtius, E. R. *European Literature and the Latin Middle Ages*. Translated by Willard R. Trask. 1953. Reprint. New York: Harper & Row, 1963.

Dickens, A. G. *The English Reformation*. New York: Schocken Books, 1964.

Donnelly, R. C. "The History of Defamation." *Wisconsin Law Review* (1949): 99–119.

Doughtie, Edward. "The Earl of Essex and Occasions for Contemplative Verse." *English Literary Renaissance* 9 (1979): 355–63.

Drew-Bear, Annette. "Face-Painting in Ben Jonson's Plays." *Studies in Philology* 77 (1980): 388–401.

———. "Face-Painting in Renaissance Tragedy," *Renaissance Drama*, n.s. 12 (1981): 71–93.

Eisenstein, Elizabeth L. *The Printing Press as an Agent of Change: Communications and Cultural Transformations in Early-Modern Europe*. 2 vols. Cambridge: At the University Press, 1979.

Elias, Norbert. *The History of Manners*. 1939. Vol. 1 of *The Civilizing Process*, translated by Edmund Jephcott. New York: Urizen, 1978.

———. *Power and Civility*. 1939. Vol. 2 of *The Civilizing Process*, translated by Edmund Jephcott. New York: Pantheon Books, 1982.

Elton, G. R. *Reform and Reformation: England, 1509–1558*. Cambridge, Mass.: Harvard Univ. Press, 1977.

Ferguson, Arthur B. *The Indian Summer of English Chivalry.* Durham, N.C.: Duke Univ. Press, 1960.

Finkelpearl, Philip J. *John Marston of the Middle Temple: An Elizabethan Dramatist in His Social Setting.* Cambridge, Mass.: Harvard Univ. Press, 1969.

Fisher, F. J. "The Development of London as a Centre of Conspicuous Consumption in the Sixteenth and Seventeenth Centuries." *Transactions of the Royal Historical Society,* 4th series, 30 (1948): 37–50.

Fletcher, Angus. *The Prophetic Moment.* Chicago: Univ. of Chicago Press, 1971.

Foucault, Michel. "Nietzsche, Genealogy, History." In *Language, Counter-Memory, Practice,* edited by Donald F. Bouchard, translated by Donald F. Bouchard and Sherry Simon. Ithaca, N.Y.: Cornell Univ. Press, 1977, pp. 139–64.

———. *Discipline and Punish.* Translated by Alan Sheridan. New York: Random House, Vintage Books, 1979.

———. "Prison Talk." In *Power/Knowledge: Selected Interviews and Other Writings, 1972–77,* edited by Colin Gordon, translated by Colin Gordon et al. New York: Pantheon Books, 1981, pp. 37–54.

———. "Two Lectures." In *Power/Knowledge: Selected Interviews and Other Writings, 1972–77,* edited by Colin Gordon, translated by Colin Gordon et al. New York: Pantheon Books, 1981, pp. 78–108.

Garfinkel, Harold. "Passing and the Managed Achievement of Sex Status in an Intersexed Person." In *Studies in Ethnomethodology.* Englewood Cliffs, N.J.: Prentice-Hall, 1967, pp. 116–85, 285–88.

Geertz, Clifford. "Ideology as a Cultural System." In *The Interpretation of Cultures.* New York: Basic Books, 1973, pp. 193–233.

Glatzer, Paula. *The Complaint of the Poet: The Parnassus Plays—A Critical Study of the Trilogy Performed at St. John's College, Cambridge, 1598–99—1601–02, Authors Anonymous.* Salzburg: Institut für Englische Sprache und Literatur, 1974.

Goffman, Erving. "The Nature of Deference and Demeanor." In *Interaction Ritual: Essays on Face-to-Face Behavior.* Garden City, N.Y.: Doubleday, Anchor Books, 1967, pp. 47–95.

———. *Strategic Interaction.* Philadelphia: Univ. of Pennsylvania Press, 1969.

———. *Relations in Public: Microstudies of the Public Order.* New York: Harper & Row, 1971.

Greenblatt, Stephen. "Improvisation and Power." In *Literature and Society,* edited by Edward Said. English Institute Essays. Baltimore: Johns Hopkins Univ. Press, 1980, pp. 57–99.

———. *Renaissance Self-Fashioning, from More to Shakespeare.* Chicago: Univ. of Chicago Press, 1980.

Greene, Thomas M. "Roger Ascham: The Perfect End of Shooting," *ELH* 26 (1960): 609–25.

———. "The Flexibility of the Self in Renaissance Literature." In *The Disciplines of Criticism: Essays in Literary Theory, Interpretation, and History*, edited by Peter Demetz, Thomas Greene, and Lowry Nelson, Jr. New Haven: Yale Univ. Press, 1968, pp. 241–64.

———. "*Il Cortegiano* and the Choice of a Game." *Renaissance Quarterly* 32 (1979): 173–86.

Greenlaw, Edwin. "Elizabethan Fact and Modern Fancy." In *Studies in Spenser's Historical Allegory*. Baltimore: Johns Hopkins Univ. Press, 1932, pp. 59–103.

Hale, J. H. "Castiglione's Military Career." In *Castiglione: The Ideal and the Real in Renaissance Culture*, edited by Robert W. Hanning and David Rosand. New Haven: Yale Univ. Press, 1983, pp. 143–64.

Hanning, Robert W. "Castiglione's Verbal Portrait: Structures and Strategies." In *Castiglione: The Ideal and the Real in Renaissance Culture*, edited by Robert W. Hanning and David Rosand. New Haven: Yale Univ. Press, 1983, pp. 131–41.

———, and David Rosand, eds. *Castiglione: The Ideal and the Real in Renaissance Culture*. New Haven: Yale Univ. Press, 1983.

Harper, Fowler V., and Fleming James, Jr. *The Law of Torts*. Boston: Little, Brown, 1956.

Heinemann, Margot. *Puritanism and Theatre: Thomas Middleton and Opposition Drama under the Early Stuarts*. Cambridge: At the University Press, 1980.

Henning, Roslyn Brogue. "The Paideia of a Renaissance Gentleman: Castiglione's *Book of the Courtier*." In *Renaissance Men and Ideas*, edited by Robert Schwobel. New York: St. Martin's Press, 1971, pp. 107–20.

Hexter, J. H. "The Education of the Aristocracy in the Renaissance." In *Reappraisals in History*. New York: Harper & Row, 1961, pp. 45–70.

———. "The Myth of the Middle Class in England." In *Reappraisals in History*. New York: Harper & Row, 1961, pp. 71–116.

Hogrefe, Pearl. "Elyot and 'The Boke Called Cortegiano in Ytalion.'" *Modern Philology* 27 (1930): 303–9.

Hollingsworth, T. H. *Historical Demography*. Ithaca, N.Y.: Cornell Univ. Press, 1969.

Hooper, Wilfrid. "The Tudor Sumptuary Laws." *English Historical Review* 30 (1915): 433–49.

Hurstfield, Joel. *The Queen's Wards: Wardship and Marriage under Elizabeth I*. Cambridge, Mass.: Harvard Univ. Press, 1958.

———. *Freedom, Corruption, and Government in Elizabethan England*. Cambridge, Mass.: Harvard Univ. Press, 1973.

Jackson, Sir Charles James. *English Goldsmiths and Their Marks*. London: Macmillan, 1921.

James, M. E. "The Concept of Order and the Northern Rising of 1569." *Past & Present* 60 (1973): 49–83.

Jameson, Fredric. *Marxism and Form.* Princeton: Princeton Univ. Press, 1971.

_____. "Marxism and Historicism." *New Literary History* 11 (1979): 41–74.

Javitch, Daniel. "*The Philosopher of the Court*: A French Satire Misunderstood." *Comparative Literature* 23 (1971):97–124.

_____. "Rival Arts of Conduct in Elizabethan England: Guazzo's *Civile Conversation* and Castiglione's *Courtier.*" *Yearbook of Italian Studies* 1 (1971): 178–98.

_____. "Poetry and Court Conduct: Puttenham's *Arte of English Poesie* in the Light of Castiglione's *Cortegiano.*" *MLN* 87 (1972): 865–82.

_____. *Poetry and Courtliness in Renaissance England.* Princeton: Princeton Univ. Press, 1978.

_____. "*Il Cortegiano* and the Constraints of Despotism." In *Castiglione: The Ideal and the Real in Renaissance Culture,* edited by Robert W. Hanning and David Rosand. New Haven: Yale Univ. Press, 1983, pp. 17–28.

Kearney, Hugh. *Scholars and Gentlemen: Universities and Society in Pre-Industrial Britain, 1500–1700.* Ithaca, N.Y.: Cornell Univ. Press, 1970.

Kelly, Francis M. "Queen Elizabeth and Her Dresses." *The Connoisseur* 113 (1944): 71–79.

Kelso, Ruth. *The Doctrine of the English Gentleman in the Sixteenth Century.* In *University of Illinois Studies in Language and Literature* 14 (1929): 1–288.

Kent, Joan. "Attitudes of Members of the House of Commons to the Regulation of 'Personal Conduct' in Late Elizabethan and Early Stuart England." *Bulletin of the Institute of Historical Research,* vol. 46, no. 113 (1973): 41–71.

Kerrigan, William. "The Articulation of the Ego in the Renaissance." In *The Literary Freud: Mechanisms of Defense and the Poetic Will,* edited by Joseph H. Smith, M.D. Psychiatry and the Humanities, vol. 4. New Haven: Yale Univ. Press, 1980, pp. 261–308.

Kinney, Arthur F. "Rhetoric as Poetic: Humanist Fiction in the Renaissance." *ELH* 43 (1976): 413–43.

_____. "Humanist Poetics and Elizabethan Fiction." *Renaissance Papers 1978,* pp. 31–45.

Lanham, Richard. *Revising Prose.* New York: Scribner's, 1979.

_____. *The Motives of Eloquence: Literary Rhetoric in the Renaissance.* New Haven: Yale Univ. Press, 1976.

Latham, Agnes M. C. "Sir Walter Raleigh's *Instructions to his Son.*" In *Elizabethan and Jacobean Studies Presented to Frank Percy Wilson in Honour of His Seventieth Birthday.* Oxford: Clarendon, 1959, pp. 199–218.

Lehmberg, Stanford. *Sir Thomas Elyot: Tudor Humanist.* Austin: Univ. of Texas Press, 1960.

Levi-Strauss, Claude. *The Savage Mind.* Chicago: Univ. of Chicago Press, 1966.

Lewis, C. S. *The Allegory of Love.* 1936. Reprint. Oxford: Oxford Univ. Press, 1958.

Lievsay, John L. *Stefano Guazzo and the English Renaissance, 1575–1675.* Chapel Hill: Univ. of North Carolina Press, 1961.

Lucas, Paul. "Blackstone and the Reform of the Legal Profession." *English Historical Review* 77 (1962): 456–89.

Lukacs, Georg. "Class Consciousness." In *History and Class Consciousness,* translated by Rodney Livingstone. Cambridge, Mass.: MIT Press, 1971.

MacCaffrey, Wallace. "Place and Patronage in Elizabethan Politics." In *Elizabethan Government and Society,* edited by S. T. Bindoff, Joel Hurstfield, and C. H. Williams. London: Athlone, 1961, pp. 95–126.

McConica, James. "Scholars and Commoners in Renaissance Oxford." In *The University in Society,* edited by Lawrence Stone. 2 vols. Princeton: Princeton Univ. Press, 1974, I: 151–81.

Marotti, Arthur F. "Countertransference, the Communication Process, and the Dimensions of Psychoanalytic Criticism." *Critical Inquiry* 4 (1978): 471–89.

Mason, John E. *Gentlefolk in the Making: Studies in the History of English Courtesy Literature and Related Topics from 1531 to 1774.* Philadelphia: Univ. of Pennsylvania Press, 1935.

Mauss, Marcel. *The Gift.* Translated by Ian Cunnison. 1954. Reprint. New York: Norton, 1967.

May, Steven W. "Tudor Aristocrats and the Mythical 'Stigma of Print.'" *Renaissance Papers 1980,* pp. 11–18.

Mazzeo, Joseph A. "Castiglione's *Courtier*: The Self as a Work of Art." In *Renaissance and Revolution: Backgrounds to Seventeenth-Century Literature.* New York: Random House, Pantheon Books, 1965, pp. 131–60.

Montrose, Louis Adrian. "Celebration and Insinuation: Sir Philip Sidney and the Motives of Elizabethan Courtship." *Renaissance Drama,* n.s. 8 (1977): 3–35.

————. "Of Gentlemen and Shepherds: The Politics of Elizabethan Pastoral Form." *ELH* 50 (1983): 415–59.

Neale, Sir John. "The Elizabethan Political Scene." In *Essays in Elizabethan History.* New York: St. Martin's Press, 1958, pp. 59–84.

Nietzsche, Friedrich. *The Genealogy of Morals.* Translated by Francis Golffing. Garden City, N. Y.: Doubleday, Anchor Books, 1956.

O'Day, Rosemary. "Ecclesiastical Patronage: Who Controlled the Church?" In *Church and Society in England: Henry VIII to James I,* edited by Felicity Heal and Rosemary O'Day. London: Macmillan, 1977, pp. 137–55.

Ong, Walter J. "Oral Residue in Tudor Prose Style." In *Rhetoric, Romance, and Technology: Studies in the Interaction of Expression and Culture.* Ithaca, N.Y.: Cornell Univ. Press, 1971, pp. 23–47.

————. "Voice and Opening Closed Systems." In *Interfaces of the Word: Studies in the Evolution of Consciousness and Culture.* Ithaca, N.Y.: Cornell Univ. Press, 1977, pp. 305–41.

Osborn, James M. "Sidney and Pietro Bizari." *Renaissance Quarterly* 24 (1971): 344–54.

————. *Young Philip Sidney, 1572–1577.* New Haven: Yale Univ. Press, 1972.

Osgood, C. G. *The Voice of England.* New York: Harper & Bros., 1935.

Parks, George B. "The First Draft of Ascham's *Scholemaster.*" *Huntington Library Quarterly* 1 (1938): 313–27.

————. "The First Italianate Englishmen." *Studies in the Renaissance* 8 (1961): 197–216.

————. "The Genesis of Tudor Interest in Italian." *PMLA* 77 (1962): 529–35.

Prest, Wilfrid. *The Inns of Court under Elizabeth I and the Early Stuarts, 1590–1640.* London: Longman, 1972.

Prouty, C. T. *George Gascoigne: Elizabethan Courtier, Soldier, and Poet.* New York: Columbia Univ. Press, 1942.

Read, Conyers. *Mr. Secretary Walsingham and the Policy of Queen Elizabeth.* 3 vols. Oxford: Clarendon, 1925.

————. *Lord Burghley and Queen Elizabeth.* 1960. Reprint. London: Jonathan Cape, 1965.

Rebhorn, Wayne. *Courtly Performances: Masking and Festivity in Castiglione's "Book of the Courtier."* Detroit: Wayne State Univ. Press, 1978.

Ruutz-Rees, Caroline. "Some Notes of Gabriel Harvey's in Hoby's Translation of Castiglione's *Courtier.*" *PMLA* 25 (1910): 608–39.

Ryan, Lawrence V. *Roger Ascham.* Stanford: Stanford Univ. Press, 1963.

————. "Book IV of Castiglione's *Courtier*: Climax or Afterthought?" *Studies in the Renaissance* 19 (1972): 156–79.

Saccone, Eduardo. "*Grazia, Sprezzatura,* and *Affettazione* in Castiglione's *Book of the Courtier.*" Translated by Susan G. Beecher. *Glyph* 5 (1979): 34–54.

Sartre, Jean-Paul. *Anti-Semite and Jew.* Translated by George J. Becker. 1946. Reprint. New York: Schocken Books, 1965.

Saunders, J. W. "The Stigma of Print: A Note on the Social Bases of Tudor Poetry." *Essays in Criticism* 1 (1951): 139–64.

Schnerr, Walter J. "Two Courtiers: Castiglione and Rodrigues Lobo." *Comparative Literature* 13 (1961): 138–53.

Sheidley, William E. *Barnabe Googe.* Boston: Twayne, 1981.

Siegel, Jerrold E. *Rhetoric and Philosophy in Renaissance Humanism: The*

Union of Eloquence and Wisdom, Petrarch to Valla. Princeton: Princeton Univ. Press, 1968.

Simon, Joan. *Education and Society in Tudor England*. Cambridge: At the University Press, 1967.

Starnes, D. T. "Shakespeare and Elyot's *Governour*." *University of Texas Studies in English* 7 (1927): 112–32.

Staton, Walter F. "Roger Ascham's Theory of History Writing." *Studies in Philology* 56 (1959): 125–37.

Stern, Virginia. *Gabriel Harvey: His Life, Marginalia, and Library*. Oxford: Clarendon, 1979.

Stone, Lawrence. "The Educational Revolution in England, 1560–1640." *Past & Present* 28 (1964): 41–80.

———. *The Crisis of the Aristocracy, 1558–1641*. Oxford: Clarendon, 1965.

———. "Social Mobility in England, 1500–1700." *Past & Present* 33 (1966): 17–55.

———. "Office under Queen Elizabeth: The Case of Lord Hunsdon and the Lord Chamberlainship in 1585." *Historical Journal* 10 (1967): 279–85.

Strong, Roy. *Splendor at Court: Renaissance Spectacle and the Theater of Power*. Boston: Houghton Mifflin, 1973.

Struever, Nancy. *The Language of History in the Renaissance: Rhetorical and Historical Consciousness in Florentine Humanism*. Princeton: Princeton Univ. Press, 1970.

Trafton, Dain A. "Structure and Meaning in *The Courtier*." *English Literary Renaissance* 2 (1972): 283–97.

———. "Politics and the Praise of Women." In *Castiglione: The Ideal and the Real in Renaissance Culture*, edited by Robert W. Hanning and David Rosand. New Haven: Yale Univ. Press, 1983.

Vance, Eugene. "Signs of the City: Medieval Poetry as Detour." *New Literary History* 4 (1973): 557–74.

Veeder, Van Vechten. "The History and Theory of the Law of Defamation." *Columbia Law Review* 3 (1903): 546–73.

Vogt, George McGill. "Gleanings for the History of a Sentiment: Generositas Virtus, non Sanguis." *Journal of English and Germanic Philology* 24 (1925): 102–24.

Ward, B. M. *The Seventeenth Earl of Oxford, 1550–1604*. London: John Murray, 1928.

———. "Further Research on *A Hundreth Sundrie Flowres*." *Review of English Studies* 4 (1938): 35–48.

Whigham, Frank. "Ideology and Class Conduct in *The Merchant of Venice*." *Renaissance Drama*, n.s. 10 (1979): 93–115.

———. "The Rhetoric of Elizabethan Suitors' Letters." *PMLA* 96 (1981): 864–82.

————. "A Lacuna in Puttenham's *Arte of English Poesie.*" *English Language Notes*, in press (Fall 1984).

White, Beatrice. *Cast of Ravens: The Strange Case of Sir Thomas Overbury.* New York: Braziller, 1965.

Williams, Neville. *Powder and Paint: A History of the Englishwoman's Toilet.* London: Longman, 1957.

————. *Elizabeth, Queen of England.* 1967. Reprint. London: Sphere, 1971.

Williams, Penry. *The Tudor Regime.* Oxford: Clarendon, 1979.

Williams, Raymond. *Marxism and Literature.* Oxford: Oxford Univ. Press, 1977.

Willson, D. H. *King James VI and I.* New York: Oxford Univ. Press, 1967.

Woodhouse, J. R. *Baldesar Castiglione: A Reassessment of "The Courtier."* Edinburgh: Edinburgh Univ. Press, 1978.

Woodward, W. H. *Studies in Education during the Age of the Renaissance, 1400–1600.* Cambridge: At the University Press, 1906.

Wrigley, E. A. and R. S. Schofield. *The Population History of England, 1541–1871: A Reconstruction.* Cambridge, Mass.: Harvard Univ. Press, 1981.

Yates, Frances. *Astraea: The Imperial Theme in the Sixteenth Century.* London: Routledge & Kegan Paul, 1975.

Youngs, Frederic A. *The Proclamations of the Tudor Queens.* Cambridge: At the University Press, 1976.

Index

effortlessness, 33–34
game, 78–81, 195n67, 218n55
leisure, 88–93
poetry described in terms of, 126
privacy, 42–43, 65
recreation, 88–93, 126
retirement, 127–30
spontaneity, 91–92
sprezzatura, 93–95
Overbury, Sir Thomas, 58, 209n57
Oxford, Earl of, 18, 173–74, 210n10, 215n33

Paradiastole, 40–42, 204n17
Parker, Matthew, 16
Parks, George B., 177
Parnassus Plays, The, 28, 55, 58, 175–76, 209n55
Pastoral, 171–75. See also *Otium*
Patronage, 9, 12, 48, 69, 86
Peacham, Henry the Elder, 41
Peacham, Henry, 132, 215n33
Pearson, R. (translator of Botero), 79
Peele, George, 79–80
Philibert de Vienne, 26
Pico della Mirandola, 1, 37, 38
Pliny, 93, 153
Prehistory. See Myths of origin
Prest, Wilfrid, 17
Privacy, 42–43, 65. See also *Otium*
Puttenham, George, 28–29, 65, 87, 139–42
on affectation, 147–48
on *allegoria* or "the courtier," 36
on *cosmesis*, 117
on deceit, 36, 99–100, 125
on decorum, 52, 66
on Elizabeth, 46, 67, 73, 86, 175
on fictional displacement, 122, 125–26, 130. See also Myths of origin
on *paradiastole*, 40–41
on pastoral retirement, 128–30
on self-trivialization, 120
on social structure, 46, 67

Quintilian, 93, 205n17

Raleigh, Sir Walter, 28, 38, 49, 127, 132, 217n49
Rebhorn, Wayne, 61, 224n43
Recreation, 88–93. See also *Otium*
Reputation by association, 131–32
Retirement, 127–30. See also *Otium*
Reverence, 65–67
Rhetoric of social combat, the, 139–47
Romei, Count Annibale, 28, 43, 45, 47, 68, 75, 156

Saccone, Eduardo, 93
Sartre, Jean-Paul, 35, 94–95
Self-trivialization. See Courtesy literature, and triviality
Shakespeare, William, 37, 46, 56, 57, 58, 83, 88–89, 97, 104, 115, 116, 142, 151–55, 170, 181, 204n17, 215n30, 216n41, 229n13
Sidney, Sir Philip, 21, 30, 75, 87, 100, 213n24
Simon, Joan, 25
Slander, 142–47. See also Rhetoric of social combat
Social mobility. See Demography
Social structure
linear and circular models, 67–71
origins of rank. See Myths of origin
rank and merit. See Stipulation of virtue by rank
Speech and silence (decorum and delay), 50–53
Spenser, Edmund, 15, 23, 58, 67, 69–70, 79, 156, 173, 174–75, 197n84, 219n58
Spontaneity, 91–92. See also *Otium*
Sprezzatura, 93–95. See also *Otium*
Stipulation of virtue by rank, 73–75
Stone, Lawrence, 6–7, 9, 15–16, 17, 56
Sumptuary regulation, 155–69

Tasso, Torquato, 171
Tel Quel group, 33
Tertullian, 215n30
Thucydides, 204n17
Trafton, Dain A., 220n4
Translation, evils of, 19

Compositor:	Innovative Media, Inc.
Text:	Sabon
Display:	Sabon
Printer:	Braun-Brumfield, Inc.
Binder:	Braun-Brumfield, Inc.